MAKING A MEAL OF IT

For my children, Duncan, Susannah and Sophie,
and their families, with love

MAKING A MEAL OF IT

Writing About Film

BRIAN McFARLANE

Introduction by Ian Britain

MONASH University
Publishing

Monash University Publishing
Matheson Library and Information Services Building
40 Exhibition Walk
Monash University
Clayton, Victoria 3800, Australia
www.publishing.monash.edu

Monash University Publishing brings to the world publications which advance the best traditions of humane and enlightened thought.

Monash University Publishing titles pass through a rigorous process of independent peer review.

www.publishing.monash.edu/books/mmi-9781925523416.html

Series: Cultural Studies

Design: Les Thomas

Cover: Les Thomas

National Library of Australia Cataloguing-in-Publication entry:

Creator:	McFarlane, Brian, 1934- author.
Title:	Making a meal of it : writing about film / Brian McFarlane.
ISBN:	9781925523416 (paperback)
Subjects:	Motion pictures.
	Motion pictures--History.
	Motion pictures--Criticism and interpretation.
	Film criticism

Printed in Australia by Griffin Press an Accredited ISO AS/NZS 14001:2004 Environmental Management System printer.

MIX
Paper from responsible sources
FSC
www.fsc.org
FSC® C009448

The paper this book is printed on is certified against the Forest Stewardship Council ® Standards. Griffin Press holds FSC chain of custody certification SGS-COC-005088. FSC promotes environmentally responsible, socially beneficial and economically viable management of the world's forests.

CONTENTS

Acknowledgments ix

Introduction x

Part I: Starters 1

Film Reviews 2

1 *My Brilliant Career* 3

2 *Nijinsky* 9

3 *Gallipoli* 14

4 *84 Charing Cross Road* 21

5 *Hope and Glory* 24

6 *Comrades* 28

7 *The Whales of August* 32

8 There's a Lot Going On in *Australia*: Baz Luhrmann's Claim to the Epic 35

9 Shakespeare's Brave New World and Julie Taymor's *Tempest* 46

10 The Odd Couple: Language and Life Lessons in *The King's Speech* 49

11 *Cloudstreet* anew 58

12 The Filmmaker as Adaptor: Fred Schepisi Takes On Patrick White in *The Eye of the Storm* 61

13 A Tale of Two Terences: *The Deep Blue Sea* 68

14 *Much Ado About Nothing*: 'Oh, what a merry war' 71

15 Shuttlecock: *What Maisie Knew* 74

16 All That Glitters ... *The Great Gatsby* 77

17 No Surrender: *Suffragette* 80

18 Taking the Plunge: *The Water Diviner* 87

19 *Sunset Song* 95

Book Reviews 98

20 *Ealing Studios* 99

21 Days of Their Lives.............................. 106

22 Some Kind of a Man: *Orson Welles: The Stories of His Life* 110

23 Conjuring the Rebel without a Pause: *The Rebel: An Imagined Life of James Dean* 115

24 A Cinema Torpid But Not Terminal: *Icons in the Fire: The Decline and Fall of Almost Everybody in the British Film Industry 1984-2000* ... 118

25 Flaunting Your Perfections: *The Original Million Dollar Mermaid: The Annette Kellerman Story* 121

26 Hepburn Springs Eternal: *Kate* 125

27 A Poignant Tale Worth Playing Again: *Ingrid: Ingrid Bergman, A Personal Biography* 129

28 Australian Screen Classics: *Alvin Purple* 133

29 *I Peed on Fellini: Recollections of a Life in Film* 139

30 The Spellbinder: *God of Speed* 144

31 'He really was a contender': *Somebody: The Reckless Life and Remarkable Career of Marlon Brando* 149

32 *Bowery to Broadway*: *The American Irish in Classic Hollywood Cinema* 152

33 'Mommie dearest' Just One Role Among Many: *Possessed: The Life of Joan Crawford* 158

34 One Man in His Time: *John Gielgud: Matinee Idol to Movie Star* 161

35 Out of the Dark: *I Found It at the Movies: Reflections of a Cinephile* 165

36 Routes of Passage 170

37 *John Wayne: The Life and Legend* 173

38 The Trouble with Ackroyd: *Alfred Hitchcock* 176

Part II: Mains 181

39 The Biography Industry: Creatures Great and Mostly Small 183

40 Local/Global: *The Bank* and *Lantana* 208

41 Mothers: Some Kids do 'ave 'em 216

42 Portraits in Celluloid 224

43 Shooting Minds 236

44 Size Doesn't Matter: Big Stupid Films. 246

45 Country Towns in Australian Films: Trap or Comfort Zone? 261

46 From Rock of Ages to Rock 'n' Roll 277

47 Softly and Tenderly 287

48 Finding Ourselves in Australian Films 296

49 A Curmudgeon's Canon: Random Thoughts on *Summer Heights High*, *The Office* and Other Nasty Pleasures 302

50 How Weird Does this Mob Still Seem? 316

51 *Kath & Kimderella*: From Box to Multiplex 324

52 The Voice of a Generation 332

Part III: Afters – or Just Deserts 345

53 A Gifted, Trenchant Friend: Lindsay Anderson 347

54 Who is Lance Comfort? 351

55 Jill Esmond Olivier: The First Wife 355

56 The Choice Fruit of *The Mango Tree* 362

57 Obituary: Sir John Mills 365

58 Merle Oberon: 'She walked in beauty ...' 368

ACKNOWLEDGMENTS

My thanks are due to the various sources and editors of the pieces for their permission to re-publish here: *The Age*, *The Australian Book Review*, *Metro*, *Meanjin*, *Inside Story*, *Senses of Cinema*, *Screening the Past* and *Sight & Sound*. The editors involved were in all cases helpful and co-operative. I also thank Scott Murray, former and co-founding editor of *Cinema Papers*, for his advice concerning my copyright in my articles from its pages.

After someone (now lost to my memory) suggested this project, I mentioned this to Ian Britain who encouraged me to go ahead with it and said he'd like to do an Introduction. I am grateful for his continued help and suggestions.

My daughter, Sophie Scully, has been indefatigable in putting the manuscript into shape, drawing on technical skills that were well beyond my capacities. I couldn't have done it without her help – and have even learnt a few new computer tricks. My huge thanks and love to her.

Once again, it has been a pleasure to be associated with Monash University Publishing, and I thank Nathan Hollier and his team for their unstinting support.

The book is dedicated to all my children and their families. The children particularly must often have felt that they could have had a more practical parent than one who was an obsessive writer. My love to them all.

Melbourne, 2017

INTRODUCTION

Reviews, like revenge, may be a dish best served cold, as they are in this collation by one of Australia's most prolific film critics. Brian McFarlane, by whom I was taught at school and with whom I later taught courses at university, has been reviewing films and books (particularly books *about* film) over the past forty years or so. This occupation has provided something of a meal ticket for him along with his teaching and scholarly research, which have also largely focussed on books and films and the relations between them. The 'meals' he's made of what he reviews are, of their nature, designed for sharing with a wide audience and prepared on the 'occasion', as he puts it, of a film's release or a book's publication. That's when reviews will make their most direct impact, helping to determine commercial sales or box-office returns. But they *can* have a higher and more enduring value, and particularly in the hands of so spritely and erudite a practitioner of the craft as Brian.

As acknowledged by Pauline Kael, doyenne of film critics in her day, there's a risk with reviews that when they're just hot off the press they may 'keep people away' from whatever they're reviewing rather than prompting readers to investigate for themselves and make up their own minds. The 'star' ratings that have become such a routine feature now of film reviewing only increase this risk; how often have I had to try to reason with friends who are resistant to seeing this or that movie simply because 'Critic X' only gave it 'one-and-a-half stars'! I suspect some of them just look at the number of stars and don't even bother to read the substance of the review –

which in the more popular media seems to be getting thinner and thinner anyway: down to a few hastily dashed-off and ill-informed lines.

The more substantial, less reductive review, especially when read at a distance in time, should have the opposite effect. We – I, certainly, on the basis of those pieces republished here – become intrigued by the sound of even the most pilloried book or movie and want to search it out to see how fair the verdict appears with hindsight and in the light of changes in taste and fashion over the years. In the course of reviewing a particular movie, Brian will often allude to half a dozen or more precursors, some of which we might never have heard of before, and, again, he will have us itching to find them on Netflix or at a DVD store. Or he will reawaken our interest in films that we, too, have seen, but long ago, and that are now just a sketchy blur in our minds. We're prompted to look at them afresh and see how they measure up to his original response, as well as to our own, dimly remembered one. Thereby an old review works as a stimulus to new, or renewed, appreciation. Far from keeping people away it's likelier to draw them in all the more.

Of course, there's much more to Brian's output than his reviews – the so-called 'starters' to his menu of offerings in this book. He has compiled whole encyclopaedias as well as a string of critical monographs on a variety of narrative modes, genres or techniques, authors, actors and directors. These works should all be on the shelves of any good general library, but less readily accessible, and so more important to reproduce samples of here, are the reflective essays that he's published in various periodicals or magazines on a miscellany of themes and trends in cinematic history and folklore. Longer, as well as more wide-ranging, than his reviews, they are grouped in these pages under the rubric, 'Mains', while under 'Afters' he has chosen to present an assortment of profiles of actors and directors, particular favourites of his with whom in some cases he forged a personal friendship. This is not mere self-indulgent confectionery; the label 'Afters' takes on an additional, and more poignant, meaning when we realise that all of the subjects of these profiles are now dead. So the profiles serve as elegies, lightly and delicately concocted ones, free of any solemnity, but not of seriousness – a distinction he impressed on me and my classmates when teaching us decades ago.

Taking film seriously, as a medium in its own right with its own distinctive language, but not solemnly, as a refined art form divorced from the rest of life, is a quality Brian admires in another of his favourites, the only recently deceased English critic, Philip French. Other, related qualities he admires in French are his 'masterly grasp' of the functions both of reviewer and critic, his capacious 'range' of reference, the 'eclecticism' of his 'responsiveness to what film has to offer', his 'gift for perceiving … recurring motifs and preoccupations across genres and decades', his 'grasp of film history', and the 'ease and authority' with which he 'situates film in the larger processes of cultural change'. It strikes me again and again that these are also the hallmarks of Brian's writings, as represented in the pages that follow. Without being derivative in any way, they incarnate the spirit of all that is finest in the traditions of film criticism worldwide – and here on our own home ground. How blessed we are in this antipodean avatar!

Ian Britain, Melbourne, June 2017

Part I

Starters

This section comprises reviews of either individual films or books related to film. The earliest derive from *Cinema Papers* in the 1970s, along with later reviews in *The Age*, *Australian Book Review*, *Metro* and the online journals *Senses of Cinema*, *Screening the Past* and *Inside Story*. The purpose of reviews is, among other aims, to guide, inform and entertain: their occasion is the release of a film or publication of a book. Many of the titles selected here reflect my interest in the adaptation of literature or drama to film.

The reviews are arranged chronologically, in the expectation that they may reveal some changes in filmmaking and writing about it. For all I can tell, they may also reveal the reviewer's attitudes changing with the remorselessly passing years.

Film Reviews

1

MY BRILLIANT CAREER

Just when it seemed that 1979 was not to be a good year for Australian films, *My Brilliant Career* arrived to restore confidence and take its place with the six best films this country had produced in the liveliest decade of its cinema history.

Gillian Armstrong's film is, with one exception, wholly true to the spirit of Miles Franklin's semi-autobiographical novel, and, in my view, greatly improves on the letter of that exuberant but over-exclamatory work. There are limits to the allowances one is inclined to make for the youth of the author (22 when the book was published in 1901) and she often mistakes girlish gush for zest. But it does have a tough-mindedness that flashes out intermittently and stays with us at the end.

The strength of Eleanor Witcombe's screenplay is in grasping and holding to the vitality and independence of Franklin's vision and shearing away its jaunty excesses. She keeps the heroine's likability and determination, and eschews the irritating slanginess and self-conscious romanticism that clog the book. In doing so, she has given director and star something really substantial and coherent to work on, and has considerably surpassed her own efforts in *The Getting of Wisdom*.

The film's explicitness about its heroine is very much Miles Franklin's. When Sybylla (Judy Davis) says to her suitor; 'Give me a chance to find out what's wrong with the world, with *me*, with everything', or, in finally refusing his proposal, 'I can't lose myself in someone else's life till I've lived my own', the words may be Witcombe's, but their tone and emphasis are Franklin's. They might make us wince if the Sybylla, created by the Armstrong-Witcombe-Davis combine, were less attractive and credible; she is a good deal more so than Franklin's wearying high-spirited heroine.

The film, like the novel, is framed by its protagonist's autobiographical intentions. Plain white credits on a black background give way to a bleak, lovely Australian landscape with a single corrugated-iron house. As wind and dust blow through open windows and doors, Sybylla, with endearing egotism, begins to read the story of her brilliant career, oblivious of the uncongenial surroundings. The film ends with the early-morning freshness of long shafts of light falling between trees and behind Sybylla as she consigns her finished manuscript to Blackwood's, Edinburgh. As she leans on a sliprail gate, the audience is left on a note of quiet optimism.

Between these framing images, the film briskly pursues Sybylla's career as she moves from the genteel poverty of home, to the more gracious comforts of her grandmother's house, to the opulence of Harry Beecham's property, Five-Bob Downs, to the slab-built squalors of the McSwats' where she goes as a governess, and back home again (if not, one feels, for long).

As it recreates these changes of setting and their importance in Sybylla's growth, the film emerges as a triumph of *mise-en-scène*. It's not just a matter of that loving attention to detail that evokes the limited pleasure of recognition. Rather, much of the film's meaning is made in the impact of changing scenes on Sybylla; in the tensions created between her and the places she finds herself in.

In the early scenes at home, for instance, the recreation of the Victorian period through ornately-framed photographs, and the jangling of the piano (as Sybylla plays) against the background of family chores establishes her separateness from – and, indeed, opposition to – her environment.

By contrast, and it is a dramatic contrast in that it works towards the expansion of Sybylla's consciousness, are the alert, economical scenes establishing the comfort and abundance of Caddagat, her grandmother's home, with its soft interiors beautifully lit (Don McAlpine excelling himself), its more formal, gracious manners, and its superior piano which Sybylla plays, properly listened to this time.

As the camera cuts from Sybylla's delight in her room (her mother's old one) at Caddagat – luxurious white rugs, pretty wallpaper, canopied bed – to her mother working in her dingy kitchen at home, the audience is not just being asked to admire Luciana Arrighi's art direction, though they certainly should do so. A point is being made about what the girl has escaped from, that is, from the debilitating poverty that has made her mother (Julie Blake) careworn and complaining, a poverty that cannot find time or place for a life of the kind which Sybylla craves. Caddagat is an opening up of possibilities for her.

The lush natural background, at Caddagat and at Five-Bob Downs, sets off and helps to account for the social graces within. In this gentler, more yielding landscape, the film suggests, it is easier to be cultivated and independent. In contrast with the swirling dust racing through open doors and windows at home, here we get views of verdant gardens lightly beckoning as seen from cool interiors. This kind of natural receptiveness to man is epitomised in an exquisite long-shot: the composition of this scene, in which fence-rails cross the foreground and Sybylla's red sunshade dominates the dappled, leafy greenness of the middle-ground through which the river runs, achieves a Monet-like impressionism. The shot seems not merely artistic, but *about* art and people in harmonious settings. The scene has a nicely-judged anticlimax as Sybylla chucks the bunch of flowers brought her by the pompous English jackaroo in the river.

The film's visual style has been stressed here because it is more than a style; it is the chief source of the film's coherence. The grandeur of the Five-Bob Downs colonnade recalls the shot of the verandah of the country pub to which Sybylla had earlier gone to find her drunken father. However, whereas the camera passes through the colonnade to yet more elegance within, in the earlier scene it pulls back from the verandah to subvert our notions of the pub's charm by revealing its ugly squatness. The striking overhead shot of Sybylla dancing, somewhat wildly, at Caddagat, contrasts with the decorum of the breakfast scene the next day, or with the soft fireside interior at Five-Bob Downs. These later scenes, suggesting the constraints that work on Sybylla, resonate with the recollection of the earlier one.

The idea of Sybylla's being wrenched out of the pleasures of Caddagat to go to work for the McSwats is underlined in the way this unpleasant news cuts into the serene image of the girl in the blossom tree. The extent of this break is made in tersely effective visual terms: 'Do her the world of good – make her think of other people,' says Granny (Aileen Britton) complacently in her comfortable sitting-room, and the camera cuts to the filthy McSwat children. The congeries of broken-down huts that is the McSwat farm is caught in a brilliant long-shot that suggests all the worst kinds of slothful incompetence; it is juxtaposed to a prettily-composed scene of Granny and Aunt Helen (Wendy Hughes) on the terrace at Caddagat.

If I am making the film's procedures sound too schematic, I don't mean to do so. What I want to point to is the intelligent way one scene is enriched by contrasts or parallels with another; the ways in which recollection of one image informs another. Sybylla's final meeting with Harry (Sam Neill) at a dam-side, where she is trying to pull a sheep out of the mud, recalls the idyllic punting scene at Five-Bob Downs. Judy Davis makes something very affecting of her efforts to explain why she can't marry Harry, and part of the tension of the scene is due to our recalling that earlier scene of pleasantness between them.

The film's sense of relationships is also reassuringly firm-minded. The feeling between Harry and Sybylla deepens satisfyingly from the first meeting which has a tension that's comic and sexual to the last when, half-reluctantly, she dismisses him. Much will probably be made of Miles Franklin's 'feminism' here (and of woman director and scriptwriter), but the film's strength is less to be found in a proselytising approach to a cause than its sympathetic understanding of a character and a personality struggling to establish and assert itself. The film is therefore equally generous in its treatment of Harry; he is allowed an impressive stillness and maturity that make his love worth having. For Sybylla, this cannot be enough, though she is aware of how nearly it is so.

Gillian Armstrong has chosen her stars well: Judy Davis and Sam Neill create a relationship that is wholly believable in its suggestions of sexuality, in the feelings chiefly withheld, but occasionally expressed in a burst of activity like the dancing at Five-Bob Downs, and in its final emotional inequality.

The one major blot on the film is the absurd pillow-fight between Sybylla and Harry which begins in the house and continues through garden and paddocks. It seems no more than an opportunity for a cameraman's virtuoso display. If it is meant to suggest a sense of sexual release for the two young people, it is incredible given the stage of their relationship. It has nothing to do with Miles Franklin, or with the rest of this lovely and touching film.

The film's other relationships are well-handled. Because they bear directly on Sybylla's growth, they contribute significantly to the film's coherence. Much of her growth can be traced through her relationships with her mother, her grandmother, her Aunt Helen, whose husband has left her, Harry's Aunt Gussy (Patricia Kennedy), and the slatternly Mrs McSwat (Carole Skinner). What she learns from her dealings with each of these is unobtrusively realised and each has her role in the drama of Sybylla's growing self-awareness. All these roles are perceptively written and played, but Wendy Hughes is outstanding: reminiscent of the early Geraldine Fitzgerald, she brings the right grace, warmth, and suppressed sadness to Aunt Helen.

Gillian Armstrong has kept her eye, and her mind, firmly on where this film is leading us. It is always sumptuous to look at, marvellously lit and composed, but doesn't suffer from Creeping Beauty; Nathan Waks' score, using Schumann's *Scenes from Childhood*, helps to create that tone of blended poignancy and resilience which is part of the film's meaning; and the editing works constantly to reinforce the film's imagistic patterns. *My Brilliant Career* is essentially about a girl's determined movement towards a maturity that will suit her, and almost everything in the film works towards delineating this process.

Cinema Papers, September–October 1979.

2

NIJINSKY

It may not be fair to hold a film's advertising against it (though I am not sure that it is totally *unfair* to consider this aspect of the packaging), but Herbert Ross's relentlessly simple-minded treatment of the life and times of Nijinsky invites it: 'Genius. Madman. Animal. God,' the posters promise, and the film's notions of psychology depend on just those sorts of facile dichotomy.

The film subscribes absolutely to the aphoristic tosh given to Diaghilev (Alan Bates) when he refuses Romola Nijinsky's (Leslie Browne) plea to take her husband back: 'You mean he's suffering from some form of mental breakdown – tragic, of course – but perhaps inevitable. The other side of genius.' Ross then dissolves from an extreme close-up of Diaghilev's eyes to those of Nijinsky (George de la Pena), strait-jacketed in a cell. The film begins and ends with this image to ensure the audience's not missing the point. Similarly, the animal/god polarity is heavily underscored by the way in which Nijinsky's near-rape of Romola to the noisily banal accompaniment of Stravinsky inevitably recalls the supposedly god-like achievements of the artist.

Not that the film ever really gives the artist's achievements much chance to make themselves felt. Whatever the schmaltzy deficiencies of Ross' previous excursion into the ballet world, *The Turning*

Point, there was real pleasure in the dance sequences themselves. In *Nijinsky*, this compensation is minimised by incessant close-ups of the dancers' faces (when, presumably, if they are to come at the audience in sections, it is their legs that matter) and, worse, close-ups of boring faces in wings and boxes. No sooner has Nijinsky done (or nearly done) his famous leap through the window in *Le Spectre de la Rose* than the film cuts to Romola's rapt (= blank) gaze.

This frustration is characteristic throughout. Romola, having pursued Nijinsky to Monte Carlo, gets larger and larger close-ups as she watches *Scheherazade*, while the ballet itself gets lost in a lot of smarty-pants camerawork. It is as though Ross simply doesn't trust his audience to be interested in what made Nijinsky famous. His appalling lack of narrative sense ensures that *Jeux* is reduced to a series of snippety flash-forwards while Nijinsky outlines his idea of the ballet to Baron Dmitri de Gunzberg. *Le Sacre du Printemps* (usually mispronounced) similarly passes for almost nothing, while Ross firmly centres his attention and camera on the outraged audience and Diaghilev's shouting for it to listen.

To be fair, George de la Pena as Nijinsky manages to be riveting when it matters most: that is, in his performance of *L'Après-Midi d'un Faune*. For once, the camera acknowledges why he is in the film and makes credible the *succès de scandale* that ensues. De la Pena is no great actor, and is not helped by Hugh Wheeler's screenplay, but from time to time he suggests the vulnerability and confusion of Nijinsky, even if the four demanding roles advertised elude him.

There is, unfortunately, nothing whatever to be said for Leslie Browne's Romola. Chosen presumably because of her Balanchine Ballet fame, she is then given a non-dancing role, an index of the film's stupidity. Her great talent (seen in *The Turning Point*) is from the knees down, so naturally *this* film focuses on her unrevealing face. Her Romola has no passion, no vitality, nothing to support the film's narrative claims for her, and she is cruelly exposed by the unrelenting close-ups that suggest only chronic cerebral inertia. Ross's casting of her seems inexplicable: the role needs an actress for sense and credibility, not a dancer in repose.

Perhaps Ross assumed that Browne's knowledge of the ballet world from the inside would rub off on the film. If so, he was wrong. He was less wrong in the case of Anton Dolin's sharp sketch of Maestro Cecchetti, who does suggest something of the discipline and obsessiveness a great ballet master needs.

In general, though, the ballet world is simplistically conceived as a succession of opulent interiors in which someone is always storming out after delivering a bitchy one-liner. The film neither takes a romantically extravagant view of the world it presents, nor does it affect to be presenting the audience with what used to be called 'documentary realism' about the glamour and grind of it all. It is simply vacuous, and not all Douglas Slocombe's lovingly-lit theatres and dressing rooms, steamers and stations, doing full justice to John Blezard's production design, can compensate for the lack of any real sense of how a kind of life works on those who live it. Ross (an ex-choreographer) and his producer-wife Nora Kaye (a former ballerina) may be supposed to know the ballet world, but if so they have not managed to imbue this film with that knowledge.

Part of the trouble lies in a screenplay which has no notion of narrative and no ear for the way people – even terribly sophisticated impresarios – speak. The script's idea of narrative, wholly embraced by Ross, is simply to move its puppets from one cultural centre to another – Budapest, Greece, Monte Carlo, Paris (1912), London,

Italy (1913), etc. – and from train or boat to theatre and hotel, until every new lush exactness of art direction becomes an irritant in itself. And in not one of these episodes does Ross *build* to any sort of tension.

The 'Cherbourg 1913' scene is a typical example. Nijinsky explains to Dmitri that Diaghilev is not accompanying them because he is afraid of the sea (a no-doubt-true bit of trivia which the film mentions often as though it meant something). On board the steamer, amid the usual boringly opulent *mise-en-scène*, Nijinsky and Romola meet again: 'M. Diaghilev, I understand, is not with us', says Romola and her influence is about to begin.

This petulant schoolgirl is, one gathers, about to pit herself against Diaghilev for the body and soul of Nijinsky. The scene registers this crucial moment in dialogue like, 'I know one thing – I'll never let him hurt you.' A telegram arrives from Diaghilev dispensing with Nijinsky as dancer and choreographer. Nijinsky weeps and bangs his head on the door and wrecks the cabin in a frenzy – but there is no suggestion of inner-ness, just athletics, involved in his display. Then, to remind the audience of the genius/madman juxtaposition, there is a shot of Nijinsky cowering in the corner, before Romola enters with, 'Everything is for the best; he's always been a monster'. There is a great deal of loud Stravinsky on the soundtrack as he Takes Her (the kind of language in which the film thinks) on the floor. Crashing climax. Cut to 'Buenos Aires 1913' and the marriage.

I defer to no one in my detestation of Ken Russell's disgusting farragos on the lives of the musical great, but for a wild moment the predictable banalities of Ross's treatment of Nijinsky's career made me think almost with longing for their nasty, vulgar liveliness. For this film is devoid of life, and crashing chords only emphasise the flatness of its conceptions.

Most of *Nijinsky* is so tedious – and I'd rather spend an afternoon in traction than watch it again – that it is difficult to do justice to its minor merits. Alan Bates as Diaghilev mostly surfaces above the morass of clichés he is given to say, and suggests an appropriate dedication to his entrepreneurial function. However, not even he can do anything with dialogue like, 'If I listened to my heart this time it might be in danger of breaking', or with the predictable zoom in on his pain as he receives the news of Nijinsky's marriage.

Bates does succeed in creating the naturalness of Diaghilev's homosexuality without recourse to obvious signposting, and contrasts effectively with Alan Badel's Baron, amusingly played as a witty old queen ('half-Admiral of the Fleet, half-maiden aunt', as he contemplates his face in the mirror). In fact, unlike most of the film, the homosexual aspects are handled with credible casualness and in the early scenes between Diaghilev and Nijinsky are especially well done – lightly, amusingly, and subsumed into their total relationship.

In the end, though, such incidental moments of truth and wit are lost in the meandering stodge which this expensive-looking film mistakes for quality – possibly even for art. It is a film without style and, therefore, without any meaning.

Cinema Papers, No 31, March–April 1981.

3

GALLIPOLI

The opening image of the film is that of a boy doing loosening and breathing exercises to commands rapped out by an old man. At dawn, in an empty West Australian landscape in May, 1915, the boy practises his sprint as his uncle times him.

'What are your legs?' 'Steel springs'. 'How fast can you run?' 'Like a leopard'. 'How fast are you going to run?' 'Like a leopard'. The boy has his answers by rote as the old man drills him. The incantation comes back to him just before the final scene as he climbs out of the trench at Gallipoli, stepping over the dead and wounded, to run madly into the line of the Turkish artillery. And the film's last frozen frame holds the boy in the heroic posture of the runner, now streaked with blood.

Between the opening and closing images, Peter Weir has considerably extended his range, thematically and aesthetically. In his earlier feature films, he seemed chiefly preoccupied with the extraordinary lurking at the edges of the mundane, with rational man confronted by matters in which his rationality no longer serves him. In *Gallipoli*, his concerns are at once less metaphysical and more sociological, less an illustration of a pre-determined thesis and more an exploration of attitudes. In spite of its title, the film is not a war epic; in fact, it deliberately refuses invitations to be so. Its first and last shots are of an individual and this proves to be more than mere artistic tidiness.

Gallipoli is not, then, a 'war film' so much as a film *about* war; about the kinds of attitudes Australians and particular individuals took towards it in 1915: about, in a broader sense, what it felt like to be Australian then – and perhaps still does feel like. The second half of the film's length is taken up with scenes of war (in Egypt and later at Gallipoli). The earlier half has to do with Archy Hamilton's (Mark Lee) career as a sprinter, his meeting with Frank Dunne (Mel Gibson), whom Archy defeats at an athletic meeting, and their 'joining up', Archy in the Light Horse, Frank in the Infantry.

The two halves of the film fit together because there are continuing ideas which Weir explores in an unhurried, unemphatic way and which gain in cogency through being pursued in different milieux. I mean ideas like competitiveness and mateship and sporting spirit as aspects of our national mythology. As well, the earlier half of the film reinforces the idea of Australia's isolation from the rest of the world and the second half dramatises the enforced surrender of that sense of isolation.

Archy's being a sprinter is a way of stressing the individual competitive aspect of the Australian character; its solitariness is created in Russell Boyd's glowing images of the austere blankness of the landscape. Stronger than the competitive urge, though, is the feeling for mateship; the friendship between rural Archy and urban, knowing Frank, which develops after Archy has beaten Frank.

This relationship is developed in a long sequence in the first half of the film, in which the two head for Perth where Archy plans to join up. Stranded in the desert at a railway siding, they are told there will be a two weeks wait for the next Perth train, 'unless you're game enough to cross the lake'. Accepting this challenge they set off across the lake's dry bed, the Aboriginal railway worker warning them, 'If the snakes don't get ya, the blackfellas will', and two incongruous figures set off in a dry, empty landscape of shimmering heat.

This landscape will have a visual echo in the desolate crags of Gallipoli, but a more important aural echo is also set up. Frank's joking reference to Burke and Wills pre-figures another doomed enterprise – the Gallipoli landing – which has also passed into the national mythology.

During their trek to Perth, Archy and Frank achieve a friendship that surmounts their different attitudes to the war 'It's not our bloody war – it's an English war,' Frank claims, and Archy counters with, 'You're a bloody coward.' But Archy's patriotism is a mindless affair. When they meet an old man with a camel in the desert, the old man hasn't heard of the war (he has never been to Perth either, but he once knew a German), and Archy tries unsuccessfully to explain to him what the war is about.

This brief scene is rich in resonance: it encapsulates Australian isolation from world affairs (and underlines this by the very nature of the terrain), muddled patriotism to an undefined cause (and this notion gets its supreme expression at Gallipoli itself), and casual indifference to another country's quarrels. There is, further, an element of preposterousness in the very notion of this discussion's taking place in a vast stretch of desert.

The two men finally reach Perth, are recruited and then separated until, months later, they meet in a field exercise in Egypt – an exercise in which Light Horse and Infantry get rid of their mutual animosity by acting as enemy to each other. An officer breaks up their friendly reunion with 'This is supposed to be warfare', so they lie down as if wounded. Major Barton (Bill Hunter), influenced by their running prowess, permits a transfer which allows them to go to Gallipoli.

They want to be part of the action, in time they get their chance, with inevitable results.

If narrative were merely a matter of plot, the film would be thin and episodic enough. It would be a more or less interesting, even touching, account of a friendship casually begun and arbitrarily ended. However, the film's texture is persistently richer than such an account would suggest.

Gallipoli is not a polemical film: it is not essentially a 'war film'; equally, it resists the label of 'anti-war film'. I don't mean that it celebrates war or that it approves of World War I and Australia's participation in it but, rather, that its interest is in the way people react to and in war. This kind of interest leads Weir to admire the feeling that grows between Archy and Frank, between Frank and his former railway-ganger mates, between Archy and his old tormentor Les (Harold Hopkins) who turns up briefly in the Gallipoli trenches.

Weir is interested in why these men go to war, why Australians, so cut off from world events, should involve themselves in Britain's military and political problems, and what happens to them when they do commit themselves to the war. That the film is concerned with individuals in war is affirmed by the striking emphasis on close-ups as opposed to the sweeping panoramic shot. (In the mock battle between the Infantry and the Light Horse, there are some stunning long shots of serried ranks, and it occurred to me that this was the last of the CinemaScope wars, but this is not where Weir's interest lies.)

In his exploration of why these Australians go to war, Weir suggests that the competitive urge (races, bets on races – on anything) is part of the Australian consciousness, that it's no more to be resisted than the sex and booze the soldiers are warned about in Egypt. The first half of the film is full of people challenging each other and of others betting on the outcome. The challenge of a war, however dimly its causes are understood, takes its place in a context of competition. Archy's first reference to joining up is cut short by his uncle's reply, 'You're under-age', but Archy counters this by talking of his uncle's youthful escapades, competition, sporting spirit, enterprise: war offers a wider opportunity for their display.

Also, for all Frank's cynicism about its being 'England's bloody war', the ties of empire are still there, strongly, if not articulately, felt. In one charming domestic episode, Uncle Jack reads to Archy's younger brothers and sisters and, while the Australian wind whistles round their isolated farmhouse, the children listen rapt – to Kipling. The point is unobtrusively made that Kipling is as much part of this scene as the kerosene lamp. When a soldier with a drum is led on to the sportsground on a wooden horse, bearing the legend 'Join the Light Horse', it is not incongruous for another poster to proclaim, 'The Empire needs you.'

Isolated or not, Australians are reading about Gallipoli. The connection between Archy and Frank is first established by their reading of newspaper accounts of the war: Archy's cutting about Gallipoli is kept, significantly, in *Every Boy's Book of Sport and Pastimes*; Frank is reading a newspaper at the railway camp in the next shot. People are responding to the 'baptism of fire on the rocky slopes of Gallipoli', even if they are not sure where those slopes are.

In the marvellously-lit scene of night farewell as the troopship leaves Perth, the soundtrack has snatches of 'For England, home and beauty' as well as 'Australia will be there'. The men may be marching to different drums, but one of them is clearly the drum of empire. This is not to say that Weir and David Williamson (who wrote the screenplay) are taking a nostalgic or reactionary line: they are just implying that motives for going to this war were mixed – and muddled.

In Egypt, men from the youngest country in the world are seen playing football at the base of the pyramids and the camera offers a close-up of the Sphinx, no doubt bemused by this display of colonial competitiveness. Against this ancient backdrop, Frank claims that he's not interested in history, but in beating the Victorians at football. The competitive spirit, further seen in the Australians' haggling over Egyptian tourist junk, is finally seen as inappropriate to Gallipoli. It has taken them there, but cannot *help* them there where they are wholly at the service of the British.

The anti-British feeling glimpsed in the Australian scenes is intensified with the Australians' contact with the British Light Horse in Cairo where Frank and his mates are dismissed by British officers as 'undisciplined'. And, at Gallipoli itself, it is clear that they are to draw the Turks out of the way so as to protect the British. Officer/men resentment (hinted at as the soldiers watch Major Barton drink champagne as he listens to his gramophone) falls before the stronger resentment against the British when Barton is commanded by the British Colonel (John Morris) to order his men to advance, with bayonets at the ready but no bullets, in spite of the Turks having dug in. They are cut to pieces and the camera pans slowly over the dead and dying.

The men who are left know that the next order will send them to death, and medals, watches, rings and other mementos are left in the Australian trench when they climb out into 'the valley of the shadow of death' as the 23rd Psalm is read on the soundtrack. For a change, a freeze-frame ending means something: the final frame leaves us with a clear sense of lives cut short in utter futility.

Near the start of this review, I suggested that this film shows Weir extending his range and changing direction. In doing so, I suspect he has made his most successful film to date, and also that David Williamson's screenplay has been a major asset and influence. Williamson is not the kind of writer likely to embrace the sorts of concepts Weir explored in *Picnic at Hanging Rock* or *The Last Wave*. Nor has he ever been as tidy in his structures as *The Cars that Ate Paris* and *The Plumber* were.

Gallipoli is more loosely inclusive than the latter two, less determinedly enigmatic than the former two. It knows where it is going, without being in any particular hurry about it or without spelling out its themes. It manages to be a humane, and moving reconstruction of times past without succumbing to nostalgia. Those who wish to do so may see in it a critique of subsequent Australian involvement in world events, but this will not be crucial to a reading of the film.

Cinema Papers, July–August 1981.

4

84 CHARING CROSS ROAD

Is there any truth in the rumour that *84 Charing Cross Road* will next appear on ice? To date, what began as an exchange of letters between a lively Jewish bibliophile in New York, Helene Hanff, and an antiquarian bookseller in London, Frank Doel, has metamorphosed first into book form, from which an engaging sense of character emerged, then as a 1975 television production, next as a stage-play (London 1981, Broadway 1982), and now as a film whose production was divided between the two relevant countries.

That this unlikely best-seller has proved so media-flexible is probably due to the development of its central relationship, which is fuelled by a love of books, is several times on the verge of the consummation of meeting, and is thwarted twice by Hanff's financial problems and finally by Doel's death shortly before Hanff at last realised her dream of getting to London. The relationship is essentially a conversation in letters and the film very properly uses a good deal of voice-over and direct address to camera to convey this. As director David Jones cuts between the two, he renders both the common bibliophiliac zest and the complementary nature of the two personalities, her ebullience playing off against his humorous reserve.

Though the film's two protagonists necessarily dominate, there is a lively sense of other lives going on around them. In London, there are Frank's quiet colleagues at 84 Charing Cross. Road and his Irish wife Nora (Judi Dench), who is both slightly jealous of his epistolary rapport with Hanff and, along with the shop people, grateful for the food parcels she sends them in Britain's post-war austerity. In New York there are Hanff's acting and writing friends who create around her a relaxed sense of community. As well, there is an unobtrusively realised apprehension of time passing, from meat-queues to mini-skirts in London, from brownstone front to glassy apartment blocks in a New York troubled by student demonstrations.

Film's mobility in representing shifts in time and place permits a clear discrimination between New York (sunny, lively, cheerful) and London (muted and poky, moving from austerity to affluence). The contrasts in the film's diegetic world are created in cuts from Hanff's carelessly poured gin and tonic to the tea-making rituals of Charing Cross Road, from the Brooklyn Dodgers to the Tottenham Hotspurs, from Hanff's disorderly apartment to the Doels' neatly suburban flat. In an absurdly touching moment, Hanff's love of England links the two worlds as she listens rapt to the Queen's coronation on the radio while the Doels watch the event on television, serving their friends with ham sandwiches derived from Hanff's largesse.

The contrasts are reinforced by the film's attention to the look of the two places (the result of loving care in production and costume design in each, and of Brian West's luminous and versatile camera work) and by the acting styles of the two protagonists. Anne Bancroft and Anthony Hopkins, each playing with detailed, sympathetic understanding, complement each other perfectly and establish their growing regard in a way that is a treat for audiences who love film acting.

In its small-scale way, *84 Charing Cross Road* is a charming, civilised piece, often witty, full of the pleasurable warmth of relationships securely realised, and at certain key points, most notably Hanff's reception of Frank Doel's death, very moving indeed.

Cinema Papers, July 1987.

5

HOPE AND GLORY

1987 has proved a very good year for cinematic nostalgia. Not only has there been a lot of it but the quality has been superior. In their disparate ways films such as *Charing Cross Road*, *Peggie Sue Got Married*, *The Tin Men*, *Hoosiers* and *Radio Days* have all engaged in the remembrance of things past and, in one way or other, achieved an intelligent purchase on their material. And now *Hope and Glory*, a surprising departure for director John Boorman, joins their ranks.

Like all the films above, *Hope and Glory* has the look and sound of its period and place – England in World War II – superbly right. Like *Radio Days*, it offers essentially a child's-eye-view of a vanished world, bringing us to the verge of nostalgic indulgence time and again, then at the crucial moment undercutting this tendency with comedy or a severer truth.

The film is marvellously evocative of time and place, immaculate in its observation of the outbreak of war, of London in the blitz, of evacuee trains, of beaches fenced off with coils of barbed wire, the well-known voices of political leaders and stammering king on the radio. All of this has, of course, been done before, but not often with such wit and demystifying seriousness. And a good deal of its effect is due to its use of Bill Rohan (Sebastian Rice-Edwards), the sharp-eyed, imaginative child who stands in for the young John Boorman.

War is the greatest fun for young Bill who protests to his mother against evacuation with 'I'm gonna miss the war and it's all your fault.' He doesn't, however, and he and his gang prowl the rubble of bombed suburbia, nightmarishly lit to recall the waste land of Paul Nash's 'The Menin Road', acting out war-time clichés ('We have ways of making you talk'), and learning about sex (an orderly inspection of what is concealed by the bloomers of a girl called Pauline) and death (Pauline's mum is killed one night).

So, it is not a war film but a film about coping with war. For Bill and his friends, indeed for everyone, there is a heightened excitement that goes along with the anxieties, a sense of ceaseless activity and movement that has shaken up the lower-middle-class suburb. But what accounts for so much of the film's pleasure is not so much the careful reconstruction of the period as the unexpectedness of some of its observation.

Bill's mother, Grace (Sarah Miles), finds that, when her husband goes off ('typing for victory' in a clerical job, as he says), she likes being on her own. Her friend Mollie (Susan Wooldridge, Daphne in *Jewel In The Crown*) goes off with a Polish pilot, leaving the husband who confesses to having loved Grace but has been too poor in the Depression to think of marrying. Bill's teenage sister Dawn (Sammi Davis) meets a young Canadian corporal (Jean-Marc Barr) but, instead of falling lyrically in love with him, finds she wants him with sexual urgency. The solemnity of the King's Speech on Christmas Day is undercut by Bill's drunken Grandpa (Ian Bannen) reeling off a list of floozies he has known.

All this is given coherence by Bill's watchful attempts to make sense of adult sexual behaviour. Even his friends' games are touched with this as they 'torture' an intruder, claimed to be a Yank: 'Teach him a lesson. Think they can come over here and take our women'. Less complex than sex and death, cricket, with the arcane mysteries of the googly passed on to Bill by his father at the outbreak of war 'in case anything happens to me', is a source of continuing solace in the boy's world so lovingly and unsentimentally recreated in the film.

When the Rohan house is hit and the family is forced to move in with Grace's parents in the Thames Valley, the film assumes the look of childhood idyll. While the ridiculous old Grandpa complains of 'Too many women in my family, all hens and no cocks', Bill and his younger sister explore a wonderland of river and summer green. But even this idyll is laced with farce and tensions.

As Churchill announces 'the end of the beginning' on the radio, the riverside greenery is just touched with autumnal gold. Ah, one thinks, a rites-of-passage movie, but the nostalgia for childhood itself is recognised for what it is. Childhood is seen as a time of incomplete understanding and the film is wry and tough enough to see that adults mostly botch things as well.

Hope and Glory resonates with echoes of other films. One recalls those Hollywood England films of the 1940s in which Britain was seen as moving towards a cross-class consensus, a community spirit replacing old divisions. There is an air-raid shelter sequence which recalls *Mrs Miniver* where the little ones had *Alice in Wonderland* read to them: here, the shelter is so dankly repulsive no one can bear to go into it. There is even a German pilot rounded up in a suburban allotment by an incompetent policeman to 'place' comically Mrs Miniver's heroic behaviour in similar circumstances. And there are echoes of John Schlesinger's *Yanks* in young Dawn's succumbing to the Canadian, and of many other British or Hollywood accounts of embattled Britain.

But *Hope and Glory* is both funnier and more affecting than any of these, largely because (for the most part) it keeps Bill at its centre, and because of its tonal delicacy. 'In all my life nothing has ever matched the pure joy of that moment', says the mature Bill's voice on the soundtrack. This tremulous pronouncement is not the result of some deep spiritual experience: it is the child's heartfelt response to the bombing of his school. 'Thank you, Adolph', shouts one of the little boys on this occasion in which the tone of the film is so beautifully epitomised. Nostalgia is not often so much fun.

Cinema Papers, November 1987.

6

COMRADES

In 1834 six Dorset labourers were arrested, not for forming a Friendly Society, which was their right, but for the swearing of illegal oaths. As a result of the trumped-up charge (glancing reference is made to the King's brother and the Orange Lodge, with its secret oaths and meetings), the Tolpuddle six were transported to Australia. They were pardoned two years later as a result of agitation from the London-Dorset Committee and others.

Their story is rightly seen as a landmark in the trade union movement and Bill Douglas's film pays austere tribute to the solidarity of the working class then and, by implication, urges such rigorous coherence now. Against a background of changing seasons, as lowering skies and sodden roads give way to the lushness of spring and the gold of summer harvests, Douglas invokes a life of grinding work and of desperate poverty as well as, say, the sudden gaiety of a sailor dancing a hornpipe at the village fair. That is, he is careful and honest enough not to depict these lives as joyless: they are too rooted in home and family and community for that. Rarely, though, has the sheer arduousness of physical labour been so convincingly depicted on the screen: the film takes work and working lives with absolute seriousness, in ways that recall both Hardy and Brueghel.

The first half of this immensely long film slowly and painstakingly builds up the background to the arrest of the six labourers. There is an intense realism, visual and almost tactile, it seems, in these scenes of haymaking, of carpentry, of sparse family meals, but ultimately it is not realism which Douglas is primarily after. What in fact he seems to have sought is a genuinely epic quality, achieving a Brechtian interplay between realistic enactment and distancing observation. One is moved by the individual lives dramatised before one, but is constantly made aware of the element of illusion so potently at work in their presentation.

The chief means by which this is effected is the use of an itinerant lanternist, who arrives in Tolpuddle after seeing the brutal suppression of an outburst of machine-smashing by labourers whose wages have been cut to below subsistence level. The lanternist, played by a Douglas regular, Alex Norton, turns up in various guises, most often in connection with the film's insistence on the apparatus of illusion. He is, for instance, a silhouette artist in colonial New South Wales, an outback photographer whose heliotypes are inadvertently destroyed, as well as engaging with other pre-cinema optical devices and presenting various theatrical performances. As well, there are carefully composed and magically lit shots of silhouetted figures, a fluted glass door which reveals three different images, depending on the angle of viewing, and an animated map which records the journey from England to Botany Bay.

Douglas himself has claimed: '… what I wanted to suggest was the *magic* of things, rather than just depict them accurately'. The lanternist is sometimes part of the action (e.g., as a policeman), sometimes a commentator on it. In the latter role, one of his functions is to draw attention to the fictional, magical elements of the narrative process. Douglas achieves a real involvement with the lives presented but never lets the viewer forget that that is what he is: a viewer manipulated by processes of illusion-making.

The second part of the film is set in Australia and pursues the fortunes of the transported Tolpuddle Martyrs. It is still absorbing but it is so in more conventional ways. One works on a chain-gang making an outback road; one evades seduction by the rich widow who has concealed news of his pardon; one is bought by a fop; and so on. It is more obviously a many-stranded narrative, individual protagonists replacing the earlier sense of a class at bay, and with some predictable anti-colonialist swipes. It is also more obviously spectacular than the British section: this is partly perhaps the result of a shift to a bolder landscape, but is more subtly to do with the loss of the delicate balance between realism and the display of illusionism that has characterised the film's first half. The acting has become bolder, with somewhat florid cameos from James Fox (as the Governor), Vanessa Redgrave (the widow), and Arthur Dignam (the fop), and though these have their pleasures they belong to a different tradition from the more nearly minimalist acting styles of the Dorset section.

However, all this, in the context of the film as a whole, is not much more than a quibble. Further, the film ends back in London with a celebration of the return of the Tolpuddle Martyrs, one of whom, George Loveless, in close-up on a darkening stage, calls on 'every working man in England to shake off that supineness … that leaves them in the position of slaves'. And he thanks the lanternist who has 'told the story today – it was almost as if he had been present throughout himself'. The film ends unequivocally on the didactic note it has so frequently struck before. Not just in dialogue, but in the sudden juxtapositions created by editing (between, for example, the establishment clergyman urging 'us to be satisfied with our lot' and the chapel congregation singing 'We'll win the day'), in the willingness to hold shots so long that we begin to notice the length (the images of the chained men whom the film insists we remember), in the use of the lanternist's devices. The lanternist may trade in illusion but, in the end, it is a version of reality he brings to his audiences.

Even the casting seems part of the didactic intention. The heroes and their families are played by largely unknown actors: they might be anyone and their importance is to represent a class rather than individuals. They are supported by 'stars', most of whom appear briefly as oppressors of this class, the exceptions being Michael Hordern as Pitt, a leading member of the Committee that secures pardon for the men, and John Hargreaves as the convict who fails to escape, having been warned that he can't achieve anything alone.

Douglas has made a major film in *Comrades* and, if the British cinema is indeed to enjoy a renaissance of some kind, one would like to think such a film might be in its forefront. However, it is uncompromising in ways which will probably not ease its commercial path: its first two-thirds resists the conventional lines of narrative; it is prepared to risk slowness and didacticism, and it keeps exposing its own apparatus. For those prepared to stay with it, it is also one of the richest film experiences of the year.

Cinema Papers, January 1988.

7

THE WHALES OF AUGUST

Nothing very much happens in *The Whales of August*, in the way that nothing very much happens in a Chekhov play. That is, the surface of the lives it depicts is disturbed only by the minutiae of everyday living and the deeper currents that threaten this are ultimately deflected, leaving the surface nevertheless subtly changed.

In Lindsay Anderson's film, the lives that matter are those of two old sisters, Sarah (Lillian Gish), hopeful and romantic, and Libby (Bette Davis), blind and acerbic, living out their daily rituals on an island off the coast of Maine. Sarah tends the garden and prepares meals and, in the film's 'crisis', wonders if she can go on looking after Libby who 'was always a difficult woman at the best of times', according to their cheerful, flirtatious neighbour Tisha (Ann Sothern). The crisis passes when Libby gives in to Sarah's yearning for a picture window, a gesture to the future, and two gnarled hands reach out to each other across the screen. In the superlative last segment of the film, the two old ladies walk slowly down to the point, wondering if the whales have all gone. 'You can never tell,' is Libby's quietly life-affirmative answer.

If this sounds like sentimentality, that is my fault. Sweetness and strength, not sentimentality, are the film's hallmarks. Anderson, the director of *If*… and *O Lucky Man*, is not interested in a variation of

On Golden Pond. He offers old age without quavers or quaintness, and without compromise in the sense that there are no young people to offer obvious contrast and no attempt to smarten up the film's pace, which is unhurried but never slow. The pace is mimetic of the lives represented, the odd pause and stillness are as important as movement.

The film's control of *mise-en-scène* is masterly, whether of the warm, beautifully lit, pine-panelled interiors or the serenely lovely exteriors. In the former, the camera moves with unfussy fluency to rest upon the relics of a lifetime; in the latter the moonlight shimmers on and shadows drift across the waters of the bay in ways that are instinct with drama rather than mere pictorialism. The eye is again and again struck by the sheer beauty of the compositions, but it is a beauty that tells us about the lives lived in this place, not just the result of formal virtuosity.

Ann Sothern, Vincent Price, as a Russian emigré of romantic if doubtful provenance, and Ford alumnus, Harry Carey Jr, as a local handyman, provide the most engaging support to the two incomparable performances at the film's core.

From Lillian Gish and Bette Davis, Anderson has wrought performances which miraculously and aptly seem to sum up their whole careers. The fact of their belonging to two different acting generations and traditions – one the greatest silent screen actress, the other arguably the greatest talkies star – is made to work in the film's favour, as are their on- (and off-) screen personae. The endurance and purity one associates with Gish, the tenacity and abrasiveness of Davis, are at the service of roles which draw on both and which extend them in ways that are beautiful to watch. Gish's celebration by candlelight, with a glass of port and a rose, of the anniversary of her wedding to her long-dead husband, and Davis's stroking her face with the locket and strand of hair of *her* late husband are as moving as anything either has ever done.

It is not often the cinema offers actresses in their eighties full-length roles, let alone roles which do them so much honour. Neither has had such an opportunity in nearly 40 years and they rise magnificently to the occasion. Anyone interested in the cinema's acting traditions will want to see *The Whales of August*; so will anyone interested in seeing the spectacle of life subtly transformed into the stuff of drama.

Cinema Papers, November 1988.

8

THERE'S A LOT GOING ON IN *AUSTRALIA*

Baz Luhrmann's Claim to the Epic

You've got to admire the cheek of a director who calls his film simply *Australia*. It implies that what is going on in it is comprehensive enough, or at least symptomatic enough, to evoke the continent at large. Can it possibly live up to such a grandiose announcement of intention? There have been plenty of films named for cities (*New York, New York* [Martin Scorsese, 1977], *Barcelona* [Whit Stillman, 1994], most recently *Paris* [Cédric Klapisch, 2008]), but summoning a city seems a modest enterprise compared with a country or a continent (please sort us out, Senator Palin). D.W. Griffith in 1924 and Robert Downey Sr. in 1986 had a go with *America*: neither director is today remembered for his attempt to aggrandise the personal into the national.

What we indubitably get in Baz Luhrmann's new film is Australia as landscape – but landscape of a restricted kind. Does Luhrmann believe that it is only Dorothea Mackellarland (all 'sweeping plains' and 'ragged mountain ranges' and 'droughts and flooding rains') that the world at large will recognise as Australia? What he shows us is gorgeous beyond the shadow of a doubt – gorgeous, that is, to look at on a huge screen rather than to live in. It is, though, hardly the

'Australia' that most of its inhabitants will know intimately, living as we do in our urban fastnesses, but the pictorial arts have done their bit in instilling it as one of the sites of our yearning.

Perhaps it's really a love story at heart, a love story in a huge setting that overpowers its fragile forays into intimacy. The film is wildly overlong at 165 minutes (are directors paying attention to my efforts to have films limited to ninety minutes and to their losing a finger for every minute over?), and, whatever its virtues, none of the film's preoccupations is developed in such a way as to earn this running time. As a love story, and I'll come back to this, *Australia* might easily become Luhrmann's *Ryan's Daughter* (1970), and look what *that* did to David Lean's career.

But maybe Luhrmann's real concern, the subject of portentous captions fore and aft, is the plight of Australia's Aborigines and especially the tragedy of the 'Stolen Generations'. Or the clash of the conflicting values of Aboriginal earth knowledge and white man's greed and insensitivity? Or the idea of English upper-crust hauteur being humanised by rugged Australian values? Or the notion of Australia's being pulled into nationhood by its response to foreign invasion?

Clearly this is a film in which a lot is going on, and further examination may indicate that Luhrmann has bitten off more than he can chew in the course of one, albeit mammoth-length, film. Coherence and dramatic development may be imperilled in the process.

None of the above is written in the spirit of one soured off by the massive hype that has surrounded this film, as if it were perhaps to put the Australian industry on a new international footing. I write as one who has greatly admired Luhrmann's output to date. Think of the mixed modes of *Strictly Ballroom* (1992, musical crossed with mockumentary procedures), the transplanting of Shakespeare, verbally intact, from old Verona to twentieth-century Venice Beach, California, in *Romeo + Juliet* (1996) and the hybrid pyrotechnics of *Moulin Rouge!* (2001). These are, each in its own way, the work of a risk-taker, of an iconoclast with the courage (and capacity) of his iconoclasm, from concept to execution. Luhrmann has been that rare phenomenon in Australian cinema: one who has been willing to upset preconceptions and follow his own imaginative convictions with panache and persuasion.

His new film, though, may well be his most conventional to date, in spite of all the high-sounding verbiage that has been spilled in its promotion. For instance, the press kit tells us:

> Australia is a metaphor for the feelings of mystery, romance and excitement conjured by a distant, exotic place where people can transform their lives, spirits can be reborn, and love conquers all.

Luhrmann himself has said of his wish to make an 'epic' of the kind he loved as a child:

> I wanted to create a cinematic work that would be similarly inclusive because I feel passionately about having more inclusiveness in our lives. Bringing people together brings comfort to the heart and soul in this unpredictable world.[1]

Well, in box-office terms he may well be proved to have achieved his aim, but in doing so I'd say he has sacrificed the dash and daring and sharpness of his earlier films.

Revisiting the epic

I've written elsewhere of what seems to be a resurgence of popular genres in recent Australian cinema,[2] drawing attention to the antipodean spin given to the likes of the western, the musical, the teen movie and the biopic. In view of this, I was interested to see what Luhrmann would make of the epic, a costly genre not common in Australian filmmaking. I wonder, though, whether he has actually made anything new and distinctive of the genre, and on the whole the answer seems to be 'no'.

It's not actually clear what he means by epic, citing as he does such disparate works as *Gone with the Wind* (Victor Fleming, 1939), *Lawrence of Arabia* (David Lean, 1962) and *Titanic* (James Cameron, 1997). Does he use the term simply to summon up very long, sprawling, expensive works? If so, then, yes, *Australia* qualifies. If, however, it refers to a work in which 'the style is appropriately elevated to the greatness of the deeds'[3] that carry the narrative, then that requires only a qualified answer here. So does the extent to which the film conforms to the Brechtian idea of 'the objectivity of epic narrative',[4] in which the events are put before us so as to encourage criticism rather than acceptance of the social conditions represented in the drama. To turn more specifically to the idea of the 'film epic', Jeffrey Richards has recently argued for the importance of the way historical epics give 'the events a contemporary resonance by constructing them as an explicit commentary' on the events of the period in which they are made.[5]

It is not Luhrmann's fault if the film has been trumpeted in ways that would have made the Second Coming seem disappointing, but, as he is on record as wanting to produce a work in the epic mode, it is not inappropriate to consider what that might mean and how far the film lives up to such expectations. If *Australia* does exhibit epic characteristics, its lineage is less those films to which the descriptor is usually applied than that of the large-scale Westerns. Its cattle drive inevitably recalls *Red River* (Howard Hawks, 1948) and its scenic grandeurs invoke the memory of such Fordian masterworks as *The Searchers* (John Ford, 1956) and *Cheyenne Autumn* (John Ford, 1964), the interracial conflict of these latter also echoed in *Australia*. There is even a cultured outback drunk, Kipling Flynn (Jack Thompson), whose lineage stretches at least back to Thomas Mitchell in *Stagecoach* (John Ford, 1939).

But while there are some stunning shots of a vast herd of cattle as it is being driven to the port of Darwin, as a 'Western epic' the film lacks the power and threat of *The Proposition* (John Hillcoat, 2005), the previous Australian film which sought to revitalise the Western genre in a new location. Essentially, the film shows interest in some Big Themes but doesn't sufficiently articulate them in terms of character and action.

A curious lack of chemistry

How does *Australia* measure up as a love story? It clearly counts on the star power of Nicole Kidman and Hugh Jackman in this respect, but they are at the service of a screenplay that delineates and motivates them too meagrely. As everyone probably knows by now, Kidman plays a haughty English aristocrat, Lady Sarah Ashley, who comes to Australia in 1939 to see what her husband has been up to and to sell their huge outback property, the aptly if not subtly named 'Faraway Downs'. She arrives in Darwin, where she is appalled at some very macho Australian behaviour that at one point involves her lingerie being scattered in the dusty street. To get to 'Faraway' she is driven by Jackman, a very independent type, not about to be cowed by an uppity English milady, and who answers only to 'Drover', a name that announces his work and perhaps his legendary status.

There is something very familiar in the way these two are being set up as a potential couple. You can almost imagine how the initial scenario might have read: 'There was antagonism between them from the start', as if they were some latter-day John Wayne/Maureen O'Hara duo. When Drover is not making such suave remarks to her as 'I wouldn't have it on with you if you were the only tart left in Australia', he is offering philosophical gems like 'In the end the only thing you really own is your story, so live a good one'. He is also presented, in all his rugged masculinity, as a man of liberal principles, correcting Sarah when she speaks of 'the natives'. She will naturally come to rely on his drover's capacities when she decides to move her cattle to Darwin to be shipped off for food for the troops, thus outwitting unscrupulous neighbouring cattle baron King Carney (Bryan Brown), who has his eye on 'Faraway'. Drover, in his turn, will come to admire Sarah's resilience and her maturing sympathies. At least, that's what the screenplay (the work of such distinguished hands as Ronald Harwood, Richard Flanagan and Stuart Beattie – a cook or two too many?) seems to have in mind.

Sarah and Drover simply don't work as a romantic couple, and this is as much due to the scripting as to the curious lack of chemistry between them. Kidman does well enough as Lady Ashley stalking about her English stately home in her stylish riding attire, barking out orders. She is described by someone as 'a genuine aristocrat' when she arrives in Darwin, and someone else, to signal the tough new world she's come to, pronounces her 'Not a bad-looking sheila'. One of the film's oppositions is epitomised there in the contrasting modes of appraisal. This will be echoed, again none too subtly, in Drover's long-held wish to 'mate an English thoroughbred with an Australian bush brumby', for which of course we read the two leads.

Kidman's initially convincing accent soon wobbles somewhat, and disappears altogether with a speed that is scarcely credible. And talking of 'speed', her changes of heart are too arbitrary: you'd think that, in so long a film, there would have been time for a more believable softening of her brittle imperiousness. Jackman certainly looks like a leading man, is given a chance to display his well-muscled torso, and is a persuasive action hero, dealing authoritatively with cattle and stroppy pub types, but the script just doesn't give him much help with the more intimate moments. Their first kiss, ushered in with huge close-ups, is curiously devoid of passion, and there is a sex scene shot discreetly enough not to offend your Auntie Joan. As if to compensate for this, it is followed – and this sort of editing move is par for the film's course – by a wild tracking shot that takes in the post-'wet' renewal of the landscape.

The look and feel of Australia

The landscape of outback Australia is perhaps peculiarly amenable to the epic treatment. Again and again, the film offers vistas of craggy outcrops and endless dusty tracts (or of Darwin harbour) that are simply breathtaking to look at, but one becomes tired of having one's breath taken away so predictably. By this I mean not only that one begins to intuit a vast panorama coming on, but also the ways in which these shifts of scale are rendered. A comparatively small moment will almost inevitably cut to a huge long-shot that seems to take in an area the size of Tasmania; not only that, cinematographer Mandy Walker can't resist pulling up for these wide overhead shots, so that the camera's procedures assume the status of nervous tic. This sounds ungrateful for some imposingly lit and composed vistas, but accompanied, as they too often are, by David Hirschfelder's too-emphatic musical score, you begin to feel you are being coerced into admiration.

As to the look and sound of the film, the production and costume design by Luhrmann's partner and collaborator Catherine Martin are less strikingly in evidence than in some of their earlier films but still contribute substantially to the film's pleasures. Personally, I have little knowledge of how women were dressing in the period of the film, but Martin's designs skilfully differentiate among Kidman's elegant raiment (on and off horseback), the ladies of the Darwin social ascendancy, and the Aboriginal women in their unassuming dresses. And as to production design, Martin gives 'Faraway' a look of credible English influence at work in an unlikely setting, describing how she set out to 'achieve the major textural changes the homestead undergoes from the dilapidated state we first see it in, to the green oasis it eventually becomes'.[6] Similarly, her recreation of various Darwin settings (in Bowen, Queensland, to be exact) in the period leading up to the Japanese invasion gives off an air of both authenticity and foreboding. Her work in fact is the key continuity with Luhrmann's earlier films, and award nominations are surely as inevitable as they are deserved.

The sound of the film is less securely achieved, whether in some false notes struck in the dialogue or in the utterly eclectic scoring which takes in Cole Porter's 'Begin the Beguine', 'Waltzing Matilda', snatches of Beethoven and, I was assured, Elgar, as well as the symbolically charged 'Over the Rainbow'. Whereas musical eclecticism had served *Moulin Rouge!*'s drama and fantasy so well, here it gives a merely distractingly polyglot effect. Nevertheless, one of the most memorable moments in the film is that set in the open-air cinema at

Darwin with *The Wizard of Oz* (Victor Fleming, 1939) playing, and Judy Garland's singing of that song to that mixed audience hints at possibilities and longings that confer an emotional intimacy and a thematic potency that ring truer than the film's bigger 'statements'.

The idea that the epic film should resonate with contemporary importance has perhaps been paid too heavy-handed a service in *Australia*'s dealings with Aboriginal life and its representation. The concept of the 'Stolen Generations' is one of the significant ideological issues of our time, but the film's explicit foregrounding of it in opening and closing captions suggests that the liberal point of view hasn't been tellingly enough dramatised in the film's narrative texture. In fact, it has. The character of Nullah (Brandon Walters), the 'half-caste' child, who is always in danger of being snatched away into the care of no doubt well-meaning even if misguided missioners, encapsulates the sense of non-belonging. Even so, the film feels a need to let him emphasise his problem of not 'belonging' anywhere, as if it didn't trust the drama of the narrative to make this point. This is not to question the film's liberal sentiments, chiefly articulated by Drover, whose Aboriginal wife has died because 'white' hospitals wouldn't treat her tuberculosis, or in the pitiable abuse to which 'half-caste' children (cries of 'creamy') are routinely subjected. Further, one applauds the eloquent presence of such notable Aboriginal actors as David Gulpilil, as Nullah's grandfather, often depicted in iconic postures that recall Gulpilil's first appearances in *Walkabout* (Nicolas Roeg, 1971); David Ngoombujarra, memorable pawn in the legal game of *Black and White* (Craig Lahiff, 2002), as Drover's offsider; and, very winning, young Walters as the child caught in the middle. Their performances make redundant the spelling out. It is a pity because it is the situation of Aboriginal life and beliefs in the society that has marginalised them that gives the film its chief claim to the epic in the Brechtian sense.

As suggested earlier, the love story and the mixed-race conflict are only two of the film's narrative elements. As well, there is a drama about inheritance, the brittle Sarah determining to save 'Faraway Downs' with the help of Drover. There is the Anglo-Australian theme, not merely sketched in the Sarah–Drover skirmishes, but also in the mixed attitudes to the arrival of an English aristocrat and in the Aussie bully trying to take over the English-owned station (and from whom had the English owner taken it over in the first place?). The threat of war brings of course a heightened tension to all the plot's strands, without actually imbuing them with a coherence of purpose that would give shape to the film's epic intentions. The attack on Darwin is brilliantly staged and shot, but its function as the plot's *deus ex machina* is both oddly arbitrary and strangely muted.

One doesn't want to sound grudging about so eagerly awaited a film event from a major Australian filmmaker, and there are certainly things to admire about *Australia*. Compared though with the way Luhrmann made riotous eclecticism work so enchantingly for him in the patent artificialities of *Moulin Rouge!*, I have to say that, for me, the eclecticism in narrative motifs, casting and music of the new film remains a collection of scattered ambitions and effects. The breath, as I said earlier, is often taken by the film's physical grandeurs, but the heart is rarely stopped.

Metro, No. 159, 2018.

Notes

1 *Australia*, production notes, p.3.
2 Brian McFarlane, *'Groupings and Gropings in Australian Cinema: Adi Wimmer's Australian Film Cultures, Identities, Texts'*, Overland, no. 193, Summer 2008, pp.95–96.
3 Sylvan Barnet et al., *A Dictionary of Literary Terms*, Constable, London, 1964, p.60.
4 M.H. Abrams, *A Glossary of Literary Terms*, 4th edition, Holt, Rinehart and Winston, 1981, p.52.
5 Jeffrey Richards, *Hollywood's Ancient Worlds*, Continuum, London, 2008, p.1.
6 *Australia*, op. cit., p.5.

9

SHAKESPEARE'S BRAVE NEW WORLD AND JULIE TAYMOR'S *TEMPEST*

Anyone who remembers Julie Taymor's 2000 version of *Titus Andronicus*, Shakespeare's first published play, will not be expecting a reverential treatment of what is reputedly his last, but the film does move more or less inexorably to the play's final wisdom: 'The rarer action is/ In virtue than in vengeance'. *The Tempest* is a difficult play, fraught with tensions which resonate perhaps even more forcefully in our time than in Shakespeare's. But over-all it is pervaded by a sense of 'lastness', of moving almost painfully towards resolution of what may have seemed irreconcilable conflicts, as if its author shared with Miranda her view of a 'brave new world/ That has such people in't'.

This is not a play with a powerful forward narrative thrust, in the manner of, say, *Macbeth*; *The Tempest* is more ruminative as it draws its several threads together. There is, though, a lot going on, with three main arenas of action, all taking their starting point from the eponymous storm and resulting shipwreck which brings upheaval to the worlds of Prospero and Miranda, of the slave Caliban, and of the royal castaways. Over these diverse groupings hovers the figure of Prospero himself, as puppet-master and magician, standing metaphorically perhaps for the playwright with his own command over his created drama and appraising the values of the life he has lived.

The Tempest has attracted filmmakers of maverick hue. The two most recent screen adaptations are Derek Jarman's in 1974 and Peter Greenaway's *Prospero's Books* in 1991. Actually, Jarman's film, despite some bizarre trappings (e.g., Elizabeth Welch, as a 'goddess', leading a chorus of sailors in 'Stormy Weather'), offered a surprisingly plain reading of the text. Greenaway was essentially more venturesome, and to eloquent effect, virtually setting the whole film in Prospero's mind and stressing his manipulation of all the other characters, to the point of speaking most of their lines. Above all, he had a legendary stage Prospero, John Gielgud, at the centre of this imaginative and resourceful filmmaking, which made us see the original work in a new light – surely the real goal of adaptation.

Taymar's *Titus* created the network of jealousies at work in the Roman Empire with a fine visual sweep that brought the saga of revenge-begetting-revenge to potent screen life. The film was often breathtaking in its panoramic compositions or sudden close-ups, boldly juxtaposing ancient Rome with 1930s music or with young punks drinking beer from cans. Flamboyant stuff certainly, but preferable to that reverence before the idea of Shakespeare that stifles imagination.

Now, with *The Tempest,* she calls on some of the same cinematic daring, if not perhaps with quite the same success in tackling a more complex play. The abiding challenge in filming Shakespeare seems to me the reconciling of the screen's remorseless demand for a level of visual realism with the equally remorseless artifice of the iambic pentameters. Sometimes Taymar overdoes the realism effect, filling the screen with wonderful shots of daunting terrains (various Hawaiian locations), then cutting to a huge close-up of a face or to a wild flight of fantasy, as in creating Ariel's ubiquitous exercise of his powers.

The centrepiece is of course Prospero – or Prospera, as she has become in Taymar's view of the play. In Helen Mirren's incarnation, she is utterly dominant physically, whether depicted on a rocky outcrop against the sky or observing the results of her handiwork as (the adolescent) Miranda and Ferdinand respond to each other. No one else in the film has anything like such a presence (except maybe Caliban, whose skin looks like a parched lake-bed), and she speaks the lines with the authority of wisdom and experience as the many close-ups attest, with some touches of unexpected humour. The issue of gender has often been raised in relation to this play which seems to insist on the absoluteness of patriarchy, but Taymar mines it provocatively, and Mirren is persuasive enough to ward off accusations of mere trendiness.

The other contemporary resonance is in the way the play touches on matters of post-colonial critique. At the most obvious level, Caliban has been relegated to the most inhospitable parts of the island and the African actor Djimon Hounsou projects the anger and poignancy of the subjugated 'native'. At film's end he too is embraced in the new spirit of reconciliation, just as Ben Whishaw's androgynous Ariel is given his freedom. The autocrat Prospera has given way to a new spirit of understanding and forgiveness, surrendering her more-than-human powers by hurling their symbol, her staff, into the sea.

Some of the beauty of the verse is sacrificed to the film's visual flamboyance, starting with the brilliantly staged shipwreck, but film *is* a visual medium. If sometimes the stunning vistas seem too artfully composed, the compensation is in close-ups which do brilliant service to the play's intentions – and words.

Australian Book Review, May 2011.

10

THE ODD COUPLE

Language and Life Lessons in *The King's Speech*

On the face of it, novelist J.M. Coetzee wouldn't seem to have much common ground with the problems of the British royal family, but I was struck by this sentence from his *Diary of a Bad Year*: 'The rule of succession is not a formula for identifying the best ruler, it is a formula for conferring legitimacy on someone or other and thus forestalling civil conflict.'[1] In the case of George VI, he never expected the line of succession would push him into top spot and he was ill-equipped for the job, but he worked hard enough and lived long enough to justify this baton-passing process.

His main problem was a very bad stammer that made public occasions especially harrowing for him, exacerbating a natural shyness. In coming to *The King's Speech* (Tom Hooper, 2010), I had the unusual experience of finishing the book of the same title just one hour before seeing the film.[2] This complicated the experience of the film for me in some interesting ways. The book had only recently become available and had been written in the wake of the film, so it is not an adaptation from page to screen, but rather an elaboration in light of the research surrounding the film's central subject matter. I found it difficult to view the film without thinking of what the book revealed about the king and his speech therapist. Should this have been irrelevant or not?

A complex intertextuality

In 2009, BBC Radio 4 aired a play called *A King's Speech*, which dealt with Lionel Logue's work in the matter of the Duke of York's (later King George VI's) speech difficulties. This led his grandson Mark Logue to 'appreciate that his life and work could be of interest to a far wider audience beyond [his] own family'. The following year, this episode in royal history was made the subject of an ambitious Anglo–Australian production now called *The King's Speech*, to be directed by Hooper and with an all-star cast drawing on the acting strength of the two producing countries. In 2009, Iain Canning, the film's producer, approached Mark Logue, and in the spirit of adviser – 'Logue Family Consultant' is his credit – he conducted wide-ranging research into his grandfather's role. Drawing above all on Lionel Logue's 'vividly written diaries' and his correspondence with the Duke/King, Mark came up with the absorbing book that details a remarkable, if little-known, byway of British history. Whether the film influences one's reading of the book, or whether it is the other way round, the two make for some very provocative comparisons. An interesting sidenote: David Seidler, the film's screenwriter, is planning a stage version in 2011.

The story's appearance across radio, film and stage is only one of the intertextual influences at play in one's viewing of the new film. The historical events that form the background to the personal story are themselves significant in recent history, and have been the subject of innumerable studies that, to varying degrees, many viewers will have in mind. As well, though, several recent films have drawn their narrative inspiration from true events. The most obvious example in the present context is Stephen Frears' *The Queen* (2006), a shrewd and compassionate study of monarchy under stress. Perhaps some viewers will also recall the popular 1978 television miniseries *Edward & Mrs Simpson*, which dramatised Edward VIII's abdication (with a definitive impersonation from Edward Fox) and the unwilling succession of 'Bertie', who was pushed into assuming the throne as George VI.

A more recent point of reference is director Tom Hooper's previous film, *The Damned United* (2009), based on the 44-day tenure of Brian Clough as manager of top football club Leeds United. Those who have seen this film may have in mind Hooper's way of making absorbing drama from true events. In *The Damned United*, he dramatised Clough's takeover from the club's legendary manager Don Revie: Clough disliked Leeds' dirty style of play and determined to change its image. In other words, there was an interest in the processes and repercussions of 'the line of succession', a matter near the heart of *The King's Speech*. More generally, one thinks of how other films have dealt with actual events, including such recent examples as *Balibo* (Robert Connolly, 2009) and *The Special Relationship* (Richard Loncraine, 2010), in which the unstructured interplay of everyday life is fashioned into drama.

My point is simply this: we rarely come to a film with no prior knowledge of its matter, and perhaps even more rarely does any film exist in a vacuum, without setting up echoes of other films, other texts, other events. Indeed, *The King's Speech* may have a richer and more varied intertextuality than most.

History boys

Apart from all the resonances of other film texts that make themselves felt in *The King's Speech*, behind its character drama there is the palpable sense of a tumultuous historical background. At the personal level, the austere, authoritarian figure of the 'sailor king', George V, was no one's idea of a loving father. While he may have loved his family, he had no skill in making his affection felt, which cannot have given poor stammering Bertie much confidence. At the public level, as England recovered first from World War I and then from the Depression, George V died.

Furthermore, the country stumbled into the crisis of the abdication. Edward VIII, very popular with the people (and especially with the ladies, several of whom had been his mistresses), fell for American divorcee Wallis Simpson. In his famous renunciation speech he told the anxious nation that he could no longer continue as king without 'the woman I love by my side', thus catapulting the diffident and unwilling Bertie into the limelight of top job. His unwillingness was partly a matter of congenital shyness, but it was hugely exacerbated by his speech defect. With the woman *he* loved by his side (by then Queen Elizabeth and later the Queen Mother) and with the help of Logue's therapy, he persisted and became a much respected monarch, giving the nation something like moral leadership through the grim days of World War II.

Bertie and Logue are the key figures in the personal drama of the film, but those other historical personages – George V, Queen Mary, Edward VIII, Mrs Simpson, Queen Elizabeth, the prime ministers Chamberlain and Churchill, and others – all bring memories of their roles in recent history. The filmmakers have necessarily given coherent presences to all of these figures in the film, and chosen carefully what to stress and what to soft-pedal about them. Personal and public histories are what the film goes to work on.

'We've become actors!'

George V hates making the Christmas Day broadcast, complaining in the film that these days of the emerging 'wireless' require kings to be vocal actors. This will of course be one of the film's key motifs in view of Bertie's fear of public utterance. The film's opening image is, appropriately, a close-up shot of an old-fashioned radio microphone. The announcer (a witty cameo from Adrian Scarborough) intones 'the new invention of radio' by way of introducing the Duke of York, Bertie (Colin Firth), who is standing by looking very apprehensive. Despite the comforting presence of his wife Elizabeth (Helena Bonham Carter), the speech is a disaster. After Bertie's physician recommends the relaxing powers of smoking and a mouth full of marbles, Elizabeth seeks out Australian speech therapist Lionel Logue (Geoffrey Rush). And thus the film's central drama is set in motion.

Logue insists that he will 'need trust and total equality', leading Elizabeth to tell him, 'You're awfully sure of yourself.' This sequence is followed by brief contrasting interludes of domestic intimacy: Bertie with his wife and daughters, and Logue with his wife and sons. These segments seem to be the film's way of announcing the total (dramatic) equality that must exist between its two protagonists, if not quite in the way that Logue imagines.

The real heart of the film is, then, in Logue's dealings with the future monarch. It is Logue's function to help Bertie become the sort of 'actor' his father has in mind, and the film is essentially structured around meetings between the two men, in which Logue helps Bertie to overcome his speech defect, and public occasions, where Bertie's progress as a royal actor can be observed. The dramatic impulse is in

Bertie's gradual mastering of the techniques Logue has taught him; perhaps surprisingly, these involve therapeutic bursts of four-letter words that prove cathartic for dealing with Bertie's frustrations. All this is treated without sentimentality as Bertie moves towards greater public confidence, culminating in a wartime Christmas speech. Hooper and Seidler avoid the inviting trap of the feel-good, in the interests of the genuinely inspirational.

In Colin Firth and Geoffrey Rush the film has two of the world's best actors at this moment, and both are at their best here. Firth, incomprehensibly overlooked at the Oscars last year for his grief-stricken academic in *A Single Man* (Tom Ford, 2009), has given a string of venturesome performances over the past decade, not trading on his looks as many a similarly equipped actor might have done. His subtle, heartbreaking work in *A Single Man* is possibly outdone here by his complexly nuanced study of the man who would be king despite his reluctance. The way frustration shades into aggression, the way it softens in response to Elizabeth's wifely solicitude, the way it registers a cautiously growing confidence on state occasions: in these and other situations Firth offers a wonderful display of what film acting can achieve.

There is a very interesting shift in the way the film presents Logue's character in comparison with the figure that emerges in his grandson's book and its primary source material – Logue's own diaries. The film coarsens Logue from his very first appearance, when he comes out of the toilet to greet the Duchess of York. The mere act of his calling the Duke 'Bertie' is a prime example of what I mean: certainly in Mark Logue's account, his grandfather made clear that the Duke would have to visit his rooms in Harley Street for treatment, but he would never have insisted to the Duchess that it has to be 'my game, my turf, my rules'. It is, in the light of the social reality of the time, unlikely that Logue would have been quite so quick to assert his equality as he does in Rush's compelling and vivacious account of the man.

The filmmakers have clearly decided that, for the sake of dramatic contrast, they would make Logue a much less respectful character than he seems to have been. As Mark Logue writes in summary, 'Indeed, to a modern reader, the tone Logue adopts when writing of the King can seem fawning.' This raises the question of what responsibilities filmmakers have to the actuality of their historical subjects, as distinct from those that might pertain to the case of adapting a fiction. This will not matter to viewers who don't read the book just before seeing the film, but those who do will bring to the latter a strong sense of a much more deferential Logue – just as determined to do his job to the best of his ability, but within the parameters of a historically more probable commoner-royal relationship.

One sees what Hooper and Seidler were up to in this matter. There is actually specific reference to the King's ignorance of how 'the people' live and how little they know of his life. It's as if the film wants to explore this gap of understanding, to suggest a common humanity, a common capacity for friendship. Perhaps, too, the filmmakers want to point to the way the colonies were losing any residual subservience to a distant monarchy. If so, this function is proleptic: many Australians would still refer to England as 'home' for a decade or more after the events of this film. What concerns me here is the degree of licence the 'adapter' of a real-life situation can reasonably take in order to make, say, a political or other cultural point. Such concerns inevitably followed my response to Rush's engaging performance, which seems to have little to do with the actual man's demeanour and attitudes.

The film's two stars are surrounded by a very impressive cast that brings the other historical figures (less problematically) to life. Helena Bonham Carter has done nothing so fine since *The Wings of the Dove* (Iain Softley, 1997), steely determination and wifely solicitude vying for precedence in the interests of Bertie's growing confidence, with a nicely waspish aside about Mrs Simpson's 'certain skills, acquired in an establishment in Shanghai'. Eve Best is an astonishing look-alike as the basilisk-eyed divorcee whom the Duchess ignores; Guy Pearce is an aptly handsome, feckless Edward; and the parents are magisterially incarnated in short studies by Michael Gambon as George V and Claire Bloom as Queen Mary, who falls to her knees in obeisance before Edward when her husband dies. There are also Derek Jacobi (Archbishop Lang), Jennifer Ehle (Mrs Logue), David Bamber as a theatre director making snide remarks about 'the colonies' when amateur actor Logue auditions for Richard III, and a vocally uncanny Churchill from Timothy Spall. I mention all these people because this is one of the most strongly cast films in years, and because there is complex interest in considering the extent to which the actors' personae are melded to what we know of the public figures they are representing.

The King's Speech might have become a mere Sunday-night TV drama, but it doesn't: it is persistently engrossing as it avoids cosiness and maintains a capacity to disconcert. In addition to the major virtues of acting, the film also has Eve Stewart's production design (a role she also filled on Hooper's *The Damned United*) and Jenny Beaven's costumes, which together evoke period and class associations with unerring eyes for detail. Just look at the Duchess idly flicking through the pages of *The Illustrated London News* as she waits for Bertie to finish his session with Logue, or any of her discreet ensembles in their pastel shades. These are creative talents that know what they're about – as does the film at large.

Metro, No. 168, March 2011.

Notes

1 J. M. Coetzee, *Diary of a Bad Year*, London, Viking, 2007, p.14.
2 Mark Logue & Peter Conradi, *The King's Speech*, London, Quercus, 2010.

11

CLOUDSTREET ANEW

Whereas the miniseries, most often based on revered literary texts, has been a staple of British television for fifty years, I could count on the fingers of a damaged hand its Australian counterparts. In fact, the miniseries in general, as distinct from serials that run for a longer or shorter period, seems never to have been as common here, though *The Dismissal* (1983) remains an Australian small-screen highlight. (As for those derived from novels the count is even sparser.)

However, last year delivered the goods in *Rake*, and 2011 may just be about to lift the miniseries score significantly: we've had the excellent *Paper Giants*, ostensibly about the founding of *Cleo* magazine but in fact an incisive study of changing cultural mores; we are promised a lavishly-cast version of Christos Tsiolkas's *The Slap*; and now, in mid-year, comes *Cloudstreet*. For my money, this may be the most adventurous miniseries ever made here.

Since it was published in 1995, Tim Winton's *Cloudstreet* has rightly won a key, or even the dreaded 'iconic', place in the annals of Australian fiction, including first place in *ABR*'s Favourite Australian Novel poll, in 2010. In its ambition and its scope, it aspires to an epic quality, a tract of time and place put before us for our contemplation as well as the more customary novelistic pleasure of emotional involvement. It is also, though, intensely poetic in its insights into how people relate to time and place.

At its heart are two families on their uppers, each with a major accident in its past, each of which will have an offspring that wants to break away from the family cycle. Otherwise, the families have little else in common when their fates bring them to live in a rundown house on the Swan River, near to Perth, in the decades after World War II. The house, inherited by the Pickles family and tenanted by the Lambs, assumes a presence in the novel, one that overrides the two disparate lifestyles practised by the families that share its roof – and yard. Further, the narrating voice of the novel goes beyond mere omniscient functionality, offering the reader strange and evocative perspectives on the lives of these families – and, indeed, on the very nature of family and of life itself.

So, what is television to make of this? The short answer is a great deal. For over a decade, there were attempts to film *Cloudstreet*, from a screenplay by Ella Fontana. Now, in the more expansive format of the 6-hour miniseries, Winton himself has worked with Fontana to produce a script that preserves the novel's over-all narrative trajectory, while also making something essentially new. Various characters, including some of the children of each family, are reduced to shadowy figures; some events are telescoped in the interests of dramatic impact; and the time-frame of the novel's twenty years has been reduced to ten, and there is less sense of 'size' as a result. The miniseries concentrates more fixedly on the house, the damaged boy, Fish Lamb, and the parallels, whether for contrast or comparison, between the two fathers, the two children who leave the nest (though 'eyrie' in some ways evokes it more vividly), and, most poignantly, the two mothers.

That still gives it plenty to go to work on, and director Matthew Saville, with much notable television and the taut, multi-plotted feature, *Noise* (2007), behind him, and with a slew of gifted collaborators, has made of the filmed *Cloudstreet* a television event both memorable and rare. By 'rare' I mean especially that this is a miniseries in which 'story' isn't everything. Those whose preferred TV tipple is Friday Night Crime will find it too reflective for their taste. I don't suggest that it is short of plot: the two families still converge on the house, the slovenly one offset against the more industrious one, though that makes it sound schematic, which it is not; Quick Lamb heads for the outback and Rose Pickles for the city before both return to set up with each other; and so on. What I mean is that here is television quite daringly espousing the poetic, in terms both visual (the house itself in its shabby grandeur) and verbal (Ron Haddrick's voice-over which inducts us into places beyond what meets the eye).

Without a vestige of sentimentality, the miniseries becomes a study in reconciliation. Rose and Quick, married in the nick of time before their baby is born, unite the unlikely pair of families, and Saville has chosen to end on this note rather than the book's image of the two mothers together in the garden. The last line is given to the adult whom Fish never fully becomes, but for me the moment that lingers is that in which, at the wedding celebration, the unbending Oriel Lamb (Kerry Fox) takes sluttish Dolly Pickles (Essie Davis) to dance. If this beautiful impulse of reaching out doesn't move you, you may not be a very nice person.

Australian Book Review, June 2011.

12

THE FILMMAKER AS ADAPTOR

Fred Schepisi Takes On Patrick White in *The Eye of the Storm*

It takes real nerve to come out of a film based on a famous novel and declare unreservedly that you enjoyed the film much more than the book. I mean, books came *first*. Literature, as a study, preceded film by *decades*. Adaptation of novels into film brings out the cultural cowardice in so many of us. Could you imagine anyone daring to 'prefer' a film version of, say, Charles Dickens' *Great Expectations* or Henry James' *The Portrait of a Lady* to their illustrious predecessors? Well, courageously, that is what I'm about to do.

Much of the reputation of the 'new Australian cinema' of the 1970s was derived from somewhat decorous films adapted from respected Australian novels, preferably set in the past and most often with a coming-of-age narrative line. Fred Schepisi, having made his name with *The Devil's Playground* (1976), from his own screenplay, next adapted Thomas Keneally's *The Chant of Jimmie Blacksmith* (1978), again writing the screenplay himself, and no one could have thought of this as 'decorous': set in the past certainly, the film, however, confronted issues central to contemporary Australian life. Schepisi went on to direct several impressive films derived from literary sources: *Plenty* (1985), from David Hare's exploration of a woman's attempt to come to terms with life in post-war England; the very smart and witty *Six Degrees of Separation* (1993), from John Guare's play; and best of all, *Last Orders* (2001), the beautiful, affecting version of Graham Swift's novel. And now he's taken on Patrick White.

In his function as adaptor – whether as director or screenwriter or both – of other men's fictions, Schepisi has shown a respect for the antecedent works without letting this topple into a crippling reverence. The movies he has made from novels and plays suggest a filmmaker who has found something to excite his attention in the original and to suggest cinematic strategies for rendering this 'take' on the original. In the case of *Jimmie Blacksmith*, he and Keneally both made painfully clear the fact that Jimmie, at the end, belongs nowhere, but, whereas Keneally arrives at this point via an austere choice of words, Schepisi does so through a passionate arrangement of images. In the case of *Plenty*, screenwriter David Hare (adapting his own play) is on record about Schepisi's wish to retain more of the original dialogue, but the film never feels like a mere conversation piece, even though it doesn't undervalue the impact of the eloquent spoken word. It moves fluently between past and present in cinematising Susan Traherne's (Meryl Streep) adjustment to the present as she comes to terms with her wartime experiences as a Resistance worker. In the process of rendering this, the film also works as an allegory of England's loss of direction and prestige in the decades after the war. In relation to *Plenty*, Schepisi acknowledged the importance of Streep's star power in getting the project adequately funded and distributed. That is, there is more at stake than just a matter of 'transferring' a story and characters created in one medium to another.

Six Degrees of Separation is a film that makes daring demands on its audience from several points of view. Schepisi, working from Guare's adaptation of his own play, insists that we listen carefully to an incessant flow of often-dazzling talk, far more than is the case with most films. However, it is no more a conversation piece than *Plenty*, and it requires the closest attention as it darts about in time and place, depending on the minutiae of *mise-en-scène* to keep us informed about its narrative twists and turns – and about its philosophical and cultural intentions.

The matter of establishing a fluid concurrency of past and present, of here and there, is crucial not just to *Plenty* and *Six Degrees of Separation* but also to *Last Orders* and to *The Eye of the Storm*, and this feature, common to several of Schepisi's adaptations, is an area in which the screen is potentially and peculiarly adept. Playwrights and novelists risk confusion if they fragment the time continuum in this way: it presents staging difficulties for theatre and even novels that embark on such alternations of tense and that need to prepare the ground a little more thoroughly than film, in which a shift in *mise-en-scène* may reorient the viewer immediately.

This was brilliantly achieved in *Last Orders*. I had the experience of reading Swift's Booker Prize-winning novel just prior to seeing the film, and was amazed at how closely it adhered to the book's sequence of events *and* to its ways of narration, of letting bits of information slip in. It was hard for me to sort out what I knew from the book, what from the film. By this I don't mean it was a tediously non-cinematic exercise in fidelity to the original; only that, to an extraordinary degree, it sought and found cinematic means of rendering the emotional texture and elegiac atmosphere of the novel as well as its incidents and characters. It is much easier to replicate incidents and characters, far less so texture and atmosphere – even supposing the filmmaker wants to, and in my view there is no reason why he/she should feel any such obligation. It's the filmmaker's job to make something new and compelling, whether he/she is working on an adaptation or from an original screenplay; and Schepisi now has an impressive record of doing just that.

Which brings us to his latest venture in adaptation. Unsurprisingly perhaps, Patrick White has not attracted much film attention. There have been several TV versions of his plays (*A Cheery Soul*, 1966; *Big Toys*, 1980; *The Ham Funeral*, 1990); Jim Sharman made a moderately interesting film of the novella *The Night the Prowler* (1978), for which White wrote his own screenplay; and there was talk of a film version of *Voss*, to be directed by Joseph Losey from a screenplay by David Mercer, that never came to anything. Now, Schepisi has filmed *The Eye of the Storm* from a screenplay by former actor Judy Morris, and, while sticking to the over-all trajectory of White's narrative, he has honed persuasive drama from the family tensions at its heart.

For my money, Schepisi has achieved a major success in recycling a novel of misanthropic malice and irritatingly over-ornate and affected stylistic posturing, and keeping a more humane eye on the lives of the dying Elizabeth Hunter, her son and daughter, and various others who touch on the Hunters' affairs. Having just reread the book, I couldn't quite rinse out the nasty taste by the time I saw the film, but, even if it had nothing else going for it, the film lasts only two hours as distinct from the 580 pages it takes White to rub our noses into the more repellent aspects of his characters' lives before a flick of 'grace' at the end. As if that stood a chance against all that had gone before, whether lovingly rendered details of snot or shit or misogynistic observation of a woman's least attractive features.

So what, in narrative terms, is being adapted? Elizabeth Hunter, rich, once-beautiful, cruelly self-absorbed, lies moribund in her Sydney mansion (actually a Melbourne location passes for this in the film), and her two children have flown in from Europe to see her but, more important, to ensure their inheritances. Basil Hunter, *Sir* Basil, has reached a middling eminence as an actor in England, an eminence he is at pains to gloss, while sister Dorothy, now the Princesse de Lascabanes, is miserably separated from her French husband. They are not drawn by affection for their mother, and don't have much for each other. Elizabeth is tended by three nurses, named for allegory rather than life as Badgery, De Santis and Manhood; by a German Jewish housekeeper, Lotte Lippmann, who has had a past in cabaret which she puts to use in diverting the dying matriarch; and by a lawyer named Arnold Wyburd, whose wife Lal has (White is pleased to tell us, for no very good reason) a 'single pockmark on one cheek beside the nose'. The son and daughter fly in; the nurses and lawyer hover; money and jewels are at issue; and there are frequent dips into the past and away from the crucial setting of Elizabeth Hunter's bedroom.

In terms of adaptation, one notes that the film begins and ends with the younger Elizabeth (Charlotte Rampling) paddling in the shallows of an island beach, the beach where she had weathered 'the eye of the storm' and presumably experienced something approaching a state of enlightenment. In this way, the film gives a shape and a thematic emphasis of its own to its adapted narrative materials. Once Elizabeth has been established on the beach, the film cuts to her much-aged face on the pillow of her Sydney bedroom, and this is followed by two brief sequences in which Basil (Geoffrey Rush) and Dorothy (Judy Davis), in alternating shots, are seen arriving at, respectively, their hotel and club rooms. Elizabeth's curtains in fact open to our first glimpse of Basil. All three – mother, son and daughter – are repairing the ravages to their ageing bodies prior to their imminent re-meeting.

One curious aspect of the adaptation is that the character of Basil is privileged in the sense of having sole access to voice-over narration. This seems disconcerting, not because it gives him a narrational presence he doesn't have in the novel, but because it seems to imply his thoughts have greater importance than those of either Dorothy or Elizabeth. Nothing else in the film would support such a distinction, so that, in line with the reference above to Meryl Streep, one can only assume that this is intended to imply the superior star power of Geoffrey Rush. From the outset it feels like a stylistic miscalculation, at odds with the visual parity accorded both Rush and Davis, as they engage in their various affectations and self-delusions.

While on the subject of how the film goes about dealing with its precursor text, it is worth noting a couple of ways in which Schepisi and the screenplay have trimmed this overlong novel. One very simple economy is in the deletion of Sister Badgery, the least carefully detailed character among the three nurses. She exists as a presence in the novel merely by scattered references to her middle-class snobberies and her late tea-planter husband, and the film doesn't need her. The other departure, again perhaps in the interests of focusing attention during the film's two hours, is that it retains visual inserts of only Elizabeth's past, not those of Basil or Dorothy. Film, by virtue of its intense visual mimesis, instructs us about how characters look and dress and conduct themselves, in the process arguably obviating the need for filling in a lot of 'background'. In this case, Dorothy's disappointment is caught in the lineaments of Davis' taut gaze and over-careful couture, while the second-rate 'success' of Basil announces itself in Rush's too-loud bonhomie, not to speak of yachting jacket and cravat.

And very noticeably, the film avoids that final business of the novel in which the emblematically named nurse, Mary De Santis, commits herself to a new patient, and next morning finds her arms 'rounded by increasing light' as she sees to the feeding of birds in the garden. This bit of unpersuasive uplift is replaced in the film's last moments by that image I mentioned before, of Elizabeth Hunter's one moment of spontaneous joy on the island beach.

What the film has to offer is a compelling study of greed, vanity, self-interest and other assorted moral slipshoddiness. So, it might be said, has the novel, but at least in the film the mere fact of having to embody these characteristics in actual living figures (or their two-dimensional representations) endows them with a humanity that is hardly evident on the page. They may be selfish and egoistic but small moments of other manifestations will keep seeping through, endowing them with vestiges of life that escape their public facades. Mind you, it helps the film to have been so exemplarily cast: if you have Rampling, Rush and Davis at their commanding best, with other roles taken by the likes of Helen Morse (and how good to see her on the big screen again in a vivid sketch as flamboyant Lotte), Colin Friels (as politician Athol Shreve), John Gaden (as Wyburd) and Robyn Nevin (as Lal), the film is off to a good start. These actors, representative of several decades of Australian cinema, and Schepisi, one of the notable pioneers of the 1970s revival, have joined forces to effect a transition from one medium to another that leaves the earlier one trailing in its own ungenerous dust.

Senses of Cinema, September 2011.

13

A TALE OF TWO TERENCES

The Deep Blue Sea

By chance, two of the most famous 1950s plays are in the news again. John Osborne's historic rant, *Look Back in Anger*, has been successfully revived on Broadway, while Terence Rattigan's emotionally taut piece, *The Deep Blue Sea*, has been filmed by another Terence – Davies, that is. In their day, Osborne railed against the 'porcelain plates [of] the well-set table of British theatre' (John Lahr in *The New Yorker*), his arrows directed at the likes of Noël Coward and Rattigan, who in their turn were less than excited by Osborne's class-based invective. It's now at least arguable that Rattigan has outlasted Osborne; he has been much more frequently revived on stage – and on film and television – than his vituperative contemporary. Who now, I wonder, would rather watch or listen to *Look Back* than *The Winslow Boy*?

One of the great women's roles in 20th-century British theatre is surely that of suicidally-inclined Hester Collyer in *The Deep Blue Sea*. First created in London by Peggy Ashcroft, she was succeeded by Googie Withers, who then played the role unforgettably in Melbourne in 1955, opposite husband John McCallum as Freddie, her emotionally stunted lover. In 1994, film director Karel Reisz guided Penelope Wilton through a stage production, subsequently recorded on television. Hester offers rewarding scope to an actress of intelligence and passion, and Davies has found another such in Rachel Weisz, who brings to the role a depth of pain that eluded Vivien Leigh in the 1955 film version.

In bringing this lacerating story of messy relationship to the screen again, Davies has made his first fiction film since the comparably harrowing *The House of Mirth* (2000) and his finest since *Distant Voices, Still Lives* (1988). The latter comes to mind here because of the images and prevailing atmosphere of post-war shabbiness in a Britain stumbling towards renewal, but people and their unequal passions don't date and this is a matter that Rattigan frequently returned to in plays such as *The Browning Version* and *Separate Tables*. In *The Deep Blue Sea* he reputedly drew on a doomed homosexual relationship of his own.

The new film takes place within the course of one day. It opens on Hester's attempted suicide, with the gas oozing into her shabby flat and memories of her fateful meeting with Freddie (Tom Hiddleston) at the Sunningdale Golf Club, while married to judge, Sir William Collyer (an impeccable Simon Russell Beale). In her seemingly random recollections as she is losing consciousness, filmed in very fluid camera and editing moves, Davies, screenwriter as well as director, establishes economically the contrasts between Hester's meetings with Freddie, with their moments of sexual abandon, and her chaste scenes with Collyer as they sit at table, flanking his formidable mother on one occasion.

Structurally, the film recalls the way *The Iron Lady* moved between Mrs Thatcher's demented present and memories of a more potent past. Davies has trusted his collaborators – especially his three leading actors, but also his cinematographer and production and costume designers – to create Hester's bleak present and the past in which her unequal marriage to Collyer and unequal affair with Freddie are brought vividly to life. There is a sequence of entwined naked limbs, filmed with sensuous elegance, which would have been unthinkable in the 1955 film. (It's even been suggested it might have been unlikely in Britain then because of the unavailability of central heating.) These scenes outside the shabby flat where Hester and Freddie have been living together don't come under the usual heading of 'opening up' when the filming of single-set plays is concerned, but are the result of Hester's attempts to summon up those episodes in her life that have brought her to the point of turning on the gas.

For the most part, and as a by-product of these memory inserts, the film avoids the static quality of the play's long dialogue exchanges. In fact, the play now seems curiously flat on the page as one duologue follows another. Because of the film's greater mobility in time and space, the rare occasions when, say, Hester and Collyer or Hester and Freddie try to talk through their situation are accorded real prominence, and Davies allows his camera to stay unfussily on them. Two important additions to the play's cast are those of Collyer's frosty, patronising mother and Hester's father, a benignly conventional vicar. In the playing of Barbara Jefford and Oliver Ford Davies, these two parents offer insights into the ways in which their offspring have been emotionally imprisoned, just as the experience of the war has left Freddie in a state of raffish and RAF-ish immaturity.

Sharply evoking place and period (London round 1950), this superbly acted film, with its take on unrequited love, exerts the power to move even a calloused modern audience.

Australian Book Review, May 2012.

14

MUCH ADO ABOUT NOTHING

'Oh, what a merry war'

There have been more than 900 Shakespearean film adaptations of one kind or other, for screens large and small, dating back to scenes from *Macbeth* in 1898. The Stratford playwright would have become rich beyond the dreams of avarice from film rights alone. Equally, though, I think he would have acknowledged that film-makers have notched up a pretty honourable record in bringing his plays to the cinema. Certainly, such screen versions have been essentially aimed at arthouse audiences, but he might well have been pleased at some of his successes among the groundlings. Think of Zeffirelli's *Romeo and Juliet* and how well it chimed with the youthful Zeitgeist in 1968.

The most notable films have tended to be British in origin, though there are potent exceptions such as Kurosawa's *Ran* (ex-*King Lear*, 1985) and Grigori Kozintsev's *Hamlet* (1964) – or the all-star Hollywood *Midsummer Night's Dream* of 1935. This last date is significant here. There has been nothing so like Hollywood, and in some ways so like the Hollywood of the 1930s, as Joss Whedon's *Much Ado About Nothing*. For my money, there has been nothing so exhilarating in the filmed Shakespeare canon for a very long time (I nearly said 'ever').

The mention of Hollywood needs some gloss. First, the film is set in California, Santa Monica to be exact, and largely in the director's own house and grounds. This spacious setting has a kitchen with guests pottering about, bedrooms with children's toys, and so on; in other words, it's a place where life is going on. Second, Whedon clearly sees it as a sparkling romantic comedy, with screwball affiliations, making me think of, say, Katharine Hepburn and Cary Grant striking sparks from each other, as if the final clinch weren't inevitable, in the great *Philadelphia Story* (1940). And third, it is shot in lustrous black and white, so that it seems almost like a throwback to the great days of Hollywood in these genres – during the 1930s above all. The choice of monochrome (maybe cheaper, and I hear the film was made fast and economically) seems to insist on placing it in such a context.

What is most wonderful is the apparently seamless wedding of the Shakespearean verse drama with the conventions of film. It simply doesn't feel like a play, unless the several white-outs are intended to stand for the conclusions of individual acts. It moves fluidly around the large house, into the neighbouring gardens and roads, so that there is no sense of actors and action behaving in any sort of constrained, stagy way. Shakespeare's language is preserved with immaculate precision and conversational ease. The cast manages that feat of making us feel they are thinking about the matter of their dialogue as they speak, as if they are making the words up as they go along, but without any diminution of the original's wit and rhythms. We seem to be hearing conversation; it just happens to be sharper and more literate than we are often used to.

The drama of the plot relating to Claudio's wooing then public humiliation of Hero is there intact, as is the perfidy of Don John and his followers, both strands given their narrative weight. The comedy involving the dim-witted constable Dogberry and his offsiders, now cast as guards on the estate, is very funny in the performances of Nathan Fillion and Tom Lenk, as they muddle their way through CCTV findings and a very elusive grasp of grammar and vocabulary.

But at the core is the comedy of 'the merry war' between Beatrice and Benedick. This is the reason we love this play. It is they who create the emotional trajectory of what may be the greatest romantic comedy in the language, and Amy Acker and Alexis Denisof make their Beatrice and Benedick seem like descendants of that previously named film pair, who, of course, in their turn could claim Beatrice and Benedick as their ancestry. When Acker tells us, 'I'd rather hear a dog bark at a crow / Than hear a man tell me I love you', you know she's due to have her mind changed, and when she says 'Then a star danced and under that I was born', you believe her absolutely. And when it comes to what may be the play's climactic line – Beatrice ordering Benedick as a test of the love he has just been declaring, 'Kill Claudio' – she almost whispers it in his ear as he is embracing her. On stage, it is often spoken as a show-stopping line and that works well on stage. Here, it belongs utterly to that point in the relationship between the sparring, bantering pair whose realisation that each is what the other needs is at the heart of the play – and of this glorious film.

Much Ado is on limited release: it deserves huge commercial success as well as critical plaudits. Shakespeare and Joss Whedon seem made for each other.

Australian Book Review, July 2013.

15

SHUTTLECOCK

What Maisie Knew

The last twelve months have seen some notable film reworkings of classic literary texts, with *Anna Karenina* set in a theatre, a black Heathcliff in *Wuthering Heights*, and a gorgeous *Much Ado about Nothing* enacted in monochrome contemporary California. Now we have a compelling version of Henry James's novel *What Maisie Knew* (1897), which reminds one of what a good run he has had with film adaptations. Hapless as he was as a stage dramatist, James would surely have been delighted by such potent film versions as *The Heiress* (ex-*Washington Square*, 1949) and *The Wings of the Dove* (1997).

These films most often came replete with turn-of-the-century costumes and décor, of a kind to which BBC serialisations had habituated us, but *What Maisie Knew*, directed by Scott McGehee and David Siegel, is having nothing of that. This new film is set in a world of takeaway pizza and potato crisps, of mobile phones and touring rock stars; but what remains true of the century between novel and film is James's depiction of the adult negligence, corruptions, and cruelties visited on the eponymous small girl ('the little feathered shuttlecock they could fiercely keep flying between them'). One doesn't doubt that there are just as many instances now of such egoistic parents tearing each other apart and exposing children to the kinds of selfishness and solipsism of which those biologically closest to them are capable.

As Pip said of himself in *Great Expectations*, Maisie becomes a sort of 'connubial missile', if only metaphorically, between her warring parents: ageing rock star Susanna (Julianne Moore) and art wheeler-dealer Beale (Steve Coogan). The film opens on a black screen with the sound of footsteps on a wooden floor that prove to be caused by Susanna's preposterous stilettos. The image somehow alerts us to the rest of her, so that we aren't taken in by her saccharine singing of 'Rock-a-bye baby' to little Maisie. This phoney idyll is interrupted by Beale's banging on the apartment door and a slanging match witnessed and taken in by Maisie, quietly unnoticed. Throughout, she is made privy to adult vituperations that a child shouldn't have to bear but from which she learns to sort out what she can trust – and what she cannot.

What Maisie learns quite early in the film is that she can't expect full attention from either parent. Both are always offering compromised embraces, with one hand hugging her but the other more importantly engaged by their mobile phones (could there be a more resonant 21st-century symbol of preoccupation?). Maisie's best hope of steady affection is with the next partner of each of her divorcing parents, to whom she is a matter of litigation rather than primary concern. Susanna marries a hunky bartender called Lincoln (Alexander Skarsgård), and Beale takes up with Margo (Joanna Vanderham), who has been Susanna's 'help'. Margo seems at first like James's Mrs Wix with a good bleach, but Mrs Wix's function is now partly and jointly taken over by Lincoln and Margo. When the egregious Beale and irresponsible Susanna forget their parental obligations, as they habitually do, Lincoln and Margo are forced to fill the gaps and gradually come to feel for each other and for Maisie the kinds of love and affection that involve commitment to something beyond the self. Maisie, who has done a lot of peering through metal grilles and around corners, will learn to recognise where her best hopes for the future lie.

All this is written, directed, and acted with exemplary precision and assessment of the values inherent in the processes by which Maisie comes to 'know'. Henry James might perhaps have been shocked when Susanna tells Beale, in front of Maisie, 'she doesn't need you to tell her what I say is okay, asshole' (and don't imagine the profanity stops there), but I think he would have admired the coherently reimagined and stringent retelling of his painful satire. He might well have applauded such informing images as the lavishly creamy dessert that Susanna offers Maisie, as if this indulgence makes up for all that is missing in her mothering instincts, or of the insistent yellow cabs that are always dropping Maisie off at places where she may or may not be collected by whichever parent is meant to be there.

James, as one who pined for theatrical success, would surely have admired the superb acting of the stars. Julianne Moore, one of the screen's best for the last twenty years, brilliantly incarnates Susanna's endless self-absorption as she seeks to keep the decades at bay with precarious shoes and vestigial skirts, and Steve Coogan's characteristic persona, honed in his 'Alan Partridge' series, adjusts perfectly to the self-deluding Beale. Perhaps most wonderful of all is Onata Aprile's Maisie, solemn-faced and unsentimental as she comes to know more than a child should be asked to know.

Australian Book Review, October 2013.

16

ALL THAT GLITTERS ...

The Great Gatsby

One should approach a new film with an open mind, but it's very hard to do so when it has been preceded by the sort of hype that has accompanied *The Great Gatsby*. And it's not just the hype but the other threats to the open mind which include the famous source novel (one that people know about even if they haven't read it), the previous film versions, and the reputation of the new film's director.

As one who believes that an adaptation should say something new about the antecedent fiction, I'm set a serious challenge by Baz Luhrmann's *Gatsby*. I admired his relocation of *Romeo and Juliet* (1996) to Venice Beach, California, for its daring in relation to time and place while maintaining a strict adherence to Shakespeare's play; and I enjoyed the wild eclecticism of *Moulin Rouge* (2001), while drawing the line at the bloated idiocies of *Australia* (2008). So what's new about his *Gatsby*?

The main innovation here is to place F. Scott Fitzgerald's narrator, Nick Carraway, in a sanatorium, where he is being treated for alcoholism and several other disorders. As part of the therapy urged by his doctor (Jack Thompson), he is writing about his experiences, then typing them up as 'Gatsby', amending this at the end to 'The

Great Gatsby', believing him to be worth the whole 'rotten crowd'. This device allows Nick to read aloud passages of commentary on the action. It doesn't work, very often seeming redundant in the light of what we've seen, and in case we've missed the point it will sometimes appear in handwriting or typing sprawled across the screen. Further, Toby Maguire's blank-faced Nick never suggests the insights of one who 'wanted the world to be … at a sort of moral attention forever'. And no amount of quoting Fitzgerald's words will guarantee that the film will mean the same thing – if that's what Luhrmann intended.

The film's visual style, and sometimes its aural (the jazz age is suggested by rapper Jay-Z), is often wildly overblown. At best it evokes a superficial society, epitomised by Gatsby's lavish parties at which neither invitation nor host's presence is essential. Again, at best, it is not just that the treatment is excessive but that it is *about* excess, although there is a great deal more lingering over the fabulous sets and costumes (brilliant work from Catherine Martin) than we need to understand what makes Gatsby tick. Gatsby's palatial spread evokes Disneyland rather than Long Island. Too often Luhrmann has opted for a merely frantic montage of cars and clothes and décor.

In fleeting contrast with all this are a couple of wonderful long shots of the impoverished farm of Gatsby's childhood and the sepia-tinted glimpses of Gatsby at war and during his wartime romance with Daisy, which give a touch of poignancy to Gatsby's certainty that the past can be repeated. On other occasions, Luhrmann has allowed Simon Duggan's camera to fasten on such symbols as the green light across the bay (beckoning like the receding past) and the valley of ashes presided over by the 'eyes of Doctor T.J. Eckleburg' on a great billboard. What, I wonder, would anyone not familiar with the novel be expected to make of such insistences?

As for the main characters, and what they embody, there appears to be a curious disparity in the ages of Gatsby and Daisy, as played by Leonardo DiCaprio and Carey Mulligan. Individually, each creates a compelling resonance. DiCaprio, blandly inscrutable for much of the film, can quickly suggest a life of necessary subterfuge and hidden possibilities – or that his surface vacuity masks a deeper emptiness. The exquisite Mulligan, so good in *An Education* (2009), incarnates Daisy's tinkling superficiality to perfection: like Fitzgerald's Daisy, she manages to reek of money and opportunism and self-preservation without quite losing her hold on us. It is as a pair that these two pose a threat to credibility. There is an eleven-year gap in their ages, and in some shots DiCaprio looks almost like her father. This matters if we are to be persuaded of their love affair five years earlier. In other key roles, Joel Edgerton offers a compelling study in snobbish old-money brutality as Tom Buchanan, Elizabeth Dubecki makes her every moment count as the languorous Jordan Baker, and Isla Fisher's sluttish Myrtle, in red fishnet stockings that precede her first entrance down stairs, resonates with a coarser world.

Luhrmann has taken a slim, elegant book and made a fat film from it. Some of Fitzgerald's more ornate prose may invite the film's stylistic hyperbolae, and the film has a certain blockbuster appeal, but as for what it's all about, who knows? It looks great, but at heart this is not a *great* Gatsby.

Australian Book Review, June 2013.

17

NO SURRENDER

Suffragette

It may have been no more than a coincidence that Michelle Payne, the first female jockey to win the Melbourne Cup, was wearing the colours of the suffragette movement of one hundred years ago. The moment was an irresistible milestone for women, however, while also recalling what ground-breakers those other purple-green-and-white wearers were. And, most poignantly, Payne's win echoes another famous horse race, the Epsom Derby of 4 June 1913, when the suffragette heroine Emily Davison threw herself under the King's horse in a suicidal gesture to draw attention to the cause of women's suffrage.

Sarah Gavron's film *Suffragette*, shown during the British Film Festival and on general release from Boxing Day, comes at the end of a year of high-profile British films, several of them featuring strong women who refuse to be subject to gender discrimination and choose to ally themselves to causes that demand moral probity. Think of Imelda Staunton as the Gay Pride activist in *Pride* or Alicia Vikander as Vera Brittain in *Testament of Youth*, two obvious examples. To this list we can now add Carey Mulligan's Maud Watts, the heroine of *Suffragette*, a fictitious incarnation of many brave women of a century ago.

I'm ashamed not to have had more detailed historical knowledge of the movement, of the suffragists whose non-violent responses to inequality were replaced by the suffragettes who found that mere words were not enough. Those who, like me, feel they would like to know more about these events of the early twentieth century may be interested to read Brian Harrison's *Separate Spheres: The Opposition to Women's Suffrage in Britain* (1978), which traces the complexities of the struggle.

Considering its central importance in the struggle for women's equality, film-makers' interest in the subject has been sparse indeed, and this is all the more surprising because, as the novelist Tessa Hadley wrote recently, the suffragettes 'couldn't have had half their effect without photography.' A compilation of early footage, *Suffragettes in Silent Cinema*, was released in 2003, but details of its production and distribution are hard to find. In 2015, to coincide with the new feature, Bryony Dixon and Margaret Deriaz have made a more ambitious compilation under the title *Make More Noise: Suffragettes in Silent Film*, its title derived from words spoken by Emmeline Pankhurst.

Other than these serious attempts to chronicle film's attention to the movement, there is a segment in the Boulting brothers' 1947 film *Fame Is the Spur* involving the suffragette wife (Rosamund John) of the film's protagonist, a politician who loses his way idealistically. His wife, on the other hand, dies for her cause, following a hunger strike and force-feeding in Holloway Prison. This is quite a way from *Mary Poppins* (1964), in which Mrs Banks (Glynis Johns) cosily aligns herself to the Votes for Women cause.

Until *Suffragette*, the only serious attempt on screen to come to terms with the movement seems to have been the BBC mini-series

Shoulder to Shoulder (1974). In six episodes of seventy-five minutes each, the series was able to be more inclusive than the new film and to take a more sustained interest in the characters of the chief activists, with each episode highlighting one of them. Perhaps the most moving is 'Lady Constance Lytton,' in which Judy Parfitt gives a harrowingly felt performance as the eponymous aristocrat who allies herself to the cause, insists on being treated with the same cruelty as the other women who are arrested, and dies for her pains – and her integrity.

Watching *Shoulder to Shoulder* again forty years later, one realises how unlikely our free-to-air channels today would be to risk holding viewers' attention over six weeks with such material. It is of course stirring in the ultimate outcome of the movement, and this note is ushered in by the robust chorus of Dame Ethel Smyth's inspirational hymn to the movement's efforts, 'The March of the Women,' but it is also uncompromising in its treatment of the rigours and brutalities to which the women were exposed. The greater length of the series enabled it to explore more amply divisions within the ranks, and within the Pankhurst family, between those who shied away from the idea of violence as a means to their end and those who supported the cry of 'action, not words.'

'You're my wife. That's what you're meant to be,' says Sonny Watts (Ben Whishaw) in a casual but firmly spoken line at the start of *Suffragette.* It's not that Sonny is especially patriarchal; he's just giving voice to the received wisdom of the time and place (London, 1912) – received, that is, by at least the male half of the population. The film's next image of this 'wife,' Maud, finds her working in a vast, hideous laundry where the female workforce is under the direction of the brusque male voice of their bullying employer. What will follow is the story of a group of working women who unite to join the fight for women's rights, these to be symbolised by their being given the vote.

Maud Watts's journey from subdued wife and mother and bullied employee to political activist who will suffer greatly from her efforts is at the film's centre, but the film doesn't make the mistake of seeing hers as a purely individual struggle. Abi Morgan's screenplay keeps its focus on both Maud's potentially tragic situation and the wider and growing storm of protest against the manifest inequity of a system that can allow a male public figure to declare with unquestioned authority that women are well represented by husbands, brothers and sons. A sudden explosion of activity, the result of stones being thrown to the accompaniment of shouts demanding 'votes for women,' pushes the film's narrative into the activism of the streets.

Part of *Suffragette*'s skill is in its juxtaposing of such episodes with the quieter but no less persuasive conflict in the Watts's cramped home, where Maud tries to interest her husband in the women's cause. The fact that Sonny is not any sort of brute imbues with real pain the later moments when he, unable to do his job, maintain their home and look after their child, is forced to give his son up for adoption. Neither Morgan's screenplay nor Sarah Gavron's direction goes in for a facile melodramatic development in the dramatisation of Maud's situation. Rather, they have settled for a realist approach in the time-honoured tradition of much of the best of British cinema, from its war and postwar days through the 'new wave' films of the late 1950s and early 1960s.

This is not to decry the potential power of melodrama but simply to indicate a different approach. There is real power in the way the film depicts Maud's gradual radicalisation in the women's movement, as she observes various kinds of cruel discrimination in her workplace and indeed on the streets and in high places. Against this growing awareness of the larger issues at stake is the gradual escalation of tension in her home, leading to some unbearably poignant moments as Maud is torn between her growing commitment to the cause, which will eventually lead her to prison, and the collapse of her family life. She becomes increasingly ready to speak out for the beliefs that have taken hold of her, and the life of poverty and struggle that have brought her to this point.

In a very moving scene – moving because it relies on Carey Mulligan's quietly tense delivery rather than any touch of sentimentality or high drama – she speaks, in place of an injured colleague, before an audience of men including Lloyd George. Here, unprepared for rhetoric, she gives a compelling account of how she has been forced out of education and, at a very early age, into employment where she was eventually paid thirteen shillings a week for the same work that earned men nineteen shillings.

While Maud is being torn between the claims of domestic life and the wider loyalty to the women's movement, the film provides a cleverly sustained build-up of the way the suffrage cause is drawing public attention to itself. Stones are thrown through windows; outrage follows the announcement that those in power follow a 'no votes for women' agenda; police intervene to curb crowds of angry women; and the montage of brutal treatment that follows seems to be based on no lack of historical evidence. Posters and newspaper headlines reveal when, but not where, Emmeline Pankhurst is due to address a crowd, and the police attempt to find out where this is to take place and to intervene.

All this is, in a sense, a build-up to Meryl Streep's star persona but more importantly to the woman whose name, perhaps above all others, is associated with this tide of history. In one of the film's obvious set-piece highlights, Streep, as Pankhurst, appears on a balcony to address the crowd of women below. As police move threateningly towards the scene, she memorably tells the listeners, 'We don't want to be law-breakers, we want to be law-makers. Never surrender!' These words, almost identical to those spoken by Siân Phillips in the same role in *Shoulder to Shoulder*, carry the weight of history with them. Streep, as immaculately English as she was when she played Margaret Thatcher in *The Iron Lady* (2011), does a great star turn, and it is difficult to think of an English actress who would have done it with more effortless authority. This is just one remarkable scene, however, and the real burden of the film is carried by Mulligan, supported by Anne-Marie Duff, Romola Garai, Natalie Press and Helena Bonham Carter as fellow foot soldiers in the cause and, on the male side, by Whishaw and Brendan Gleeson as a humane, somewhat blinkered police inspector.

But the credit belongs above all to director Sarah Gavron and her screenwriter Abi Morgan. Their film does justice to what was an appalling injustice and to the women who fought to remedy it – and they are a likely pair of collaborators for the enterprise. Remember Gavron's feature debut, *Brick Lane* (2007), with its poignant account of a young Indian woman in London tempted by a love outside her marriage to a kind, older man? It was a film made with unsentimental sympathy and a sharp perception of what goes on in relationships, both of which qualities she brings to bear on the new film. And Abi Morgan's writing credits include not only *Brick Lane*, but also *The Iron Lady*, in which she managed to be both fair and sympathetic to Thatcher, and *Shame*, which starred Carey Mulligan, the central figure in *Suffragette*. These three have now worked together to make a film that is both an absorbing entertainment and one that gives rise to serious thought.

Without ever descending into mere didacticism, a persuasive case is made. It is all the more persuasive for daring (as indeed did *Shoulder to Shoulder*) to imply that aspects of the suffragette action, such as stone-throwing, might have alienated some of the activists' potential supporters. We are often reminded, and rightly so, of other crucial twentieth-century tragedies and matters of social and political importance, and that makes *Suffragette* seem doubly overdue. *Suffragette* reminds us of what those women stood for and what they sacrificed – and what they achieved. As novelist Sarah Crompton has written, 'Each generation takes a view of the suffragettes that suits its needs. The story is both of its time and timeless, a history that mustn't be forgotten and whose sharp lessons will always be relearned.' Stories, on page or screen that tell of heroic struggle for justice can't be told too often, and *Suffragette* fulfils this function with clarity and passion.

Inside Story, 15 December, 2015.

18

TAKING THE PLUNGE

The Water Diviner

'You can find water, but you can't even find your own children,' says Eliza 'Lizzie' Connor (Jacqueline McKenzie), weeping, to husband Joshua (Russell Crowe); these are her last words before she leaves their outback home and drowns herself in the dam. This is the line that propels the narrative of *The Water Diviner* (2014), which Crowe directed. The action opens in 1915, an auspicious date in Australian history, so we have a premonition of what may have happened to the Connor sons and where the rest of the film may lead us. But it's not quite as straightforward and obvious as that may suggest.

The Water Diviner is one of several recent films that bear the disclaimer 'Inspired by true events', and it seems to me a more honest and accurate statement than the more usual 'Based on a true story'. A 'story' is a constructed thing, most often with a beginning, a middle and an end, whereas what happens in real life tends to be a much messier, more disorderly affair – a matter of events, sometimes evincing cause-and-effect connections but just as likely suggesting an arbitrary lack of these. Filmmakers may then impose *their* order, create *their* story, out of these events, and this is what Crowe has done here, drawing on the journey of a father who went searching for the remains of sons who had died at Gallipoli.

Crowe's directorial debut is ambitious. He has not settled for a trim, linear narrative; instead, the film hurtles about in time and place, between large-scale action and intimate personal motives and relationships. He also plays the demanding central role of Connor, whose journey takes him into territory that is challenging both physically and psychologically. In the process, Crowe contrives to create his most restrained performance in years, seriously engaging our sympathetic attention for his emotionally driven character.

Two landscapes

Before the film's title is announced, there are vast panoramic views of two harsh-looking landscapes, thrillingly captured by Andrew Lesnie's cinematography. The first is introduced with the caption '20 December 1915, Gallipoli' and provides the setting for some spectacularly staged military action, with the camera then picking out a montage of gunfire and soldiers in silhouette before resting on an in-trench booby trap ironically juxtaposed with an innocent chess set. It is announced that the ANZAC troops have been evacuated, and the legendary feat of courage and ultimate failure, as a military exercise, is introduced. Preceding the second panorama is the caption 'North Western Victoria, four years after Gallipoli', and in a vast overhead shot a solitary man and a dog are identified. He is Joshua Connor, and he is divining – successfully – for water in this parched countryside. What, we wonder, has this to do with the inserts of ANZAC troops in action? At this point, the film's title appears, and we soon understand that water will have a key role in the film, as will the often-contrasting agendas of army and individual. These apparently disconnected landscapes that dominate the film's opening episodes induct us thematically into what follows.

Connor's return to his isolated home after his discovery of water precipitates his wife's comment (quoted earlier) and her subsequent death while he is fixing a windmill. There is a brief montage of church, coffin and confrontation with Father McIntyre (Damon Herriman) inside the church. The priest maintains that, as she had committed suicide, Lizzie cannot be buried in consecrated ground, and, in his grief, Connor's motivation for the rest of the film is set in place. He will go to Turkey in search of their three lost sons, whom we've glimpsed as children in a flashback featuring a dust storm, with the film ultimately characterising Connor as a devoted father.

The search

The motif of the search for a missing family member or other loved one has provided the basis for some notable movies. Most recently, Canadian–Indian co-production *Siddharth* (Richie Mehta, 2013) presents a poignant drama centring on a father's (Rajesh Tailang) hunt for his twelve-year-old son (Irfan Khan), who has gotten lost in a distant city. Perhaps most famous of all, however, is John Ford's masterpiece *The Searchers* (1956). The film's title announces not merely the idea of a quest but also where the essential conflict is to be located: in the inner life of protagonist Ethan Edwards (John Wayne), who is looking for his niece (Lana Wood / Natalie Wood). He pursues the Comanches who had kidnapped her, and in the process he finds not only her but something about himself as well. Like *Siddharth* and *The Searchers*, Crowe's film is focused on the machinations of the search, but his central character emerges as more open to experience than viewers might have guessed from his simpler responses at the start of the narrative.

A good deal of credit is due to Andrew Anastasios and Andrew Knight's screenplay, which satisfyingly interweaves personal issues, larger matters of bureaucracy, and hostilities lingering in the post–World War I years, with bursts of action. Anastasios' research even led to the finding of a letter from a man named Cyril Hughes, a Lieutenant Colonel who was an integral part of the Imperial War Graves unit bringing order to the abandoned battlefield at Gallipoli, in the years immediately after the First World War.

In that letter was an intriguing line – 'One old chap managed to get here from Australia, looking for his son's grave.' That single line was 'all the inspiration needed'[1] to get the film's story moving. The long central section of the film is taken up by Connor's search, the obstacles he meets, the relationships that are forged in the process, those who help and those who hinder his venture, and how he is affected by the experience. In general, the screenplay works skilfully to maintain a satisfying complexity among these strands, and Crowe directs his leading actors, including himself, to do justice to this.

This year, 2015, is of course timely for commemorating the birth of the ANZAC legend, and *The Water Diviner* takes its place among several other re-creations and reimaginings of World War I events. One aspect of the film's ideological cast is its critical representation of the British as they make their presence felt in Connor's quest. This may well be more a matter of twenty-first century thinking than of how it was felt at the time, but that is always a given when film (and society more broadly) comes to terms with historical events – *The Searchers*, for instance, was as much about 1956 USA as about 1868 Texas, where the action is set. Maybe there was a lot of anti-British bitterness at the time, following the Gallipoli defeat, but more to the point in relation to *The Water Diviner* is the attitudes towards war that it expresses now.

For instance, the British War Office in Istanbul, where Connor's journey has brought him in 1919, is obstructive, its representative unable to give him a permit to travel to Gallipoli in spite of his having lost three sons there in 1915. The British officers here are depicted as unsympathetically imperious in their demeanour, offering finally a brusque 'Go home, Mr Connor.' When Connor leaves the office, he finds a Turkish nationalist rally in progress, with shouts and placards to the effect of 'Get out, English!' The film's attitude towards the UK recalls the chilly light in which Peter Weir's *Gallipoli* (1981) depicted the distant nation. In Crowe's film, the lack of imperial support for Connor's mission is emphasised by its being preceded by the intertitle 'Imperial War Graves Unit, Gallipoli, 1919' as well as by the fact that the Australian Lieutenant-Colonel Cyril Hughes (Jai Courtney) is working towards 'locating our dead'. Nonetheless, the film doesn't hammer an anti-British prejudice: the point is made sharply enough in this early scene in the War Office and in the wider context of the street demonstration. This approach no doubt reflects a twenty-first century sense of the slackening of Anglo–Australian ties.

Fathers and sons

A crucial encounter in Istanbul involves a small boy, Orhan (Dylan Georgiades), who runs off with Connor's bag while he is trying to arrange passage into Gallipoli. Orhan proves to be no ordinary street urchin, however. Connor's pursuit of Orhan leads to a hotel run by the boy's mother, Ayshe (Olga Kurylenko), who is at first curiously reluctant to take the Australian as a guest. She has refused to accept the death of her Turkish husband and, consequently, Orhan accompanies Connor in the hope that he will also find the boy's father when he recommences his search.

There is perhaps something conventional about the woman's initial hostility towards Connor, but her situation is made more complex by the conflict between her European nationality and her Ottoman life in Istanbul, especially the presence of her brutish Turkish brother-in-law, who insists on his right to marry her following his brother's death. The relationship that develops between Connor and Ayshe is not unexpected but, later, when they discuss their marriages while sitting by an underground river (yet another instance of water imagery), their relationship adds a further structural element in the film. This is reinforced as the engaging young Orhan comes, in time, to view Connor as a substitute father – underscoring the film's theme of connecting fathers and sons.

The film's balanced point of view, along with its rich interplay between character and idea, is also felt in the rapport that grows between Connor and the Turkish officer Major Hasan (Yılmaz Erdogan). He tells Hasan about his sons: 'I promised their mother I'd find them.' When Connor arrives at Gallipoli by boat, and without a permit, Hughes tells him he can't stay, but relents to the point of sending him food and blankets when he sets up a campfire on the beach. An officer asks, 'Why do it for one father who can't stay put?' and Hasan answers: 'He's the only father who came looking.' And it is also Hasan who brings Connor the news that one of his sons has been taken prisoner and is still alive.

Finding and after

Obviously, the film gradually moves towards the moment when Connor confronts his remaining son. He has told Ayshe: 'I steered my sons to manhood – and I failed them.' Hasan has emerged as his chief helper and, when they escape from a train attacked by Greek guerrillas, they make off with two of the attackers' horses and Hasan leads Connor to where the surviving son, Arthur (Ryan Corr), is to be found. It would have been easy for Crowe to build up to this moment, the climax of the search, in full melodramatic mode, and that might have worked. However, he has directed it with a restraint that makes it more moving, commands our attention and affords us easy emotional access. We learn that Arthur has been working on a windmill for his captors, though the film does not clarify whether he had built it, and the scene recalls the earlier windmill on the Victorian farm from which the three brothers had ridden away. Connor has to persuade Arthur to leave when, weeping as he recalls the death of his two brothers, he responds, 'I'm not coming back.' Connor accepts the blame – 'I didn't lift a finger to stop you' – but now insists, 'Either we leave here together or we die here together.' The tenderness and truth of feeling in this scene more than compensates for the lack of a big emotional outpouring. There is also a pleasing symmetry in the way father and son escape via an underground river beneath the windmill where Arthur has been working, recalling how we first saw Connor at work earlier in the film.

Later, when Connor returns to the hotel, Orhan leaps into his arms – but, here, the film likewise resists a predictable romantic clinch for Connor and Ayshe, instead gesturing quietly to their future together. In fact, the personal aspects of the narrative are done with a subtlety that highlights, by contrast, the images of war interspersed throughout the film. Certainly, Crowe has not flinched from depicting the hideousness of trench warfare. For instance, a scene of three men lying wounded, with one crying out, are both taxing enough to the viewer and oddly disconcerting because it is not clear whose images these and a good many others of battle scenes are. Connor was not there, and the film doesn't specify whether these are just in Connor's mind or if he's recalling what he's been told. This is not a major flaw but, in what is for the most part a carefully plotted film, meticulous about matters of viewpoint, it does briefly challenge credibility.

Over-all, however, there is an impressive sense of control in the film's varied narrative and imagistic interests, whether in the large, spectacularly shot action sequences, in scenes in which relationships are developed, or in the recurring water motif that reminds us of where Connor's story all began. Crowe can be well pleased with his debut as a director. He paces his film satisfyingly, he largely avoids temptations to employ cliché and tear-jerking, and his cast and other collaborators have worked his will to generally impressive effect. The film emerges as both a compelling account of a complex search and an intelligent reworking of the national mythology in this significant year.

Metro, No. 184, Autumn 2015.

Notes

1 eOne, *The Water Diviner* press kit, 2014, p. 5.

19

SUNSET SONG

It's just possible that the remainder of 2016 may produce a more memorable film than *Sunset Song*, but I doubt it. Certainly none so far has moved and enthralled me as Terence Davies' latest has, and it makes me wish again that he didn't keep us waiting so long between films. It was the semi-autobiographical *Distant Voices, Still Lives* (1988) that established him as a major figure, and in the new century there was the brilliant, painful adaptation of Edith Wharton's *House of Mirth* (2001), the eloquent documentary of growing up in Liverpool, *Of Time and the City* (2008), and a moving version of Terence Rattigan's *The Deep Blue Sea* (2011). In my view, there's more sense of piercing emotional truth in his films than those of almost any other working director.

And his latest, *Sunset Song* is no exception. It is essentially the story of a life, of a Scottish girl called Chris Guthrie, who as a teenager in Aberdeenshire shows serious academic interest and promise. The film opens on a sumptuously shot field of waving corn from which Chris emerges – she's been lying there – and then cuts to her in a Latin class where she is asked to say something in French because she is said to have an immaculate accent. So, two crucial matters have been established: her aspirations and the land whose enduringness will outlast all that follow which will include family griefs and the havoc of World War 1.

The film cuts from Chris and her schoolfriend running happily along a forest road to the interior warmth – and what seems domestic harmony – of the Guthrie family: father (Peter Mullan) and mother (Daniela Nardini), and an older brother Will (Jack Greenlees). Suddenly, with shocking arbitrariness the puritanical Guthrie beats Will for 'taking the Lord's name in vain'. We are made aware that we are in a patriarchally run household that momentarily shatters the luminously beautiful images the film has so far dealt in – and that inevitably reminds us of Pete Postlethwaite's often brutal father in *Distant Voices*. Even more painful are the cries of the mother in childhood, when she has given birth to twins upstairs. There's nothing gratuitous about the film's moments of violence; they are presented as the almost inevitable outcome of a patriarchal community in which women do what they are told. Chris, for instance, will never get to realise her idea of becoming a teacher, and the mother, played with moving grace by Nardini (of *This Life* fame), will find that she can no longer bear the crudity of enforced sex and pregnancy.

It's strange to be talking about the film as if it were full of incident. Actually, it is poetic, reflective, interested in tracing how individual lives respond to the challenges of the seasons, to the rigours of climate and to the bursts of emotional savagery on either individual or national levels. The incidents that happen are generally those that account for a daily working life, so that when something more obviously dramatic occurs it brings with it the sort of shock that everyday life, rather than the movies, has accustomed us to. In between such moments, there is, for instance, the touching sense of a bond between Chris and Will, reminding us of how rarely the affection between brother and sister gets serious cinematic mileage. One of their memorable scenes is that of the harvesting when the father propels the horse-drawn machine along and the siblings' task is to gather the hay into stooks.

This may be just idiosyncratic of me but such scenes often reminded me of Breughel's unforgettable paintings of rural life. Another such echo came to me in the sequence of the marriage of Chris and Ewan (Kevin Guthrie), a friend of her brother's, when the whole sequence has a similar painterly beauty, a rendering of real joy that recalls such community occasions in Breughel again. More to the point, though, is that Michael McDonough's cinematography, whether focused on the splendours of the natural world or the realities of everyday life or the later grimness of war, is stunningly eloquent from first to last shot. I mentioned the wedding sequence, which creates a sense of real joy (complete with singing of 'Auld Lang Syne'), and the last third of the film enacts the wonderful sense of the love and the heartbreak it will involve.

Perhaps it could be claimed that this last third, dramatising the trauma of war, needs more detailed treatment, but the performances of all concerned, particularly that of Agyness Deyn as Chris, more than carried me through effortlessly to its poignant last moments in which Chris's voice-over as older woman acknowledges what she has always believed, that 'Nothing endures but the land'. You may be moved, but you will not be depressed.

Australian Book Review, *Arts Update* 5 September 2016.

Book Reviews

20

EALING STUDIOS

By Charles Barr

There have been books about M-G-M, Columbia and Warner Bros., and no doubt someone is currently working on an in-depth treatment of the entire output of Monogram Studios in the 1930s and 1940s. But most such works have only offered sketchy histories (mittel-European *émigrés'* rise to mogulhood, the rise and fall of major stars, a glance at the studio's chief genres, etc) and even sketchier credits for the company's films.

Not many of these books have been able to give much sense of the studio's working habits, and less of the informing vision and creative procedures of those talents that gave the studio product its distinguishing qualities. Walter Pidgeon's recollection (in *The M-G-M Stock Company*) of dropping in for late afternoon drinks in Clark Gable's or Fred Astaire's dressing-room to chew over the day's work may point to the matiness at M-G-M, but it doesn't give us much insight into the films.

Charles Barr's book about Ealing is important for a number of reasons. While offering an essentially critical account of key films in the Ealing output, it also gives us a fuller sense of how these films came to be made (and to be made as they were) than any other attempt I know to anatomise a studio. Secondly, he argues a case for the achievement and limitation of the Ealing films, and does so with a rigorous intelligence. Thirdly, he is writing about a British studio, and such an enterprise is long overdue. If accounts of Gainsborough, Two Cities Films, London Films and British Lion are to follow, I hope they will be written by Barr, or at least by someone who has read and profited by his *Ealing Studios.*

The notion that Ealing's films 'reflect and project some kind of universal truth about the England of the time' is probably a common, and almost certainly a fond, delusion. Barr's opening chapter perceptively places the Ealing phenomenon, which belongs primarily to the decade immediately after World War II, in the larger context of the nation at war and then adjusting – socially and politically – to post-war stresses and changes: 'At Ealing, the instinct of [Michael] Balcon and his colleagues for gauging the feelings of an audience – or, it may be, the coincidence of their feelings with those of that audience – was reliable enough to keep the studio buoyant into the fifties; indeed, to be regarded by this time as something of a national institution.'

That last phrase – 'something of a national institution' – perhaps pinpoints the limits of the Ealing achievement. It suggests something cherished, like Vera Lynn, to the point where certain kinds of more demanding development seem not merely precluded, but undesirable as well. It may account for the fact that Ealing's most astringent director, Alexander Mackendrick, had to go elsewhere to give vent to his darkest insights and, as well perhaps, for his failure ever to get into his stride anywhere else (*The Sweet Smell of Success* was, in the event, a brilliant beacon illuminating nothing.)

Ealing's 'creative élite', according to Balcon, was 'a group of liberal-minded, like-minded people … [who] voted Labour for the first time after the war.' They had their place among the Herbivores, or gentle ruminants, identified by Michael Frayn as 'the do-gooders, the readers of the *News Chronicle*, *The Guardian* and *The Observer*, the signers of petitions; the back-bone of the BBC.' For these, the *Festival of Britain* 'was the last and virtually the posthumous work'. Their mild and attractive virtues will be gradually pushed aside by 'the brasher values of the Carnivores', including *The Daily Express* and the incoming Conservative Government.

I have over-simplified Barr's placing of Ealing in the post-war scene, but in doing so I want to stress some of the important points he makes. First, that 'Ealing is the voice of a certain consensus: one voice among many.' The Ealing voice can still be heard because it expressed its gentle values in dramatic terms. Secondly, it was of the essence of these values – wry, humorous, modestly democratic, in the end unadventurous, too closely linked to a community in danger of cosiness – that they should not be able to withstand bolder, coarser onslaughts.

It is significant that the Ealing heyday should seem equally far removed from the internationally financed blockbuster, such as *The Bridge over the River Kwai*, or the home-grown naturalism of *Room at the Top*. The glamour attached to the former, and the crude thrusting life of the latter, are light years from the Ealing spirit, characterised as it was by 'the relation between the stories told on the screen and the experience of the studio itself'.

Barr's astute account of a minor Ealing film, *Cage of Gold* (directed by Basil Dearden), sums up the crucial conflicts explored by the studio's films: 'The film dramatises questions of ambition and security, austerity and glamour, co-operation and competition, which were vividly present both in British society as a whole at this time, five years after the war, and in the small society of Ealing.' Jean Simmons' final choice of a serious young doctor, James Donald, over a dashing ex-RAF officer, David Farrar, is very much an Ealing answer to the conflict of values. It is a pointer to the studio's affectionately remembered successes and the tendency to inbreeding which will finally help to do for the studio.

Barr traces Ealing's history from its cheerfully inconsequent prewar comedies. (dominated by George Formby), through its entry into the war and the gradual emergence of the Ealing touch, epitomised in the movement from the still officer-dominated *Convoy* of 1940 to *San Demetrio London* (late 1943), 'the consummation of Ealing's war effort', a quiet celebration of unostentatious heroism and team-effort; through the 'mild revolution' that produced the remarkable string of post-war films that account for most people's view of 'typically Ealing'; to the decline and collapse of the middle '50s. Films like *Barnacle Bill* and *Davy* (1957), and *Dunkirk* (1958), exhibit the characteristic Ealing virtues in attenuation and stagnant non-response to a changed scene.

The book is not, however, essentially an historical account. Most of it is taken up with detailed and searching accounts of films which are centrally important to the Ealing achievement: Robert Hamer's *It Always Rains on Sunday* and *Kind Hearts and Coronets*; Mackendrick's *Whisky Galore!*, *The Man In the White Suit* and *The Ladykillers*; Charles Crichton's *Hue and Cry* and *The Lavender Hill Mob*; Basil Dearden's *The Blue Lamp*, and Henry Cornelius' *Passport to Pimlico*.

There are other directors and other films that have their place in the story, but it is perhaps the films I have named which, above all, established the distinctive Ealing touch. This is not to say that they are all alike, but that they share certain definable characteristics. Though Hamer may be seen as the most elegant stylist, or Mackendrick as the most sharply aware of the tensions in the Ealing 'climate', or Crichton and Dearden as the most affectionately and reliably Ealing in their responses, it is, ironically, Cornelius' sole directorial effort at Ealing which offers the quintessential expression of the studio's values and their inherent limitations. As Barr writes in defining the 'liberating nature of the basic device' (i.e., that Pimlico is found to be part of the Duchy of Burgundy): 'Given the "fantasy" premise, the story proceeds in a naturalistic style, in real or at least realistic settings. It creates a blend of fantasy and realism, and of wartime and post-war feeling ... Within this framework, Ealing can play the daydream of a benevolent community and can partly evade, partly confront in a more manageable form, those awkward 'post-war' issues, social and personal, with which it has hitherto been somewhat glumly trying to deal.'

That sense of 'liberation' is obviously integral to the narrative and philosophical procedures in Ealing's major comedies, as well as in minor works like *The Halfway House* (1944), *Another Shore* (1948), *A Run for Your Money* (1949), and *The Love Lottery* (1954). In the most serious films, including some of the best comedies, the urge towards liberation is held partly in check by a restraining urge to containment within the existing social framework. In Pimlico, the insulated community savours briefly the freedom of 'damn[ing] braces', but ends by succumbing to the 'deep-rooted nostalgia for consensus'. There is, as Barr notes, something sad in this ultimate shying away 'from the conflicts that come up in an "open" society rather than [following] them through clear-sightedly'.

The sort of 'cosy retreat' offered by *Pimlico*, the failure not merely to resolve the conflicts it is aware of, but in the end even to acknowledge that such conflicts are organic and possibly fruitful, if confronted with sustained energy and intelligence and mutual understanding, characterises all but the very acutest of Ealing films. By these I mean the Mackendrick films, where the thinking is tougher, the issues pushed further and realised with more telling visual precision.

Even in Mackendrick's films the ideal of the community, strengthened by awareness of its contrarieties, loses some of its vitality as we move from *Whisky Galore!* through *The Man in the White Suit* to *The Ladykillers*. Barr's account of the latter finishes aptly enough by pointing to the way, in the end, we see 'the inertia triumphant in a quaint little England where all alike, deep down, are innocents, a colourful neighbourhood community, with Jack Warner in charge, though hardly needed. And Mackendrick leaves for New York, to make *Sweet Smell of Success*.'

This is a frustrating book to review in a small compass because, though the main sweep of its argument is clear, it is not so bound by a thesis that it fails to do justice to particular films. Consequently, its accounts of several of these deserve detailed notice. It is as alert to the quirky and individual in the Ealing films as it is to their underlying similarities and continuities. It differentiates perceptively between the films that essentially reflect and romanticise certain aspects of the national character (e.g., love of the quaint and the old, as typified in T.E.B. Clarke's scripts) and those which subject these traits to a more critical scrutiny.

Sometimes Barr's analyses of the films make them sound less like fun than one had remembered them to be, but, in general, they testify to his claim for *Pimlico*. 'I don't think that this is a case where one risks destroying a gossamer web of wit by ponderous analysis.'

Barr writes elegantly and argues cogently. He is perhaps more consistently alive to the intellectual structures of the films than to the visual renderings of their ideas, but he discriminates with admirable firmness and subtlety among the levels of achievement, separating the inspired from the journeyman, the tough-minded from the self-indulgent. He also practises this discrimination as usefully within, as between, films.

If Ealing 'petered out', the book does not. It is still sharp when writing of *Dunkirk*, one of the studio's last films, in which Barr finds 'a recognition that Ealing cannot recreate that spirit and that united community any longer. The impetus has run out ...'. The impetus, that is, that united Britain in war and Ealing in a remarkable series of films of which this book is a fitting record. It is a book for film scholars and for anyone who is interested in what made some of the best British films British.

Cinema Papers, No. 20, March–April 1979.

21

DAYS OF THEIR LIVES

Katharine Hepburn by Barbara Leaming

Liz, An Intimate Biography of Elizabeth Taylor by C. David Heymann

Elizabeth Taylor by Donald Spoto

As well as appearing in one film together, Joseph Mankiewicz's steamy version of *Suddenly Last Summer*, Katharine Hepburn and Elizabeth Taylor had several other things in common. Whether one liked them or not, they were indisputable stars for several decades, both having done time at the luxurious MGM penitentiary. And in their distinct ways, each was a great beauty, though it must be said that Hepburn has worn better; bones will out.

Also, they were both multiple Oscar-winners (Taylor twice, Hepburn four times) and both – this is what the biographies thrive on – were singularly gifted in choosing men who would make their lives unbearable. A major difference is that Taylor kept marrying them.

Taylor is probably underrated as an actress and overrated as a person. As soon as you hear adjectives like gutsy, feisty, and outspoken applied to someone, you can be sure you are in the presence of a major bore. Two biographies of Taylor in as many weeks have been too much for me.

Heymann's is the salacious one. It is full of details of Taylor's career as a serial bride and of what she liked in men (no details are deemed too private), of her homosexual father's liaisons, or her lifelong search for father figures and how it has ended with her marrying a man young enough to be her son. For Heymann, Taylor's film career is a mere irritant which gets in the way of detailing her endless quest for emotional truth. Spoto, not averse to raking the muck as his biographies of Hitchcock and Olivier have shown, is curiously discreet about Taylor. I can only assume he didn't know some of the dirt I now know from reading Heymann; it's just not like him to suppress it.

He makes some attempt to understand what it was like to have no sense of an ordinary childhood, to be a graduate of MGM's studio school ('Ten minutes of arithmetic ... inserted between costume fittings'), to grow up having your every wish attended to, and to become obscenely rich. He is, however, so near idolatry in his view of the shy, violet-eyed beauty who grew to be fat, raucous, loudmouthed and terminally ignorant, that he seems scarcely aware of what his evidence is adding up to.

For Taylor, life itself appears to have become nothing more than a big movie. Her role changed from time to time: gorgeous but lonely teenager, child bride followed by every other sort of bride, loving mother who sometimes saw her children, AIDS campaigner and companion to the dying. The problem is that, as these latest two biographers suggest, consciously or otherwise, she really didn't know anything other than the movies, and that, when movie-type solutions proved inadequate, things simply fell apart for her.

Spoto seems genuinely to admire her acting and is sharp about how *Cleopatra* which brought her together with that rhetorical bore,

Richard Burton, changed the face of Hollywood. He also writes well enough to make one wish he'd said more about her best films, such as *National Velvet*, *Giant* and *Cat on a Hot Tin Roof*.

Heymann, on the other hand, can't be bothered wasting time on tedious stuff like that when there are perfectly good life-threatening illnesses, drunken brawls and drug abuse, marital punch-ups and raunchy *bons mots* to be paraded. His book is also marked by appalling proof-reading and a chronic vagueness about time (first indicated by his reference to Howard Duff as one of Hollywood's biggest stars, along with Garbo, in the early war years).

The definitive biography of Taylor (and as a special treat to myself, I'm not going to read it) will be one that makes a coherent attempt to account for the gap between Velvet Brown and the blowsy woman who is now mainly famous for being famous. There may well be an element of 20th-century tragedy about Taylor but neither Heymann nor Spoto, in their separate ways, comes near to documenting this.

Hepburn deserves well of a biographer and up to a point she gets it in Barbara Leaming, who has also written a notably compassionate study of Rita Hayworth. However, her Hepburn book is an oddly unbalanced affair. 'Kate', as she was always called, is not even born until page 128 and doesn't make it to Hollywood until page 272. Since that is where her coruscating career took off, this does seem like a long time arriving. At the other end of the book, a mere 16 pages are allotted to the years between 1967 and the present day.

Perhaps the latter ellipsis is meant to suggest that Hepburn's significant life was over when Spencer Tracy died just as they finished their ninth film together, *Guess Who's Coming to Dinner?*. Tracy, it must be said, seems to have been a vile man: a career drunk, bad-tempered, whingeing, timorous, asking an enormous amount of two excellent women – wife Louise as well as Hepburn – and offering very little in return. What, of course, he did offer Hepburn was the on-screen chemistry of a partnership that greatly enriched our film-going lives. Even so, Cary Grant gave her a better run for her money in *Holiday* and *The Philadelphia Story.*

The other great love of her life, once she had disposed of her nice, kind, hapless husband, Ludlow Smith, was the director John Ford, another boring drunk who just happened to make some of the best films of the century. In her own way, vastly more intelligent, better educated, and more morally appealing than Taylor, Hepburn was just as incompetent in dealing with dreadful men. Taylor's most likeable husband was the gentle-mannered Brit Michael Wilding and she could hardly wait to be rid of him; ditto Hepburn with poor Luddy.

Leaming makes a conscientious attempt in the first 200 pages to trace Hepburn's development against a background of East Coast strivings, in professions and feminist causes, and of family suicides. The telling of Taylor's absurd life might have responded to comparable researches.

The Sunday Age, 25 June 1995.

22

SOME KIND OF A MAN

Orson Welles: The Stories of His Life

By Peter Conrad

By chance the other day, watching British director Herbert Wilcox's toe-curling 'Scottish' whimsy, *Trouble in the Glen* (1954), one of Orson Welles's worst films (one of anybody's worst films), I was struck anew by the fact that, even when Welles could not save a film, he was always sure to be remembered in it. Here he plays a Scottish laird, long absent in South America, who returns to take up the castle he has inherited and, failing to bring a castful of theatrically canny Scots to heel, admits his errors and ends by presiding – benignly, but still presiding – in a kilt, yet. A romantic liaison and an appalling little girl taking her first post-illness steps may be intended to warm our soured hearts, but it is the massive figure avoiding the worst punishments for hubris that grabs what is left of our attention.

As it always did. Has anyone else known so unerringly what to do with a close-up? Is there anything more deviously engaging in film than that first shot of Harry Lime's face suddenly visible in a dark Viennese doorway in *The Third Man* (1949), unless it's the same face smiling subtly again but this time almost imploring his old friend to shoot him in the sewers at the end? Or Charles Foster Kane's lips dominating the frame as he suspires 'Rosebud' at the end of *Citizen Kane* (1941), or Falstaff, still smiling gamely but with eyes registering the pain of rejection, in *Chimes at Midnight* (1966)?

These are the kinds of images and memories with which Peter Conrad's wildly ambitious non-biography is bursting. Dismissing at the outset any claims to biography, he offers the unravelling and exploration of a very complex man in whom contradictions were juxtaposed only to be worked out again and again in one of the most audacious careers of the twentieth century.

Welles's life was chronically messy. He had three failed marriages, most famously with Rita Hayworth, whom he starred with (and shot, shattering her image the while) in *The Lady from Shanghai* (1949). He never considered the possibility of immortality through any of his children, to whom he must have been the most haphazard father. He recreated the facts of his early life to suit his own myth-making purposes, and he seems to have 'conducted his private life as if it were an extension of the roles he played'. Perhaps there was more chance of coherence on film or stage; but, again, he so serially botched the financial arrangements underpinning his artistic enterprises that it is a wonder most of them got made at all. What kind of ineptitude can have allowed him to junket off to South America and leave *The Magnificent Ambersons* (1942) to be hacked about by RKO? On the other hand, what kind of tenacity was needed to keep his idiosyncratic version of *Othello* (1952) afloat as he raced off to act in other people's films to provide the wherewithal for his own?

Conrad's densely argued, profusely illustrated (by examples, rather than the sparse photographs) weavings and diggings find both grandeur and poignancy in the sheer magnitude of Welles's aspirations.

The achievements are unique and undeniable: fifty years on, *Kane* is still regularly voted 'the greatest film ever made' (see *Sight and Sound*'s ten-yearly round-up of critical choices); *The Magnificent Ambersons* one of the most rigorous exercises in nostalgia ever made; *Touch of Evil* (1958), which he directs and stars in, as the corrupt detective Quinlan, to whom Marlene Dietrich (erstwhile sawee in his magician's act) delivers what may be Welles's best epitaph ('He was … some kind of a man'); and heartbreakingly Falstaff in his own magisterial reworking of strands from five Shakespearean plays in *Chimes*. These would be enough to ensure his place among those at the top of cinema's creative pantheon.

There is poignancy in the way his artist's intransigence and wheeler-dealer incompetence frustrated so many of his endeavours. Conrad, in telling the stories that make up Welles's life, knows that there is at least as much of Welles in the ones that didn't get made, above all perhaps in his abortive attempts to film *Don Quixote*. By this time, he was too fat to play the knight and was settling for Sancho Panza, but, as Conrad notes, it was a case of 'the mind of Quixote in the body of Sancho'. There was about Welles, at this time, an aura of the ruined romantic, the 'blinkered enemy of modernity'. And it is hard not to be moved by the idea that, unable to finance his own projects, he was forced to act in other people's often lesser works. It was one thing, as racketeer Harry Lime, to pick up *The Third Man* and run with it, so that it now seems as much Welles's film as director Carol Reed's, but his hired-hand work didn't always find such distinguished company. He made, for instance, a film by Michael Winner – though, while he is on the screen, even this, *I'll Never Forget What's 'is Name* (1967), rivets the viewer.

Conrad brings a formidable battery of talents to the daunting challenge he has set himself in illuminating the man through the work, and, if I concentrate on the films, that's because these are what we have continuing access to. These are the 'stories' in which the life is unfolded, fragmentarily, for certain, but also inexorably. Conrad is clearly saturated in Welles's oeuvre and consequently can dart about it with confidence, grasping at explanations or throwing up hypotheses. He chooses to trust not history but 'myth, with its cruel cyclical justice, its rises and falls and eternal returns which reassure us that, although everything is mutable, nothing changes'. So did Welles, who valued stories most because they preceded the teller – and outlasted him.

One is struck often by the astuteness of Conrad's insight and phrasing: of the bleaching of Hayworth for *Shanghai*, he claims Welles made 'her look like a photographic negative of herself'; or about the function of Welles's voice-over for *King of Kings* (1961): 'Visually we are restricted to what happens in the present, but words can foretell the future.' His intellectual range and grasp, hurtling across millennia, continents and media, often amazes, even if it also sometimes wearies; and the strategy, the use of films *et al* as fragments of autobiography, is demanding, as Conrad dips in and out of the Wellesian decades. There are no footnotes and, while it is flattering to be expected to know all that Conrad knows, there are times when I would have valued a gloss on some more than usually arcane reference.

It is not that Welles began at the top and the rest was downhill all the way; rather, it was hard to maintain the *Kane* plateau. He is an artist (and near the end of his life he, movingly, wondered if art had been enough) whose art and whose life may well be summed up as a labyrinth without a centre, as Borges suggested. The circularity of the stories of his life is encapsulated in the bookending figures of Kane, whose youthfully aggressive zest settled into prosthetic old age, and Clay, in *The Immortal Story* (1968), whom age has forced to turn to youth for vicarious and voyeuristic gratification. They are not the beginning or end of Welles's career but between them they encompass most of it. Like Conrad's book, they evoke the man and the life rather than merely describe them.

Australian Book Review, March 2004.

23

CONJURING THE REBEL WITHOUT A PAUSE

The Rebel: An Imagined Life of James Dean

By Jack Dann

Almost everyone who matters in this book is dead before the wrinkles set in. Not just James Dean, but Monroe, a brace of Kennedys, Pier Angeli – and Elvis Presley, still alive at the end, needn't feel smug, with barely a decade to go after the book's cut-off, Bobby K's assassination date, June 1968. It's as though the whole cast is dying to be legends, famous at least.

Dann has a great idea for a novel here: what if James Dean hadn't died in that car smash in 1955: but it's as though he doesn't quite know how best to use it. There are two main second-chance strands. In post-1955 Hollywood, he goes on to play the parts later taken by Paul Newman (described, in a nice aside, as looking 'rather sour' at Elvis's wedding), but Dann tires too quickly of what kind of actor/star Dean might have become and has him turn his charisma to politics. In this career path, he ends up defeating Ronald Reagan as Governor of California – and just think what possibilities might have ensued from that.

The main problem of *The Rebel* is that Dean, however mesmerising he was on screen and however potent thereafter as a symbol of youthful revolt, remains a hollowness at the centre of the book. The first half looks as if it's to be the biography of Dean's penis and its whereabouts: it involves endless phone calls to Marilyn, to Pier and others, and, considering what happens to them all, you can only conclude that too much sex is bad for you. Or too much talking about it, which they do – endlessly.

The friendship with director Nicholas Ray, director of *Rebel Without a Cause*, the film that crystallised Dean's appeal and legend, is more interesting for the imagined future it conjures up, and the proposed film with Elvis is a provocative idea. The Hollywood-centred earlier part of the book is much the more entertaining, but even here Monroe is apt to overshadow Dean as a *character*. And 'characters', not historical figures, are what Dann makes them. Dean 'giggles' too often; his love life, including hints of ungay gay incidents in the past, is monotonous, at least as a spectator sport; and there doesn't seem enough going on in his head to account for the second half of the book.

The shadow of Monroe hangs over all this. She is the book's fulcrum. Dean gets caught up with the Kennedys whom he blames for Monroe's death, and the Kennedys, perhaps wondering how much he knows, woo him. Somehow, though, Dean as political groupie (he takes up with '60s activists), then as Kennedy campaigner, then as Californian gubernatorial candidate just doesn't persuade the reader. This Dean was more interesting before the car crash than after. Don't say legend-making doesn't know what it's about.

There is a powerful element of fakery in both acting and politics, the difference being that it's what acting is *meant* to be about (except if, like Dean or Monroe, you fetch up at Lee Strasberg's Actors' Studio where you've got to *live* it all). Dann, and one does sometimes stumble over the similarity of the two names, executes some lively set-pieces to focus the parallels between the worlds: here a political rally, there a Hollywood wedding. But he is not generally much concerned with leading us to draw conclusions about what is important in life, or even in lives.

At one point Dean accuses a lover of engaging in 'pop psychology'. Well, the book itself is not free from this taint. Dean has a recurring dream about his mother in a coffin on a train. It is she who 'calls him back' on the night of the accident; 'Momma' is the last word of the book; and Governor Dean receives news of his estranged father's death with affectless calm.

As for that other icon who so effortlessly summons up the era, Elvis too, we learn, loved his mother best of all. It would take a stronger authorial voice behind the banal and endlessly profane dialogue of the protagonists to make one care about what this might all mean. The really disappointing thing is that the eponymous 'rebel' doesn't seem to have the core of feelings or views to justify the title or the legend. Better, hire the DVD of the Ray film.

The Age, *Review*, 5 June 2004.

24

A CINEMA TORPID BUT NOT TERMINAL

Icons in the Fire: The Decline and Fall of Almost Everybody in the British Film Industry 1984–2000

By Alexander Walker

In this account of the efforts of an English-speaking cinema to keep its head above water, especially as it crosses the Atlantic, Australian filmmakers and readers may feel a sense of *déjà vu*. Again and again, in its crowded narrative, Hollywood emerges as the villain, sometimes intentionally so, sometimes because of its bloodless conquest of the screens of the world.

It is not enough, though, just to blame the Americans for their self-interested interference in the British film industry and Alexander Walker doesn't. If Hollywood is cast as chief villain, incompetent British institutions, persons and attitudes are seen as its henchmen, and they also get it in the neck from this knowledgeably fractious commentator.

Walker was film critic for London's *Evening Standard* for an astonishing 43 years until his death in 2003, in a tradition of distinguished British newspaper reviewers including Dilys Powell, Richard

Winnington and Philip French, people of serious, wide-ranging erudition.

Among this impressive line-up, Walker was perhaps the most industry-savvy. Forever sitting on committees, firing off letters to politicians and other functionaries, he used his high profile to keep his readers informed about what native filmmakers were up to. This book completes his trilogy on the changing state of British cinema: the others are *Hollywood England* (1974) and *National Heroes* (1985), surveying the 1960s and 1970s respectively; and like them *Icons* is as much about politics and business as films. Money – how to get it and what to do with it – is the recurring motif.

He has a remarkable grasp of the movers and shakers of the period under scrutiny. At its start, Goldcrest looked like the hope of the side, with successes like *Gandhi* to its credit, but a series of expensive flops (*Revolution*, *Absolute Beginners*) put paid to its aspirations. Similarly, the enterprising Palace Pictures, after a hit with *The Crying Game*, also came a cropper in the early '90s. Walker is astute about how these and others coped with the Thatcherite '80s (at least, they had something coherent to oppose) and how they lurched through the '90s, when Tony Blair's doomed concept of 'Cool Britannia' proved as delusive to their hopes as that single swallow is of summer.

Deals, taxes, take-overs, sell-outs, and acronyms that strain the memory are confidently appraised. Confidently, if not always perhaps fairly; but, then, it is easier to be memorable than judicious. Though I generally trust Walker's *aperçus* and recollections, there are times when the absence of footnotes irritates. Perhaps he would have added these if he'd lived to see this publication; and he would have got rid of such errors as misdating *Chariots of Fire* (1981, not 1983) and '[Leigh's] *Looks and Smiles*', instead of [Loach's], but such slips are nothing compared to that of National Heritage Secretary, Stephen Dorrell, who named the Jury president of Cannes Film Festival, 1995, as 'the distinguished Frenchman, Jean Moreau', a gaffe lovingly reported by Walker.

The book has a huge cast, some of whom, such as Kenneth Branagh and Emma Thompson, step revealingly into the spotlight, but many of the others are 'suits' not known to the general public – and, in general, the public is lucky in this respect. Many of these others, often influentially connected to potential moneybags for filmmakers, wouldn't know a good film if it struck them blind, and, in the convoluted narrative of hopes raised and dashed, one often feels that these chaps (and Virginia Bottomley, replacing Dorrell, sounds chappish to me) don't really take films seriously. They take revenue seriously, however, and so does Walker. In fact, he reserves his most atrabilious attacks for the failed promise of the National Lottery money, spread over films he too easily dismisses as flops.

Walker is usually ready to praise when he sees reason (e.g., *The Full Monty*'s success), but it is not always clear just what he expects of British films. He wants them to be truly indigenous *and* to appeal world-wide (where have we come across that?), to be critically lauded *and* to make pots of money. His bleak subtitle (differently rendered on the title page) doesn't seem to hold up when one thinks of such diversely rewarding films as *Wonderland*, *Topsy-Turvy*, *Sexy Beast*, *Bridget Jones's Diary*, or *Shakespeare in Love*. Is the junk factor higher than in the Hollywood output? The English patient suffers bouts of clinical depression but it doesn't seem terminal.

The Age, *Review*, 23 April 2005.

25

FLAUNTING YOUR PERFECTIONS

The Original Million Dollar Mermaid: The Annette Kellerman Story

By Emily Gibson (with Barbara Firth)

There is something peculiarly off-putting about a book whose opening sentence reeks of inaccuracy. 'In 1952, the first Technicolor water spectacular film *The Million Dollar Mermaid* thrilled the movie-going world.' I'm not talking about anything arcane here; just the sort of factual stuff anyone can check on the Internet. Esther Williams, star of *Mermaid*, the Annette Kellerman biopic, had appeared in about ten films since 1944's *Bathing Beauty* that might have qualified as 'water spectacular films'. Not to harp, but one's confidence is further undermined in the Foreword by co-author Firth's uninflected boast that, in 1964, she 'was invited to join the Ladies Committee of the Sydney Opera House Appeal Fund, which was at that time the most prestigious committee in Sydney,' rising in time to be its 'honorary public relations officer'.

None of this bodes well. There may well be material for a serious, even inspirational, biography of Kellerman, but this is not it. She was certainly a notable swimmer, overcoming infant rickets and leg braces, with steely determination, and no doubt it took tenacity to achieve what she did. She found success on three continents, as champion swimmer and diver, and as inventor of the one-piece bathing costume, which sought, like her aquatic displays, to combine the sexually provocative with the impeccably artistic. She had a brief popular career in silent films, and a fleeting resurgence of her réclame in her native Australia in World War 2.

How likable does she seem to have been? On the basis of this soppy biography, not very. There is the potential for local-girl-made-good, triumphing over setbacks, but there is ultimately – or even early on – something wearisome in her relentless seeking of new 'challenges'. Apart from her aquatic skills, she tries her hand (and the rest of her famously revealed body) at ballet, motoring, tennis (a pro accompanied her on tour during this craze), highwire-walking, singing and (ill-advisedly) buckjumping. She is even said to have written books, though there is no evidence of her ever sitting still long enough to *read* one. She's a real goer and no mistake. If it weren't such a terrible thing to say about anyone, I'd say she saw herself as 'feisty'.

During all this non-stop activity, she is partnered by Jimmie L Sullivan, at first her manager as she embarks on a career on the vaudeville circuits, then as her long-suffering husband. While she is away from him in England, she realises 'how "really grand" Jimmie was. She remembered all the kind sweet things he'd done for her.' Thus, in the language of Mills & Boon, is their 60-year-long marriage ushered in and it never gets any better. No cliché is left interred: 'It was a classic example of opposites attracting'; 'They look happy but it's obvious she's the boss'; and so on, as she drags the quiescent

Jimmie in her wake. At one point he's asked what it was like being married to her, famous as she then was, and he is loyal and discreet. Personally, I wouldn't have risked lunch with her, let alone marriage.

Her film career embraced what sound like some of the silliest films ever made. For the most part they have been 'lost', as has so much early cinema, so one has to rely on the second-hand accounts offered here of such epics as *Neptune's Daughter* (1914), the ridiculous-sounding *Daughter of the Gods* (1916), in which she is attacked by an army of gnomes, jumps into a pool of 'slavering, open-mouthed crocodiles' and falls in full armour from a horse into the sea, and *Queen of the Sea* (1918), in which she is chained in a dungeon, attacked by live ferrets and escapes death from revolving knives. And she has the nerve to be critical of the Esther Williams biopic!

Her kind of film, and her kind of star, had finished its vogue by the 1920s, but she seems to have become locked into the idea of celebrity and finds it hard to be out of the limelight. She stops at nothing, even writing (deplorable) songs to entertain an uncritical audience of troops in the early 1940s. Much of her life sounds absurd at least in the coy, cliché-ridden style of this biography. It is sparing in the matter of sources; much of it reads like fanzine speculation resting on only the flimsiest evidence, some of it provided by Annette's own memoir (unpublished and one sees why). It is carelessly proofed ('humourous' etc), is slack about following up potentially interesting figures like the director Herbert Brenon with whom she quarrelled (my heart went out to him) and who went on to a long career, and never brings to bear on Annette's tiring and tiresome exploits any of the assessing rigour it so sorely needs.

It's as though we're asked to accept Annette at her own valuation of herself, whether or not she's actually being quoted. Let her, then, have the last word, in this bit of puff from an 'unknown' newspaper: 'Being the perfect woman antagonises other women. You can't be superior with them. You must be on their plane. They don't like to think you're flaunting your perfections at them.' Gosh, how true.

Australian Book Review, June–July 2005.

26

HEPBURN SPRINGS ETERNAL

Kate

By William J Mann

This year marks the centenary of Katharine Hepburn's birth. She finally came clean about her birth date when longevity was getting to be her trump card. So, what does her name mean as we approach this anniversary?

Do we think of her as one of the greatest (perhaps *the* greatest) and most enduring stars of the cinema, a name to be reckoned with from the early days of talkies through a phenomenal haul of four Oscars right up to the '90s when she was still plying her craft (and craftiness)? Does she stand in the public mind for something more substantial than this, something above and beyond being a mere star (even Elizabeth Taylor was that): for a kind of integrity, a gallant endurance, that give her stature as a woman?

Has she a place in the pantheon as a sensational, one-of-a-kind beauty? Surely she had two of the most perfect cheekbones in the history of women's faces, and a figure as lithe as an Olympic gymnast's.

Or is she now most likely to be remembered for her long-standing relationship with Spencer Tracy? If 'relationship' sounds chilly, 'romance' is wishy-washy and 'affair' reeks of headline triviality.

William J Mann's huge book (you could use it hold lift-doors apart, but it feels light in the mind) is anxious to set us straight on all these approaches, about which, hitherto, we and her previous chroniclers have all been so wrong. He admires her career up to a point, but doesn't let it take up too much space, warning us early that there won't be plot synopses or accounts of directors at work. The films, whose titles can make one weak with gratitude, are interpreted in the light of how she manipulated her public persona through them to parry the changing times.

She was a maverick in 30s Hollywood but, recovering from bouts of unpopularity, recreated herself as man's indomitable helpmeet in *The African Queen* (1951). Mann implies that she lost her nerve about some of her later choices: she may have been, more than most, the author of her own career but there were other issues at stake in the roles she played – like, for instance, what the public wanted to see and studios to make.

Having reduced the career to gap-fillers in the personal story, Mann then proceeds to demystify the woman. There are the upper-middle-class professional parents – the father she sought to please, made to sound a bully; the mother with her avant-garde notions on matters such as birth control – and the childhood in which she wanted to be not 'Kath' but 'Jimmy'.

Here Mann's pop-psychologising takes off, as he explains laboriously how all this and more (the perhaps sexually 'conflicted' brother who killed himself) went to work in Kath's conscious burnishing of her own public image. She is presented as endlessly working to create a myth of herself, with lasting fame as its overriding goal, until the later years when his 'research' leads him to find her arrogant, drink-flustered and querulous, clinging desperately to her stardom and needing to be deferred to and adored.

It is in the stuff about Tracy that Mann's agenda is made most palpable. There were earlier liaisons, none of them very *dangereuse* in the sexual sense, Mann urges us to believe. After dispensing with nice husband Ludlow Smith, she has dealings with philandering poet Phelps Putnam, with John Ford, great director and possibly vile man, and with millionaire aviator Howard Hughes, before embarking on the legendary partnership with Tracy.

And would you believe that every one of these men, Mann assures us, having himself been assured by 'irreproachable' sources, had at least furtive fumblings with other men. This is worked into a theory which assumes grid-like status over the book: Hepburn, who wanted to be a boy, really looked for apparently very masculine men but didn't much care for the carnal couplings that might have been expected from them and sought erotic solace with a series of women.

This becomes the book's obsession. Every man who approaches her life will be found to have 'conflicted' (it's one of his favourite words) attitudes to sex. Mann keeps casting doubts on whether Hepburn and they ever much went in for sex, whereas he is determined that every woman who crosses her path quickly slides from friend to lover.

The predictability of Mann's interpretations is utterly wearying. He may have unparalleled access to the secrets of gay Hollywood, but the reader can't help wondering (or 'can't help but wonder' as this sloppy stylist would say, when he's not saying 'disinterested' instead of 'uninterested') if there weren't other friends, other colleagues, who might have had different stories to tell, or at least different perspectives on the same ones. Five hundred pages of guessing whom she did or did not sleep with is more than enough; and the repeated quoting of interviewees of a provenance difficult to assess gives the whole thing a not merely tiresome but also a sleazy air.

If you have admired Hepburn's coruscating career highlights – think of *Bringing Up Baby*, *Holiday*, *The Philadelphia Story*, *Adam's Rib*, *Long Day's Journey into Night*, *The Lion in Winter* others too – then let me prevail on you not to read this fat, smug, self-important book. It doesn't do justice to what she was best at, and it makes a rather ugly meal of the rest.

The Age, 6 January 2007.

27

A POIGNANT TALE WORTH PLAYING AGAIN

Ingrid: Ingrid Bergman, A Personal Biography

By Charlotte Chandler

The very first scandal of my stainless youth was the 1950 defection of St Ingrid Bergman from wholesome Hollywood to corrupt Italy and the embraces of director Roberto Rossellini, by whom she was somewhat pregnant.

Sad and hapless girls got carelessly pregnant in those benighted days, but Ingrid Bergman! Married to that nice Swedish dentist, Petter Lindstrom, with daughter Pia, and the radiant star of a string of uplifting and hugely popular films – I mean, she was even *Joan of Arc* – she was the epitome of the 'natural', her glorious Nordic beauty at a remove from the brand-name glamour of, say, Lana Turner. I never was more shocked – up to that time, anyway.

What *now* seems shocking is the prudish viciousness of the American public at the time. Perhaps if she hadn't been 'Hollywood's first lady, the number one actress in box office for three years' as Charlotte Chandler tells us, the sense of outrage would have been less vociferous.

She became *persona non grata* in the US and did not film in Hollywood again until *Cactus Flower* in 1969, though she had been forgiven to the extent of being awarded a second Oscar in 1956 for *Anastasia*.

Hers had been an extraordinary career. Spotted by David O Selznick's agent in the Swedish romance, *Intermezzo*, she was signed to a contract, which he made a lot of money from by hiring her out for such successes as *Casablanca* ('We'll always have Paris'), *Gaslight* (her first Oscar), *For Whom the Bell Tolls*, *The Bells of St Mary's* (as a nun with TB) and Hitchcock's *Notorious*, in which she and Cary Grant had one of the longest snogging sessions in mainstream film. Chandler gives prosaic plot synopses of all the films but is essentially uninterested in saying anything about them.

How, one wonders, could she *not* have wanted to give more sense of Bergman's career highlights? Of the wonderful womanliness, comprising beauty, sexiness and tenderness? Of her way of *inhabiting* a role instead of just putting it on? Think of the ardent bride gradually revealed in her vulnerability in *Gaslight* and the access of strength she finds at the last. Or of Henrietta Flusky's long take in *Under Capricorn*, when she spills out the guilt and unpayable gratitude that have brought her to antipodean befuddlement. Or, years later, the world-famous pianist faced with her daughter's resentments in Ingmar Bergman's *Autumn Sonata*. And in perhaps her most famous role of all, as Ilsa in *Casablanca*, how many actresses might so convincingly made us aware of the conflicting claims of passion and integrity? There is a feeling not just of a generous talent but of generosity itself at work in such performances.

The watershed for Bergman was seeing Rossellini's neo-realist classic *Open City*, and deciding – wrong-headedly as it would prove –

that she needed to be directed by him. She persuaded Howard Hughes to put up the money for *Stromboli*, in which it should have been apparent that, however besotted they were with each other, neither she nor Rossellini had anything to offer the other professionally. For the rest of her life, and to her credit, she never spoke other than well of him, and she was distraught at his death.

There is some real poignancy in Bergman's loss of contact with daughter Pia who stayed in the US with unforgiving control-freak Petter, and she seems to have been a devoted mother to her three children with Rossellini. Chandler has spoken with the children, especially with the beautiful Isabella, and none of them does a 'Mommie Dearest' job on mother Ingrid.

Chandler's sub-title, 'A Personal Biography', is puzzling. Does this mean she is offering just her own view of her luminous subject? Or is she deliberately deflecting potential criticism of the vacuous and trivial comments on the actual films?

The most commonly used phrase in the book is 'told me' and a great many people have 'told' her a great deal, which she records in unmediated slabs of direct speech. Since there are no footnotes, it is hard to establish the provenance of such testimony of children, directors, co-stars and others. Sometimes she tells us the year of her discussion with Hitchcock or whoever, but more often not. Eight people are acknowledged 'With special appreciation' and dozens more have to make do simply 'With appreciation'. That will teach them not to be more forthcoming.

The author is not afraid of a cliché ('Hollywood had been everything she dreamed it would be', 'Roberto was there for her', and all heart attacks are 'massive'). At times the book felt like a 300-page article from *New Idea*, but what saves it is Bergman herself.

It sounds a wet thing to say, but she *does* emerge as a genuinely nice woman: not for her the shag-and-tell reminiscences of, say, bathing beauty Esther Williams (talk about having one's illusions shattered), she does seem by all the accounts given to have been kind, lacking in personal vanity, and with a regard for truth. In the end hers was a messy life, but with notable achievements as both actress and woman.

The villain of the story is the awful cant which set about destroying her life and career. It says something for her that she rose above it – and it says something for the world that it may have grown out of such censoriousness. Or 'moved on' as Chandler would probably say.

The Age, 12 May 2007.

28

AUSTRALIAN SCREEN CLASSICS

Alvin Purple

By Catharine Lumby

If you take a piece of paper and cut off half of the image of Graeme Blundell on the cover of this book and then inspect the left-hand side, you will get what seems to be the knowing, winking Aussie bloke of folklore. If, then, you cut off this side with your strip of paper and inspect the right-hand side of the face, you'll find something very different: a mildly watchful, somewhat timid image at odds with the other half. This laborious introduction is by way of saying, you – that is, we – should stop and think again about this film.

My own attitude to *Alvin Purple* at the time of its 1973 release was pretty much along the lines of, 'well, if it's popular that's something, but it's certainly not art.' I don't recall having wanted to review it then, and, without feeling any need to demolish it, tended to be more or less dismissive of it in later writings. So, I said to myself, what is this excellent series up to in devoting a whole book to this 'ocker' piece, mild fun as I recalled at the time, without ever feeling any need to look at it again? Now, I have to say that Catharine Lumby gives ample grounds for anyone to think again about this financial success so derided by the critics. Perhaps even to watch it again.

Above all, the book makes a potent case for the importance of seeing the film in context. This will almost always be instructive in the way we read a film. In relation to *Alvin Purple*, we should, following Lumby's lead, have in mind several key contexts. There was a powerful sense of 'liberations' in the air in the late 60s/early 70s, for example, in matters of race and sexuality, of gender stereotypes, of educational theory, of attitudes to drugs, of a changing political climate. Some of the fervours surrounding these may seem quaintly outmoded now, but Lumby recreates vividly a sense of those not so distant decades of which *Alvin* now seems so emblematic an artefact. She is very strong on 1970s obsessions, and particularly on the burgeoning feminist movement of the period.

But it is not just the social context which is so crucial to 'placing' – and perhaps even understanding – this film. The book is equally useful in recalling to us the nature of the Australian film industry at the time, though the use of the term 'industry' suggests a more coherent entity than anyone would have recognised then. Lumby draws attention to the two different strands of film-making that were finding favour with divergent demographics: the ocker comedies which had a popular following, and the period pieces which attracted critics and supposedly more discriminating audiences. As she says, 'The anti-ocker forces won out and Australian cinema took a very different turn, in the process becoming hailed as a standard-bearer for a much-touted Australian cultural renaissance dominated by arty period films.'

In such an industrial/cultural setting, *Alvin* had its genesis. As to 'industry', Lumby's account of some of the key players brings the period evocatively to life. Almost no one was more influential in 1970s Australian cinema than *Alvin*'s producer-director, Tim Burstall, and the book draws valuably on his assessments of industry directions. Other names to conjure with in regard to this film and its time are playwrights Alan Hopgood (author of *Alvin* and other screenplays) and David Williamson (quoted in reference to the critical reception of Burstall's next film *Peterson*), Alan Finney and Hexagon Productions. The aim of the latter was, at least for Burstall, to make 'a populist Australian comedy that could cash in on the new R-certificate'. In other words, industry and the new sexual licence were operating in tandem, and this would partly explain *Alvin*'s popularity. There was undoubtedly a sense of change in the air, in theatre and society at large as well as film, and *Alvin* is both symptomatic of such change and one of the means by which it infiltrated the culture.

Even more impressive in this study is the way the protagonist of the film is analysed in terms of these cultural shifts and in comparison with some of the other influential male images of the period. Two contemporary popular and contrasting such images were those of Paul Hogan and Garry McDonald (aka Norman Gunston). Hoges was 'a knockabout blue-collar larrikin', with a dim offsider, 'Strop' (John Cornell), while Gunston was a nerdish interviewer in an ill-fitting tuxedo jacket. Both of these personas offered critiques of Australian masculinities, and one of the fascinating things about Lumby's book is how she interrogates yet another incarnation of the Australian male in Graeme Blundell's Alvin. By contrast with the various kinds of assurance exhibited by Hoges and

Gunston, Alvin 'is an unassuming lower-middle class boy adrift in a self-consciously bourgeois sea'.

Blundell had been at the cutting-edge not only of such theatrical developments as Melbourne's experimental La Mama but also of the activism concerned with censorship conflicts. He'd been involved with Alexander Buzo's play *Norm and Ahmed*, which famously used the word 'fucking' on stage. He was not an actor, on the strength of his credentials, likely to lend himself to mindless ockerism; at very least his image of self-aware reticence might be said to subvert such an easy agenda. He was identified with what Lumby characterises as 'a genuine sense that the battle against censorship was part of a broader battle against politically and socially oppressive forces.' Possibly the most embarrassing aspect of his Alvin thirty years on is the truly appalling hairstyle and clothes he was required to wear: it is frightening to think these might ever again be fashionable, but vestigially useful to have them preserved on celluloid as a terrible warning to future generations.

Alvin may be the irresistible object of female sexual intentions (which would lead to the divestment of the garments just shuddered at) but Lumby's analysis prevents our adopting a simplistic attitude of outrage at the film's alleged sexism. She offers a very thorough, thoughtful, unclamorous reading of the film, taking on board what it represents of women's desires. Without reducing the film to a mere smorgasbord of '70s radicalism, she convincingly argues for *Alvin*'s being a more complex text than one might have expected. Not only does it challenge some accepted notions of masculinity, but Burstall chose Blundell to play Alvin in a way that would be acceptable to both men and women, describing Blundell's Alvin in these terms:

'He isn't the centre of the action. He's the sort of person who things happen to. He doesn't make things happen.' A protagonist along these lines is unlikely to rouse male envy or female obloquy. He is passive enough, despite his *donnée* of mysterious sexual allure, for women to feel that he is *their* target rather than them as *his*.

Lumby situates this discourse on *Alvin* as a representation of female desire in the 1970s context of a feminist polemics that made itself felt variously in the high-level argumentation of a Germaine Greer and in more populist vein in the pages of *Cleo* magazine. In their different ways, and possibly aimed at different female audiences, these and others like them insisted on women's rights, particularly in what women did with their bodies in sexual and other matters. *Cleo* was, in 1972, the first Australian magazine to launch a male centrefold – of actor Jack Thompson, hands discreetly placed (to avoid offence? or titillate the mag's readers still more?). Viewed against such background material, it is possible to reconsider *Alvin* as a comic contribution to the dialectic relating to women's sexuality which was so much a feature of the decade.

This may or may not qualify *Alvin Purple* as a progressive text, but Lumby does persuade us that it is amenable to more sophisticated assessment than it has commonly received. The 'merely' popular may in fact have a good deal to tell us about what was widely acceptable at the time. It may, as well, in the hands of a film-maker who knows what he is about, tell us things we weren't programmed to notice at the time. I don't mean that *Alvin Purple* is a neglected masterwork, and I don't think Catharine Lumby intends us to reach any such conclusion. What this admirably lucid and wide-ranging study accomplishes is to value the film for what it *does* achieve, to avoid easy put-downs and to unravel it as a sort of matrix of cultural strands. That doesn't make the film great, but it does make it interesting, and the book that pulls this off is another feather in the cap of a generally provocative series.

Senses of Cinema, February 2009.

29

I PEED ON FELLINI

Recollections of a Life in Film

By David Stratton

The tasteful title to this autobiography echoes the story once told of how the ebullient Italian producer, Filippo Del Guidice, performed the same disservice to J. Arthur Rank and survived to become a force in the British film industry. David Stratton, after looking sideways in a Venetian toilet, never looked back – despite Fellini's understandable choler.

Forty-odd years later, he is now best known as co-presenter with Margaret Pomeranz of SBS's *The Movie Show*, which survived transfer to the ABC as *At the Movies*. In fact Pomeranz doesn't enter the book until page 290, and there had been a range of film-related activities before Stratton started to be recognised in the street as a result of his television exposure. It may appear surprising to some that they have lasted so long – this middle-aged pair: a seemingly zany woman with big earrings and a somewhat uptight man in suit and tie – but the fact is that they *have* survived, not only a change in channels but the changing public tastes in movies.

She had been a producer/writer at SBS well before she and Stratton teamed up, and she claimed she'd wanted to bring out 'the other side' in Stratton, 'the funny side, the raconteur'. If that was her aim, I think it must be said that she failed, but equally that doesn't seem to have put off the viewers, who stuck with them when they left SBS in 2004, after a bitter conflict with new management there, and found a comparable niche with the ABC. It is useful to have this contretemps explained and it doesn't redound to the credit of SBS.

Stratton is one of those autobiographers who feel a need to start with the grandparents on either side of his family, work their way through the family fortunes (the grocery trade in his father's case, and for a time Stratton himself looked headed for this), chronicle the vicissitudes of education, and so on, before getting down to what made one interested enough in him to want to read about him in the first place. In his case, his obsession with film is what marked him for life and only his maternal grandmother, who took him at an early age to *Duel in the Sun*, shared this interest. We should all have had such grandmothers.

Arriving in Australia with his first wife, Margaret, in the early 1960s, he adapted to his new country and simply stayed. There's rather a lot about travels around country with friends, about looking for jobs and flats, about finding fellow film 'buffs'. (I'm always surprised to find that people who take films – or opera or whatever – seriously use this word which seems to trivialise their preoccupation.) He joined the Sydney Film Festival as a member of its selection sub-committee and in 1966 he was appointed its Director. From this point, everything else, including marriage and fatherhood, took second place in a life dominated by hurtling round the world's festivals in the interests of Sydney's, and by endless conflicts with censorship bodies.

There is no doubt that he has had a full and gratifying career. When he gave up the SFF directorship, he concentrated on writing, for whatever journals or papers asked him to, including *Variety* and, much later, *The Australian*, where he still shares the reviewing with Evan Williams, and in the 2000s, while maintaining his television presence, he has also taught Continuing Education courses in Film History at the University of Sydney. And he now contrives to do this while living in the Blue Mountains with his second wife, Susie.

I'm aware that this review is in danger of becoming little more than a list of his appointments but one of the problems with the book is that it moves with unrelenting linearity through jobs and trips and meetings. It is all more or less blameless: it slides down easily like invalid food: but it has no real edge, no sharpness, no perspective. The book's final chapter in which he talks of his commitment in relation to political and social events comes almost as a surprise. It has a tacked-on feel to it, when the book might have benefited by the integration of such attitudes into the texture of the emerging career.

My real worry with the book is to do with its platitudinous style and the frequent banality of its observations. On the foreign festivals he attended, he offers such unrevealing commentary as having done 'a fair bit of sightseeing' or having had 'quite an experience'. He has clearly met a great many interesting people, but though they may have 'hit it off' (as he often says) he never gives any sense of what made these encounters so memorable for him. I feared the writing was on the wall, as it were, when he recalled that, at his 21st birthday, 'close friends and family were in attendance'. I mean, whom did he expect? The Luton Girls' Choir? There is no ear for detecting clichés, so that we hear that Ron Moody was so funny he 'kept us in stitches' or that

Diana Dors had changed her name 'before hitting the big time' or that an idea is condensed 'in a nutshell'. It may sound merely captious to refer to such examples, but this sort of writing will for some of us be a barrier to engagement with the material. My personal linguistic Geiger, and this book reminds me of it several times, is never to trust the prose of someone who 'purchases' things rather than 'buys' them.

There is sometimes almost a touching faith in our caring about how he got to places, who met him, what kind of hotel he stayed at, and with whom he 'spent time together'. I used the word 'linearity' before, and there is too often no more than a sense of 'Then …' or 'Next …' or 'After …' when one would welcome shape and assessment. On the other hand, there are very few obvious errors ('Diana' instead of 'Dinah' Sheridan; Sylvia 'Sims' instead of 'Syms', 'Stefan' rather than 'Stephan' Elliott, Louise Fletcher won Best Actress, not Best Supporting Actress) of the kind one is apt to find in memoirs, and that is a relief. It means that the 'information' of the book can be trusted, even if one keeps wishing Stratton had more of an eye for the detail that would vivify the experience of a place or a meeting or a film. There must have been more to say about Joseph Von Sternberg or Wim Wenders or even Joan Fontaine than is on show here.

If the foregoing seems ungenerous, it is only fair to add that the author does, in however pedestrian a style (riddled as it is with acronyms), provide a clear enough account of the changes in Australian film culture over several decades. He also emerges as an amiable man, and, as one who shares his passion for film and who also rates *Newsfront* as his favourite Australian film, I'd want to acknowledge his diverse contributions to that changing culture. I'm not sure that fans of *The Movie Show*, and for all I know their name is Legion, won't prefer to listen to him rather than read him, but what he has recorded here is worth having set down.

Australian Book Review, March 2008.

30

THE SPELLBINDER

God of Speed

By Luke Davies

The title is presumably meant to be ambiguous. Not only did the protagonist, Howard Hughes, hurtle round the world in aeroplanes of his own devising, and not only did he ingest amphetamines at a rate that would finish most of us, but as well there is a sense of crashing non-stop through life itself. And 'speed', he tells us, 'shouldered some of the weight for me … helped me maintain control over a bucking project, since, control, ultimately, is all there is.'

As I read *God of Speed*, I couldn't help wondering who still knows about Hughes (1905–76). Perhaps younger readers will have seen Martin Scorsese's intermittently engrossing biopic, *The Aviator* (2004). Quite by chance, my daughter told me she was recently speaking to someone who had never heard of Merle Oberon. I can't say how shocked I was. It led me to wonder if such people will know who Hughes's famous bed-partners were (not Merle, I'm happy to say). It is one thing to say their name was Legion; it is another to say their names were also Billie Dove, Jean Harlow, Carole Lombard, Faith Domergue (Faith who? I hear you cry. Only dedicated buffs will know), among many others. Buffs will also have no trouble with Jane Greer, and how privileged they are, while the elderly will smile knowingly at the bedroom appearances of Susan Hayward, Lana Turner, Ava Gardner and Ginger Rogers – and surely everyone knows about Katharine Hepburn, but you can't help wondering how long people's memories are.

Anyway, everyone should know about Luke Davies because he is, on the strength of *God of Speed* and his earlier novel *Candy* (1997), already a major figure among Australian novelists. As one who wouldn't know smack from crack, I was irresistibly drawn into the drug-driven life of *Candy*'s young first-person narrator, and moved by its tenderness as a love story. And yes, *God of Speed* is a novel, masquerading as a sort of autobiography, and, as in *Candy*, Davies is utterly inside the mind of his protagonist, the semi-deranged billionaire, wildly successful womaniser, aviator, inventor, movie-maker and, ultimately, drugged-out recluse.

Hughes, in 1973, is holed up in a London hotel where he is waiting for his old friend Jack Real (a name to conjure with) to sleep off his jet-lag, having just flown in from the United States. The novel takes shape as Hughes compiles memories of old times, of air crashes and lovers, with which to regale Jack when he wakes. It is a formal triumph as Davies organises these snapshots of Hughes' past, making us feel privy to some sort of autobiography in progress while retaining a novelist's control. For all the talk of Hughes' 'control', it is really Davies' that is so impressive. That is, the 'snapshots' aren't just arbitrary, aren't just strung one after another in the chronological order most autobiography demands. The device of having Hughes imagine what he and Jack will talk about is a novelist's invention and it keeps us at a reflective remove from the actual events.

The flying adventures, with spectacularly evoked crash landings as well as the 1938 round-the-world exploit, are chronicled with an often astonishing sense of the sensuous thrill of being in the cockpit at great heights, or spiralling to earth when an engine has failed. The 1938 trip surfaces several times as Hughes makes landings at various stopovers, and the way the pioneer aviator deals with the pressures of flight – the physical demands it makes and its almost orgasmic rewards – compels admiration for this madly driven 'hero'. If, your parents dead, you've inherited a huge fortune at eighteen, it must be hard to find serious challenges and Davies persuades us that Hughes found his in flying.

The other great love of his life, at least until he started to fall apart physically, is that for beautiful women; that is, for some of the most *sensationally* beautiful women ever brought to the world's breathless attention. Davies does as brilliantly by this aspect of Hughes' obsessiveness as by the passion for speed. The sexual appetites and proclivities of his all-star cast are lovingly distinguished the one from the other, detailed with a carnal precision that has nothing to do with pornography. Most of these beauties are dead now, but I couldn't help wondering about the possibilities of litigation from, say, Olivia De Havilland, a still lively-minded 91-year-old, and what she might have to say about the reference to her. She, after all, took on Warner Bros and won, in the matter of suspension time's being added to contract period.

Hepburn would surely have had something to say, as Davies' prose caresses her finely honed body with a rapture that seems scarcely less than that of Hughes' recollection of what his hands had been up to. Decorum forbids me to quote here how these twin processes are achieved, except to record how Hughes sums up his time with the great love of his life: 'We were like two bony whippets going at it.' There's more sense of the Hepburn-ness of the megastar in almost any sentence of Davies than there was in the 600 pages of *Kate* (2006), William Mann's vast – and vastly awful – biography of her. His dealings with Jane Greer, *film-noir* icon as she became, are symptomatic of how he viewed most of his women. However enticing they were – and the gorgeous Greer, in whose 'lips was all the ineffable essence of welcoming', was as exquisite as any – he required of them total subservience. 'What right had she to see other men? I made her, I owned her for now.' Some, like poor hapless Domergue, pestered him for film chances, and he didn't like that either.

What sort of man then emerges from 'the cascading of memories'? A more complex one than you might think. Anyone who had the perception to notice that Hepburn was a great beauty as well as a briskly daunting companion had something going for him. On the other hand, note what he has to say about the fabulously lovely Gene Tierney (does anyone under 50 know whom we mean?) and her husband Count Oleg Cassini. Of her, he remembers 'there were bouquets of hyacinths hidden inside her', but of Cassini, 'a lowly fashion designer who should really and may well have been a fag', he is pleased to recall 'his greaseball macho pride' and speaks of their handicapped child as 'a retard'. He was perfectly vile in all sorts of manipulative ways, solipsistic to the nth degree, racist, insanely obsessive about planes, women and germs, but, as Davies creates/recreates him, a riveting raconteur and a spell-binding risk-taker. He wanted the whole world and came nearer to achieving that goal than almost anyone ever has; and he became a control freak firing off memos to ensure that the world, or at least that part of it he knew, marched to his drum.

The novel's brief chapters are interspersed with these memos. The sequence of memories is not merely haphazard and there are sometimes verbal links between the end of one and the start of the next that convince us about the processes of mind that are being dramatised here. For instance, one 'snapshot' ends with his screaming about Sinatra, 'Let me talk to the bastard! Lemme get my hands on him,' Sinatra having had *his* hands on Ava Gardner. The next slab of memory begins, 'No, I couldn't see what Gardner saw in him. Let alone why she would marry him. Because Sinatra was a greaseball.' Davies is fascinated by all sorts of things about Hughes, not just by the complex unlovable individual he lets him reveal himself as being. As well, Hughes commands attention for what he incarnates about the seemingly endless possibilities of the twentieth century – and, resonating out further still, for the extraordinary capacity of great wealth to corrupt and deaden the moral sense.

God of Speed is an Australian novel that has nothing to do with the specificities of Australia: it is, though, a *tour de force* and you can't often say as much about a novel from any source. I'm eager for his next book, even if it's about the excitements of double-entry accounting.

Australian Book Review, April 2008.

31

'HE REALLY WAS A CONTENDER'

Somebody: The Reckless Life and Remarkable Career of Marlon Brando

By Stefan Kanfer

It is not too much to claim that Marlon Brando changed the possibilities of film acting. Some would go further and call him the most important film star of his century.

True or not (and there aren't too many others who might have been, in Terry Malloy's words, 'a contender' for this accolade), there is no denying that he was hugely influential. If you're admiring, say, Sean Penn today, you might easily trace his lineage back to Brando. This doesn't mean that Cary Grant or James Stewart and other big male stars at the time became obsolete when Brando burst on the screen in *The Men* (1950). It just means that something rougher, rawer, more extemporary-seeming had in one leap staked his right to be mentioned in the same breath.

He had come into acting – both on stage and screen – when the climate was changing in the post-war years. Playwrights such as Tennessee Williams and Arthur Miller were dramatising a more savage vision of America; films, with more to lose economically, were as usual slower to come to terms with shifting social realities. But the films Brando made in short order – *The Men*, as a paraplegic casualty of the war, *A Streetcar Named Desire* (1951), *Viva Zapata!* (1952), *Julius Caesar* and *The Wild One* (1953) made much foregoing screen acting seem old-fashioned. He exhibited a threatening sensuality, a potent willingness to go out on a limb, in both physical terms and the dangerous challenge he offered to every kind of status quo.

He'd played brutal, slobbish Stanley in *Streetcar* on Broadway and repeated it on screen, legendarily bellowing for 'Stella!' and assaulting the fragile gentility of Vivien Leigh's Blanche. Was there another Hollywood star who could have carried this off convincingly – or the illiterate Mexican rebel leader Zapata, or the insolent motor-cyclist anti-hero of *The Wild One* – and then turn his attention so persuasively to Shakespeare with a subtly commanding Mark Antony? Then came the overdue Oscar for playing Terry Malloy, the battered longshoreman who has to make some crucial choices, in *On the Waterfront*.

It is too easy to say his career waned after this until the restorative of *The Godfather* in 1974, but certainly those first six remain landmarks in US film history, as does his Don Corleone performance twenty years later. Whatever failures and scandals became attached to Brando's name, Jack Nicholson is aptly quoted as saying, '... there was a reason people expected so much from him right to the end'. This book, though, doesn't really persuade us.

As far as the films are concerned, Kanfer trawls through them unrevealingly. He gives us plenty of the production history of each, though the absence of footnotes casts doubt on some accounts of on-set conflicts, follows this with straight descriptive plot recitals, and then adduces a swag of reviewer reactions.

Crucially missing is any sense of just what Brando was like on the screen. In biographies of great stage actors the author is inevitably relying on his or someone else's memory about actual performances, and often this can't be helped. But film acting is there to be looked at and analysed and assessed, for at least as long as video-recording has been around. I get the distinct impression that Kanfor doesn't trust his own judgments in this matter: he doesn't make me *see* Stanley or Terry Malloy or any of this imposing gallery of roles.

When it comes to the private life (and Brando had a lot of trouble keeping any of it that way), there is too much pop-psychologising about the lifelong effects of the abusive father and drunken mother and how these fed into either the acting or the support for liberal causes.

Maybe the difficult childhood *was* directly responsible for the oft-repeated undervaluing of the acting profession, and the deriding of the Hollywood hand that fed him so profusely, and the incapacity for sustaining relationships. But endless quotes are no replacement for authorial discrimination. Nor are lists of films or potted biographies of those who crossed the Brando path or slabs of familiar information about the film industry or the Vietnam War or, as they so endemically say, whatever.

In glib, sometimes crass style, flecked with such arcane usages as 'estrous' and 'lagniappe', he fails to do justice to one whom Molly Haskell described as 'a man "of the people" who towers above them, a man in constant tension with his own myth'. Kanfer settles for a summer beach-read instead – at best, Brando and soda.

The Age, 28 March 2009.

32

BOWERY TO BROADWAY

The American Irish in Classic Hollywood Cinema

By Christopher Shannon

Priests promoting a down-to-earth muscular Christianity; good-natured boozing fathers; saintly mothers working finger to the bone; pixilated soothsayer types: these were some of the ill-considered images of the Irish in American film that I'd carelessly let lie fallow in my mind over the decades. No longer. While there has never been an identifiable ongoing presence of, say, Scottishness or even Englishness in Hollywood cinema, those with long memories (a nice way of saying 'old people') will surely recall, nostalgically or not, the phenomenon of the Irish and American-Irish making themselves felt in a range of Hollywood films. In fact, *Bowery to Broadway* is the second book in recent years to address this matter, the other being Ruth Barton's *Acting Irish in Hollywood: from Fitzgerald to Farrell* (2006).

Whereas the latter investigated the Irish presence through tracing the careers of nine stars who had succeeded in Hollywood, Christopher Shannon's approach has been to examine a series of films, key representatives of their genres, and to focus on the ways in which

Irishness surfaces in these films. He is also concerned to 'place' these characteristic surfacings in relation to the wider sense of Irish-American cultural and political life, and *its* place, in turn, in the shifting panorama of American life at large in the first half of the twentieth century.

It's of course actors above all that stick in the mind as one summons up American movie images of Irishness. These films kept actors like Pat O'Brien, usually as a priest or some other respectable purveyor of ould-sod values, and Frank McHugh, bluff and rugged cops and others, in steady work for several decades. And there were stars too: big names like Bing Crosby, James Cagney and Spencer Tracy, from Irish-American backgrounds, and native Irish like Barry Fitzgerald, who was programmed to excite indulgent, undiscriminating laughter as soon as he spoke, and Maureen O'Hara, for whom Technicolor and the awful word 'feisty' were practically invented. I have to add a severe personal note here: neither Shannon nor Barton mentions that great beauty and remarkable actress Geraldine Fitzgerald. Faith, now, this is not good enough, to be sure.

Back to Shannon after this important digression. Shannon's excellent book – thoroughly researched, astutely perceptive and always readable – traces the kinds of Irish presence in Hollywood films from the late 1920s to the early '50s through a series of popular genres. In these films and in what he claims to be an accurate reflection of the Irish experience in America, he evokes the tension of the Irish being caught between the urge to upward mobility in the land of opportunity, on the one hand, and, on the other, the insistent allegiance to the community and family.

The book is divided into five main chapters, plus an introduction which sets out the author's intentions clearly and a conclusion that does more than merely summarise the foregoing five sections. Each of these examines a key genre from the point of view of how they render the Irish experience in their manipulation of genre conventions. Each takes its heading from a film title which resonates provocatively. In the first chapter, *Hell's Kitchen*, the title inducts us into its study of the gangster world, noting at the outset that, though 'Italian Americans won the battle to control the real-life world of gangsters, yet Irish Americans won the battle to represent the big-city gangster in Hollywood film'. In exploring films such as *The Public Enemy*, he draws persuasive attention to the clash of blind ambition and community loyalties, to the interaction of Irish-American cops, priests and gangsters on the make. In so far as the latter never (well, not if they're played by Cagney, for instance) wholly lose their hold on audience sympathies, Shannon argues that this is due to the residual influence of their ethnic community's morality working on them at some deeper level.

Boxing as a typical Irish way to US cultural citizenship is the subject of the second chapter titled, *City for Conquest* (named for the 1940 Anatole Litvak film), in which Cagney this time plays a boxer who instinctively knows that celebrity matters less than the values of family and stability, and at film's end his girl (Ann Sheridan) has also learnt this valuable lesson. Two other major stars who incarnated Irish-American pugilist stereotypes were scruffy Wallace Beery (*The Champ*, 1931, and others) and dashing Errol Flynn, whose last name qualifies him for inclusion here. In perhaps the most famous boxing film of all, *Gentleman Jim* (1942), he plays James Corbett, real-life champ, who embraced celebrity in a big way but is finally reclaimed to his Hibernian roots. You can take the boy out of the neighbourhood, but you can't take the neighbourhood out of the boy.

The other three major chapters – entitled *Bowery Cinderella* (named a bit obscurely for Burton King's 1927 film), *The Bells of St Mary's* (Leo McCarey's 1945 heart-tugger) and *Bowery to Broadway* (a 1944 musical directed by Charles Lamont) – follow the pattern of the earlier two. That is, there is a detailed account of films which archetypally enshrine the narrative and character paradigms that Shannon has identified. Once or twice you may feel that there is more plot description than is strictly necessary, but just as this cavil is about to assert itself Shannon retrieves his position with an astute analysis that goes beyond description. In his account of films starring Mary Pickford (*Amarilly of Clothes-Line Alley*, 1929) and Ginger Rogers (*Kitty Foyle*, 1940), Shannon traces the way their plot-lines move towards an affirmation of 'the cultural superiority of working-class Irish' over the more materialistic aspirations of the wider community. In *Kitty Foyle*, this point of view is encapsulated in Kitty's final choice of a classless doctor (James Craig) over an upper-class socialite (Dennis Morgan) who, bounder that he is, only wants to make working-girl Kitty his mistress.

Probably the most famous priest in Hollywood history is Father Bing Crosby, who won an Oscar for his Chuck O'Malley in *Going My Way* (1944), a character and film so popular that they spawned a successor in *The Bells of St Mary's* in the following year. Crosby's relaxed persona as the young priest sent to help out the aging Father Fitzgibbon (Barry Fitzgerald) at St. Dominic's ushered in a new film version of the Irish-American: neither gangster nor boxer, committed to his church but tolerant and easy-going, winning over delinquents by gentle persuasion. (Mind you, delinquents have come a long way since then, till we have the hoons of today.) As Shannon's analysis convincingly argues, the Crosby films established the possibility of being 'fully Irish and fully American'. The respective endings of the two films are worth noting: in *Going My Way*, he slips quietly out of the reunion he has organised of Father Fitzgibbon with his ancient Irish mother (Adeline De Walt Reynolds), Shannon noting that 'the priest/cowboy headed off to clean up another parish' (p.148), while in *The Bells of St. Mary's* he only leaves the parish, presided over by Sister Ingrid Bergman, when he has assured its future. These were images to warm the hearts not only of Irish Catholics but of Middle America at large in the troubled days of World War 2.

The final chapter, which, like the book at large, takes its title from the Universal musical starring Jack Oakie and Donald Cook as rival Irish-American showmen, is ushered in by an account of *Yankee Doodle Dandy*, Michael Curtiz's 1942 biopic of the Irish-American song-and-dance man George M. Cohan, who triumphed on Broadway in the early twentieth century. The film, which was a huge success (with Cagney again), 'helped to establish a link between the ethnic stage and the All-American screen'. Ignoring Cohan's wobbly Catholicism, the film brings him – and the Irish-American on the screen – together with President Roosevelt, through the common bond of the Democratic Party. Other film musicals with Irish-American themes are cited, and the chapter closes on the titular film whose title indeed can be seen as a metaphor for the Irish infiltration of the American entertainment scene, from Irish-American community to all-American acceptance.

Shannon's book finishes with a reflection on how things changed in the post-war era. The search for cultural identity was no longer crucial with the election of John F. Kennedy, with his Irish-Catholic roots, as President. In this America of the early 1960s, as Shannon wittily concludes, 'the dying Irish ghettos of New York, Boston and

Chicago have taken on something of the status of tribal homelands'. His study is as careful and scholarly as one could wish; it is also fresh, lucid and enjoyable, and one cannot always say as much for academic publishing.

Screening the Past, Issue 29, 7 November 2010.

33

'MOMMIE DEAREST' JUST ONE ROLE AMONG MANY

Possessed: The Life of Joan Crawford

By Donald Spoto

If your view of Joan Crawford was largely determined by daughter Christina's vindictive memoir, *Mommie Dearest*, or its campy film version, then you'd probably do well to read Donald Spoto's even-handed biography. There was clearly much more to Crawford than Christina was willing to allow. In an era like the present, when stardom may mean no more than getting your picture on the cover of *Hello!* Magazine, it is salutary to be reminded that the real thing involved dedicated hard work. As much as anyone, Crawford helped to define this twentieth-century phenomenon.

The English actress Jill Esmond, who'd known her in Hollywood in the early thirties, recalled two things about her fifty years later. When a lot of smart fashionable people like Douglas Fairbanks Jr, Crawford's first husband, and Laurence Olivier, Esmond's then-husband, would play clever word games, Esmond remembered how

Crawford would withdraw shyly to her knitting, embarrassed by her lack of education. When Esmond returned to Hollywood ten years later, no longer a rising star, divorced and with a sick child, the one 'name' of the earlier period who sought her out and treated her kindly was Joan Crawford.

These two memories encapsulate quite a bit about the woman whose life is at issue here. She came from an utterly deprived background: father walked out early in the piece; unsympathetic mother favoured a feckless son whom Joan would later support; Joan was put to work as a servant in the schools she was briefly sent to, and knew the drudgery of work in a laundry. And so on. No wonder she felt at a disadvantage among those game-players and in her own story she embodies some of the key characteristics of the American dream. By sheer single-mindedness in pursuit of her goal, she reached the top of her profession. If this made her difficult and demanding on occasion, as it no doubt did, the flip side of the public persona – the star who was always on duty – was the private woman who seems to have cared enough about people down on their luck to enter into their misfortunes and to do something about them.

Spoto's book stresses both aspects, without resorting to sensationalism or sentimentality. He charts the career trajectory so that the main 'acts' of its drama are apparent. First comes the dancing flapper of the silent screen, followed by the decade of major stardom at MGM, where she played several proto-feminist roles, as women determined to make their own way on their own terms, as well as more predictable Cinderella parts. In doing so, Spoto claims, 'Without intending to do so, [she] effectively changed the notion of stardom', acting out on screen the fantasies of vast female audiences. In her MGM films of the 30s, and her Warner Bros. films of the 40s, there is a potent sense of the confessional, of her own life with its pain and its obsessions, invested in such diverse films as the aptly-titled *Possessed* (1931) or her Oscar-winning *Mildred Pierce* (1945), right down to the faded star tormented (as you would be) by sister Bette Davis in *Whatever Happened to Baby Jane?* (1965).

Her career was everything to her, and almost until the end it was pretty remarkable, but it was achieved at a cost. It scarcely seems a coincidence that she made two films called *Possessed*, the second for Warners in 1947, for she was in many ways a woman possessed. Spoto chronicles the films in ways that stress their relevance to the life, to how they contributed to the successes and failures of her marriages (to three actors and finally, more happily, to Alfred Steele, the Pepsi king), and to difficulties with her children.

She was not, though, just the obsessive harpy her daughter created. She was honest about her humble origins, about her need to maintain the trappings of stardom, and she understood her own paranoia about this and about, say, the domestic perfections she demanded, and she was also clearly capable of generosity and empathy.

But it is the starring career that remains her legacy, and young people, who may be unfamiliar with its peaks, are strongly advised to check these out. No doubt she should have stopped earlier: the last two films, *Berserk* and *Trog*, both made in Britain, are horrors in every sense of the word. In them she prolonged her career but not her reputation; they are a long way from the angst and shoulder-pads of *Mildred Pierce*. *She*, though, was always worth watching, and Spoto's book goes some distance to making clear why.

The Saturday Age, 16 April 2015.

34

ONE MAN IN HIS TIME

John Gielgud: Matinee Idol to Movie Star

By Jonathan Croall

As the dust settles on twentieth-century acting giants, and reputations are appraised, it is at least arguable that John Gielgud emerges as the greatest. Certainly his was the longest and most varied career, spanning nearly eighty years, only death itself, when he was ninety-six, causing him to slow down. Since then his pre-eminence has seemed confirmed as one reads about him and his distinguished contemporaries.

These latter – Olivier, Richardson, Guinness, Redgrave – have all given rise to biographies but none has been as fortunately served as Gielgud. Jonathan Croall's first go at his life appeared in 2001, when it immediately set a new benchmark in the show business biography genre, especially as compared with Sheridan Morley's slipshod, dirt-dishing account of Gielgud in the same year. Now, having had access to many previously unpublished letters and other papers, plus a great deal more attention to the late-flowering film career, he has, in this second edition, made any further attempt on the actor's life redundant.

Usually acknowledged as the most eloquent speaker of Shakespearean verse, and described by his non-fan, the waspish Kenneth Tynan, as the best actor in the world from the neck up, his Hamlet, Prospero and many other key roles, set exacting standards for his successors to aim at. His Macbeth was less certain and his Othello a disaster, pointing perhaps to a lack of fierce physicality – or maybe the result of his having, as critic Ivor Brown noted, 'the most meaningless legs imaginable'. But his range was nevertheless vast, as was his influence, and Croall traces meticulously the ways in which he takes on and modernises the late Victorian idea of the actor-manager, reinvigorates the classical repertoire in London's West End, later adjusts to the more iconoclastic demands of the Royal Court theatre, eventually joins the National Theatre (where Olivier's jealousy may have delayed his participation), and becomes a familiar presence on film and television from his fifties until his death.

He hurdled the decades and changing theatrical fashions with apparent ease, and Croall has the knack of evoking vividly stage performances from the past and gives a sense of how Gielgud went about approaching these – and his screen roles. As well, he makes engrossing reading of how they were received, without descending into tiresome lists of snippets from reviews, which often makes such books wearisome. Instead, he creates a series of mini-dramas in chronicling the way the actor's work was received.

Gielgud was wary of film for a long time. Like many stage-trained actors in the early days of film, he regarded the new medium as a source of financial rather than artistic rewards, and in the 1940s his movie career seemed totally stalled. He was never going to be a conventional screen leading man, but in the latter half of his life he became a character actor *par excellence*. Playing Cassius in MGM's excellent version of *Julius Caesar* in 1952 was probably the turning-point, and he went on delivering the goods for nearly another fifty years. He claimed to have observed James Mason closely as he played Brutus and he won the admiration of Marlon Brando, who was Antony in this eclectically but excitingly cast Shakespeare film.

There were to be many film highlights in the ensuing decades, whether hinting discreetly at father Barrett's possibly incestuous leanings in *The Barretts of Wimpole Street* or moving wearily towards death as the King in Orson Welles's sublime *Chimes at Midnight.* He also starred magisterially in Alain Resnais' *Providence* (maintaining his dignity even from a lavatory seat in one sequence) and Peter Greenaway's imaginatively daring *Prospero's Books*, daring for Gielgud too, as he spoke all the dialogue and, at eighty-seven, appeared naked at one point). The list is almost unending, with television triumphs too, most memorably as Charles Ryder's bleak father in the much-revered *Brideshead Revisited* miniseries.

I stress the film and television appearances because they constitute one of the highlights of Croall's new edition in which they are now treated much more fully. He has spoken to many of those associated with Gielgud in these films, for screens large and small, as well as having viewed almost all of them, so that he is able to give vivid images of the actor's work and style.

But the career is not all. Gielgud emerges from all the research – from written or oral sources or actual viewings of the work – as a whole man, one perhaps only fully alive when working. He came from the theatre aristocracy of the Terry family on his mother's side, but he never learned how to behave in the grand manner. Consequently he seems to have been much loved and esteemed by those who worked with him, with the possible exception of Olivier, who always appeared warily in competition with him.

The cottaging scandal of 1953 is treated as an important and painful episode in the actor's life but there is nothing prurient in Croall's dealing with it. Ardently homosexual, Gielgud had several long (but non-exclusive) relationships, and these wind their way through the crowded narrative of a life full of achievement. Maybe the scandal cost him a peerage, but he was rewarded by having bestowed on him the rare Companion of Honour in 1977.

He had plenty of faults, was famously given to verbal gaffes, but was curiously devoid of malice. From Croall's 700-page account emerges a staggeringly prolific and very engaging figure – both career and man brought to brilliant life. With this and his biography of Sybil Thorndike, Croall stakes a serious claim to be the most notable theatrical biographer of the day.

Australian Book Review, November 2011.

35

OUT OF THE DARK

I Found It at the Movies: Reflections of a Cinephile

By Philip French

Whenever I've found myself in disagreement with Philip French's film reviews in London's *Observer*, I've always felt very worried, assuming I had missed a crucial point or misread a plot move. He may well be the longest-serving film reviewer in the English-speaking world; he is certainly the most honoured.

I am distinguishing here between 'reviewer' and 'critic': in French's words, 'Film reviewers work at the front line of criticism'. Reviewers who have to meet weekly deadlines and stringent word limits are the foot soldiers of the profession. Their words are tied to an occasion: that is, the opening of a new film. Some, though, combine reviewing with the more wide-ranging demands of critics, generating more reflective pieces, their authors not being subject to the pressures of reviewers. Philip French has shown a masterly grasp of both functions.

His professional background includes a long stint at the BBC and writing for various journals, as well as authoring or editing several notable books; but arguably it is his long reign at the *Observer* for which he will be most widely remembered. Carcanet Press is bringing out his collected writings in three volumes, the second of which will be devoted to his reviews. The first, *I Found It at the Movies*, gathers together a remarkable collection of his longer critical pieces.

The range is perhaps what strikes one first. There are essays on such diverse film-related themes as coal-mining or the English male, the Cold War or the Addams Family, how books are used as signifiers of film characters, or how boxers, the Spanish Civil War, or prison life have been represented in film. My randomly chosen selection of topics is meant to suggest the eclecticism of French's responsiveness to what film has to offer. He has a gift for perceiving such recurring motifs and preoccupations across genres and decades.

The diversity of such interests, and how he draws on them to focus on individual films and trends, throws revealing light on two of his major strengths. First, his grasp of film history enables him to pursue an idea not just across the decades but across national frontiers as well. Take his essay on 'Violence in the Cinema', where he digs back to *The Great Train Robbery* (1903), which exhibited the first important close-up in film. This final shot of the film depicted 'a menacing bandit firing his pistol directly into the camera'. This 1965 essay makes its way from 1903, via *The Cheat* (1919) in which a man 'branded his adulterous wife with a red-hot iron', to the fashionable Bond-age of the mid-1960s. Or take 'Venice as a Backdrop' which sprawls productively over the decades from the studio-built canals of *Top Hat* (1934), via *Summertime* (1955), in which American spinster Katharine Hepburn falls backwards into an actual canal, and the spooky use of its labyrinthine ways in *Don't Look Now* (1973), to *The Wings of the Dove* (1997), when the gorgeous setting throws the human machinations into stark relief.

Just as impressive, though, is the effortless ease and authority with which French situates film in the larger processes of cultural change. As you read some film reviewers and critics, you can begin to feel they've spent their formative years, if not their entire lives, in darkened rooms, unaware that there are other art forms, let alone politics and war and injustices of every hue – that is, *life* – going on out there. Again and again these essays impress the reader with their comprehensive attention to, and retention of, crucial cultural information.

Also, whereas one sometimes feels that reviewers have relied unduly on press kits to inform them about either relevant film history or world events and culture in its widest sense, in the case of French one feels he's actually *lived* in and responded to that greater world. Or if he was too young to have known about it at the time, as in the case of the Holocaust, he has read about it in sufficient depth to be able to place films as varied as *Pastor Hall* (1940) and *Schindler's List* (1993) in 'this complex historical heritage'. That is his phrase and it sums up his urge and capacity to contextualise. He knows that film is but one way of coming to terms with tumultuous events.

About other critics and reviewers, he is both astute and generous. For instance, he salutes Pauline Kael's 'passionate nature' and the way 'her collections are presented as reports on the state of the national morale', though I'd argue that he achieves this sort of effect more unobtrusively. Or take the 'Sunday ladies', C.A. Lejeune, writing for the *Observer* (1928–60) and Dilys Powell for the *Sunday Times* (1936–76): they are recalled with affection and admiration for their pioneering status, as he writes of their collected reviews (also published by Carcanet). Again, I am made to feel uneasy at having dismissed Lejeune too summarily for being remorselessly 'witty' at the expense of serious appraisal. French makes the point that such reviewers rarely get their due because their work is seen not in any sort of totality but only as it suits the purposes of other writers who know nothing of the 'exigencies of weekly journalism'.

The essays gathered together here reveal an historical sense that neither Powell nor Lejeune could emulate. It is not as if French writes with solemnity; nor does he parade his erudition, either about film or the other arts or the world that houses and inspires them. There is instead a bracing freshness about his perception, whether it's a matter of a film close-up or a panoramic view of the Great Depression – and the crime film. There is also an unforced wit at work. In an essay entitled, 'The Ring Cycle: Boxers in the Movies', he writes: 'Just when you thought it was safe to dismantle the ring, British movie-makers have got their gloves on again and are tapping the old claret'. This introduces a discussion initiated by the 1997 films *The Boxer* and *TwentyFourSeven*, and an analysis of why boxing pictures may be an exception to the rule that sports films are dubious box office. He goes on to say, 'Like Brecht, boxing is currently unfashionable and politically incorrect, and there is a widespread demand for its abolition', but 'despite this, boxing (and boxing films), like Brecht again, have endured.'

As well as such pieces that ramify out in surprising and rewarding directions, there are reviews of important books on film, and tributes to individual filmmakers. Tributes, that is, compounded of critical insights and sometimes of first-hand knowledge of the filmmaker concerned. His obituary for Lindsay Anderson, 'an ascetic, romantic Scot, a malcontent and an anarchist with a well-deserved reputation as a difficult man ...', is a model of assessment tempered with admiration.

Any writer on film who wants to be both rigorous and popular should study this book closely. Any reader who just wants to be better informed about film, and entertained at the same time, should do the same.

Australian Book Review, February 2012.

36

ROUTES OF PASSAGE

Stillways by Steve Bisley

The Long Road to Overnight Success by Shane Jacobson

Some memoirs follow a linear approach, from cradle to whatever; others opt for the impressionistic strategy; hybrids draw on both. Here are two actors busy in the Australian media illustrating this range, with variable results.

Bisley, a notable actor in Australian films since the 1970s, an authoritative presence in the likes of *Chain Reaction* (1980) and most recently *The Great Gatsby*, as Dan Cody, has chosen – or perhaps it chose him – a poetic, evocative response to the places and people of his childhood and adolescence. The stages in his growth up till he leaves his rural New South Wales home for a job at Woolworth's in Sydney are put before us with precision and clarity, but he never takes the somewhat plodding line of 'And then I did this and then that'. The passing of time and the changes it brings make themselves felt with often piercing freshness.

The key elements of his youthful life emerge in ways that should resonate with anyone who has shared a country background – and those who haven't will get some rare insights into what it was like growing up on a farm and in the neighbouring small towns. Electricity didn't reach his home on Lake Munmorah till 1964, when 'We cleaned the soot from years of gloom and lamplight, and suddenly there was nowhere to hide, now that the shadows had been driven out.' It is in perceptions like this one that he not merely brings the period to life but subtly encourages us to imagine what it meant.

There is nothing pretentious about this approach. All sorts of impressions of time and place, burnt on to his memory, carry the reader – this one, anyway – back. It's a time when people added 'sleep-outs' to their houses, or when it was still possible to celebrate 'cracker night' on 5 November, or when local halls offered '50/50 dancing' (when you could do the Pride of Erin and the foxtrot on the same evening). These are irresistibly present in Bisley's spare, often poetic prose that knows just what detail to fix on.

He recalls the local 'Show', that carnivalesque celebration of agricultural and country-town life (bulls with rings through their noses, fairy floss, the promise of 'The Strip Show'). With what was then more or less harmless xenophobia, he remembers 'Eye-ties' after the war and the changes this brought to good old Australian food, and he was – who was not? – a devotee of *Phantom* comics.

This may seem nostalgic – seems! I know not *seems* – but Bisley knows it wasn't all fun growing up insulated from big-city corruptions. There *was* fun certainly, and he fell in first love with schoolgirl Susan Green, but he doesn't shirk the underlying pain of his parents' difficult marriage and especially of his own fractured relationship with his father.

This was a father who would belt his kids until the older son one day knocked him down, and there is a blank double-page headed INTERMISSION at this point that marks its significance. There is poignancy towards the end when he knows he'll have to leave Lake Munmorah or he'll be 'trapped' forever, and when he realises that 'the only gift I ever wanted, [was] the one I never had – my father's love'.

Bisley's narrative (not that that's the best word for his methods) stops short of his success as an actor. He's concerned with evoking a childhood, neither wallowing in nor agonising over it. Shane Jacobson's book – more autobiography than memoir – never loses sight of the success he wanted as an entertainer and which he found as, and in, *Kenny* the portaloo man of the 2006 comedy success. It played as a mockumentary and, according to Jacobson, people constantly took him for a plumber rather than an actor.

What most concerns him in *The Long Road ...* is himself and his career and this begins to have a numbing effect on the reader. His parents' marriage broke up when he was young, but there is no sense of the sort of pain this might have caused anyone. He is so bent on describing everyone as 'wonderful' – his mum and dad and their subsequent partners, his uncles and aunties, Gang Show mates, his agent, everyone – that the reader can't help wondering if he's trying too hard to make himself likeable. Despite some half-hearted gestures towards self-deprecation, self-*knowledge* doesn't stand much chance against the claims of ego.

The style is flat and clichéd: he 'purchases' what he could just as easily buy; no one dies if he can 'pass away'; and the book is full of 'very special' people. Some will find this a grumpy response, and there are some good jokes, but, whereas Bisley may well have a new career as a writer, Jacobson really shouldn't give up his day job.

The Age, 14 September 2013.

37

JOHN WAYNE

The Life and Legend

By Scott Eyman

It is unlikely that John Wayne could – or would – have aspired to play Macbeth or King Lear on the stage, but he was undoubtedly a great film actor. He is one of those leading male stars that I think of as small-effects men: they may seem to be doing very little but that is because they have so wholly inhabited their roles that they appear to be not so much acting as behaving. Think of Cary Grant, Gary Cooper and, perhaps above all, John Wayne at his best, as in the matchless western, *The Searchers*.

Eyman's biography skilfully charts Wayne's development from handsome youth to grizzled age on screen and off, the personal and the professional both more complex than might have been imagined. His family background was difficult, with chilly mother and more sympathetic father going their separate ways when he was still a child burdened with the bullies-attracting name of Marion Morrison. When he started working in films, first in the props department and as an extra, he transformed himself into 'Duke' Morrison and that's how he always thought of himself, long after 'John Wayne' had become one of the most sought-after commodities in film.

Crucial to his whole career, indeed to his *life*, was the figure John ('Pappy') Ford, the irascible director who became Wayne's 'enduring father substitute' in the course of their nearly fifty-year association. Ford gave him a bit role in a 1928 film about the Irish Troubles, *Hangman's House*, and in the ensuing decade Wayne appeared in numerous westerns and serials for lesser companies before Ford catapulted him into serious stardom with *Stagecoach*. This was the turning point in a career in which he would become the archetypal US star, even with those who would have disdained his extremely conservative political and social views.

Other major directors would seek out his services in the certainty that his name would sell the film – and that his performance would make it worth selling. For Howard Hawks he made *Rio Bravo* and for Henry Hathaway he embodied *True Grit*, but it is in the Ford films the Wayne persona is forged. Or, perhaps it is truer to say, the Wayne of *real* life found a way of endowing with *screen* life a series of unforgettable characters whom he described as 'a little more good than bad'. Eyman understands how the strong-minded but often curiously poignant Wayne protagonists of the Ford films drew on the reality of Duke Morrison. Ford seems to have told Wayne what he wanted – from the likes of the cavalry captain on the verge of retirement in *She Wore a Yellow Ribbon*, or the boxer haunted by his past in *The Quiet Man*, or the stoically tormented romantic in *The Searchers* – then let him get on with producing the results in his own way. Wayne always described himself as a reactor, rather than an actor, but this is too easy, and underestimates the intelligence he brought to bear on complex roles.

Complex is also the word for Wayne, or Duke, in the off-screen reaches of his life. He married three times and never divorced his third wife, Pilar, because he was embarrassed at his failures as a husband, though first wife Josie always maintained that he was the love of her life. She was the mother of their sons Michael and Patrick who later had their places in Wayne's career. He was a devoted father to all of his children, as though somehow compensating for failing as a husband. Among colleagues, he enjoyed a high level of respect for his innate mastery of the filmmaking processes, and this rapport was sometimes achieved across a very sharp ideological divide, as in the case of cinematographer Haskell Wexler. There were elements of racism in some of his attitudes and he became a life-long friend of the crudely anti-Semitic actor, Ward Bond. Well, they had prodigious alcohol intake and effortless profanity in common as well as their tendency to explosive outbursts of rage.

He intoned risibly two of filmdom's worst-conceived lines. In *The Conqueror*, his Genghis Khan tells co-star Susan Hayward, 'Yer beautiful (pronounced 'byoodiful') in yer wrath Bortai', and in *The Greatest Story Ever Told*, re Jesus, 'Truly this man was the son of God [or Gard]'. But I can forgive him anything for the moment when, instead of killing Natalie Wood in *The Searchers*, he lifts her up and says, 'Let's go home Debbie', in which line all the complexity of his character, on and off screen, finds resolution.

The gentler more reflective aspects of Wayne's personality and the unexpected moments of generosity in his dealings with others get their due in this thoroughly researched and eloquently written 'Life'. And the 'Legend' lives on today.

The Age, 2 August 2014.

38

THE TROUBLE WITH ACKROYD

Alfred Hitchcock

By Peter Ackroyd

It requires little short of audacity for anyone to consider writing a further 'life' of Alfred Hitchcock. Any author planning to revisit this cinema icon (for once, the word may be earnt) should be very certain of having some new insights to offer about what lay behind the portly frame. Does the prolific Peter Ackroyd tell us much that we haven't read before?

What sort of man and filmmaker emerges from this re-telling? Like most people perhaps, he exhibits plenty of contrarieties of thought and behaviour, and a sustained attempt to come to terms with these might have made compelling reading all over again. For instance, he seems on some occasions withdrawn and reticent, on others gregariously engaging in the telling of dirty stories. He was reported as being something of a bully on the film sound stages, or in other versions a director who scarcely communicated with his actors. He seemed sexually obsessed with blonde women, but may have been entirely celibate in his long marriage after the birth of one daughter.

Revered by some and feared by others, he was one of the few directors who became as much a household name as the stars who submitted so readily to doing his will – if they knew where their futures lay.

So how does Ackroyd tell the largely familiar story? With unsurprising linearity is the answer, as he trawls through the familiar territory of the east London childhood, the early days of doing whatever came along in silent films, making his mark as director in 1930s Britain, distancing himself from associates who had helped him on his way, then heading to Hollywood in pursuit of – and finding – international fame.

Not much is made of the formative influences of his lower-middle-class upbringing: the Catholic family remains shadowy, the brother almost invisible; the oft-told anecdote of his father's colluding with a local policeman to have the boy locked in a police cell for a few minutes as a punishment is trotted out again, as are some of his own often-cruel practical jokes.

As for his dealings with the films, there are some insightful suggestions. He is interesting enough about the sorts of 'doublings' that often seemed to fascinate Hitchcock, as in the interplay between the niece Charlie and the ambivalent Uncle Charlie in *Shadow of a Doubt*, between the two *Strangers on a Train*, and, of course, most memorably in *Vertigo*, now often regarded as his masterwork.

There is too enough interesting information about the making of the films, especially of the great American post-war period, such as *Rear Window*, the set for which required 'thirty-one separate apartments, eight of them with fully furnished rooms'. And Ackroyd identifies recurring themes like that of the innocent man on the run or the preoccupation with fear – and so on.

The critical questions are: How much, if any, of the book's information is new? How much can we rely on, especially when it's a matter of Hitchcock's dealings with colleagues and famous stars, some of whom revered him while others feared and disliked him intensely? Ackroyd lists a huge bibliography but, because he uses neither footnotes nor endnotes nor any other form of attribution for the information he offers, it is impossible to know how far to trust it.

The text is littered with such useless glances at sources as 'by all accounts', 'he claimed he was told', 'Hitchcock told one biographer', 'one critic believed that', 'as one critic pointed out', 'it has been said that', 'does not seem plausible'.

There is also a plethora of casual generalisations and assumptions: did you know that 'Freudianism had become the new orthodox faith' in 1940s USA? Or that for 'half-caste', in *Murder!*, 'we can justifiably read "homosexual"'? Or that Janet Leigh, so memorably savaged in *Psycho*'s shower, had been named as 'No. 1 glamor girl of Hollywood'? None of these, nor hundreds of other snippets of 'fact' or 'interpretation' (to use both terms loosely), can be checked for accuracy, even if you had the inclination.

Perhaps Ackroyd needs to slow down. It's after all barely a year since his similarly lightweight biography of Chaplin appeared. This latest in his 'Brief Lives' series is Hitchcock-lite. It will infuriate serious scholars who will get much more satisfaction from another addition to the bibliography: Alain Kurzoncuf and Charles Barr's *Hitchcock Lost & Found*, which is a model of scrupulous research, rendered in immaculate prose that would disdain the dumb puns and slipshod locutions of Ackroyd's tome.

Does anyone, scholar or film-lover alike, want to read of how 'the binary galaxy of Julie Andrews and Paul Newman was introduced into the equation [of *Torn Curtain*]? Such a person would need to get out more – if only to the DVD store to borrow *Vertigo*.

The Age, 2 May 2015.

Part II

Mains

The articles selected for this section are longer pieces, longer, that is, than review of an individual film or book would allow. They began life in a range of journals: some devoted to film, others more wide-ranging; some on paper, some online; and usually taking a more general theme and exploring it in relation to appropriate films or books. The articles are again given in chronological order of publication; I think the later ones reflect a more benign approach, more youthful savagery having had its day.

THE BIOGRAPHY INDUSTRY

Creatures Great and Mostly Small

Laid side by side, as I am sure many of their authors would like to be, film star biographies and autobiographies take up several, good-sized shelves in any performing arts bookshop. Twenty years ago, an actor generally had to make it on the stage before he or we could expect his life to be celebrated between hard covers. So, luminaries of Broadway and Shaftesbury Avenue, from Tallulah Bankhead to A. E. Matthews, were trying to persuade us that they were as interesting off-stage as on, and certainly that they were much more interesting than we were. The 1970s changed all that. Not to have the enthralling saga of your life take its place on the shelf with all those other lives has become a tacit admission of not having made it. Mere decent reticence in the face of a dull life stops no one, nor does even merer unimportance.

For the flood of star biographies and, worse, those written allegedly by the stars' own hands, has gathered momentum through the past decade and shows no sign of abatement. Furthermore, they are getting longer (the first fruits of Stewart Granger's anecdotage[1] run to more than 400 pages) and, a still more disquieting sign, there is a new trend towards stopping mid-career. Presumably, this latter habit, as evinced by Granger, James Mason[2] and the unspeakable Shelley Winters,[3] is meant to leave us breathless with anticipation for Volume Two. This is indeed making a little go a long way, since the off-screen lives of these people often are remarkably dull – often as dull as our own, just lived in more comfort.

Film stars are so much a phenomenon of a packaging process, whereby some astute producer recognises a saleable commodity, ensures that it is handsomely gift-wrapped and employs highly-skilled minions to market it, that sometimes it is hard to know what there is to any given star apart from a seductive physical presence. This presence is, of course, infinitely more important on the screen than on the stage, which is at once more exposed to the consumer and more tactfully distant from him. How film stars look seems to me to be the one indisputably vital element in their screen *personae*; whatever else they may bring to their roles in the way of, say, intelligence, understanding, depth of feeling or experience is much harder to assess and to attribute.

This being so, it is perhaps not surprising that on the page, as distinct from the screen, they often are disappointing. The perceptiveness and sensitivity we have admired as they loomed above us in the dark must, we begin to feel, belong elsewhere – perhaps to William Wyler, shrewdly selecting the best of 50 takes, or Gregg Toland catching the upturned face in a way that softens the hard egoism.

On the basis of the nearly 20 volumes with which I have frittered away my youth in recent months, I would find it hard to adduce evidence for Gregory Peck's assertion that, 'They're not stars for no reason, you know. They're stars because they are interesting people.'[4]

One of the chief recurring elements of these works is certainly egoism. Clearly, even to get noticed to the point of being offered any role in a film takes a degree of persistence allied crucially to a powerfully egoistic belief in one's powers.

Having achieved not merely any role but the power and right to choose their roles – that is, to be a star – it is equally clear that an immense egoism, and egotism, comes into play to sustain that privileged position. Even a professional nice-guy like Peck derives gratification from the fact that, in his first film, his 'name was to go above the title – and it has never gone anywhere else since'. A monstress like Bette Davis[5] snarled and clawed her way to the roles that made her a star, and, once established, she alienated many by 'relentlessly demanding, imposing, seeking restlessly for what was best': best for the film of course too, but essentially best for Bette.

To know you are a film star is, presumably, to know that millions of people around the world want to watch you both being recognisably 'yourself' and doing something that is called film acting. It is a heady thought no doubt, and to the head, no doubt, it often goes.

More often than not, unsustained by families, education, religion or any other of the decentralising structures of their society, they are encouraged by those with a financial interest in their careers to believe their own publicity, to believe themselves the centre of their personal universes. With so many lives dependent on whether their latest film is pulling in the customers, small wonder it is that many of them give co-workers, spouses and others hell if their wishes are not fulfilled. To be as universal an icon as a film star is makes preposterous demands on the sanity, balance and humanity of the often otherwise-unremarkable human being just beneath the glamorous surface.

'Night of the few large stars'

It may be that the publishing bonanza of the 1970s (not just star lives, of course, but every aspect of cinema) is a product of a more or less starless age. Now that there are so few authentic stars left, the reading public is perhaps doubly fascinated with the big names of the past, expecting that they must have big lives attached to them. For, whatever it is that makes a star, the public knows one when it sees one. At the moment there aren't many to see: this is Walt Whitman's 'night of the few large stars.'

I remember reading in the mid-1970s that there were but 10 bankable stars left in Hollywood (Redford, Newman, etc., and one woman – Streisand). This is a black night indeed when you think of how many stars glittered on the mid-40s payroll of any one of the big studios. Can it be that present deprivation has provoked both nostalgia and the urge to literary embalmment? An urge, that is, showed by interested parties such as publishers, public and ageing stars themselves.

The reasons for the declining number of stars are complex. It is not that we, the cinema-going public, now feel ourselves above the idea of stars. It seems to me that the public still reaches out to any actor who is even half-way towards Coward's 'star quality' – towards the likes of Jane Fonda, Warren Beatty or, as the success of *On Golden Pond* suggests, towards unarguable and enduring Hollywood staples such as Katharine Hepburn and Henry Fonda. But the passing of the studio system, that very nursery of the stars; the precariousness of the film actor's life when he must negotiate each new role as part of a business deal; a decreasing willingness of newer actors to share their private lives (even a diluted or sugared version) with their public;

an increasingly sophisticated awareness of films among articulate sectors of the public that both make a cult of old stars and decry the need for contemporary ones: these are a few guesses about the reasons for the decline in stars. The mass audiences will still turn out for a *Star Wars* but not for a star turn. We are no longer 'visited all night by troops of stars': in these tough times we are lucky if our film has one star supported by Ben Johnson.

'… Preserve the stars from wrong' (Wordsworth)

Apart from Flora Robson[6] who didn't marry at all and Mae West[7] who may or may not have done so, most of these biographed girls and boys here have notched up several partners. 'I've been married five times', [Henry Fonda] said abruptly, 'and I'm goddamn ashamed of it.'[8] In most of the other volumes, the casting-off of the old and the taking-on of the new are presented as part of some restless quest for truth in human relations. Fonda's abrupt honesty on the matter – and I don't mean to be striking a moral pose about this – is markedly at odds with the usual cant offered about marriage and divorce.

On the whole I prefer Susan Hayward's direct account[9] of why she wanted to be rid of Jess Barker, 'The son of a bitch hit me', to the tasteful evasion of Freedland's account of Gregory and Greta Peck's break-up: '… the sad-looking surroundings [of their French villa] only seemed to echo the state of their relationship together. It took very little time for them both to realise that they weren't going to be able to cope and that it had come to an end.'

I don't mean to underestimate the sort of pressures that stardom, with all its demands for ego maintenance and repair, must make on relationship; nor do I want to suggest that it is easy to write about a succession of liaisons, with and without the benefit of formal ceremonies. Inevitably notions of romantic commitment get somewhat tarnished by the time the fifth or, in Elizabeth Taylor's case, the seventh marriage is reached.

The (auto-) biographers are caught in something of a bind here: on the one hand, they may wish to present their subjects as a moral mixture of Little Nell and Mother Teresa of Calcutta; on the other, they are aware that a breath – or better, a gust – of scandal will boost sales like nothing else. Responses to this dilemma are various: Shelley Winters has decided to let it all hang out and a very repulsive spectacle it makes; James Mason has opted for such discretion that it comes as a surprise to find him named as a co-respondent in Roy and Pamela Kellino's divorce or to find, 100 pages later, that he and Pamela are parting.

The point of this is to suggest that very rarely indeed does a star emerge from one of these biographical skirmishes with his or her image unsullied. Honesty will frequently be unkind to them; discretion can make them sound dull; and a flair for the salacious may diminish respect even as sales thrive. It is not just a matter of sexual behaviour; revealing other aspects of the private lives of stars rarely makes one think better of them. Claire Bloom is one exception: she writes[10] with unaffected honesty about the vanity, ambition and selfishness that, she believes, played a part in her career. So, too, is Flora Robson who emerges, miraculously, from Kenneth Barrow's daunting hagiography as hard-working, intelligent and compassionate.

The fact that the off-screen lives of so many stars seem not to be particularly interesting sometimes leads biographers into whipping up a spurious sense of drama where none exists. For women stars this usually means an affair with Howard Hughes; the men, faintly afraid that theirs is an effeminate profession, dwell on manly experiences like motor-racing or flying. Again and again, one feels how much more satisfactory these Lives would be if they devoted themselves more whole-heartedly to the activities that made the stars famous enough for us to want to read about them: that is, their work in films. Instead of the current stress on their sexual appetites and adventures, instead of white-washing their marital histories, from which processes they inevitably emerge as lesser people, they could very usefully tell us a great deal that would be worth knowing about the processes of filmmaking.

'It is the stars, the stars above us govern our conditions'

Shakespeare knew it all. For, in the history of Hollywood certainly, the influence of stars in shaping entertainment has been enormous.

Productions were built around the talents of particular stars; the greater the responsibility on a star for a film's success or failure, the more powerful became that star's wishes in the making of the film. If stars could not sell a bad or unattractive film to the public (cf. Gable and *Parnell*, Julie Andrews and *Star!*), they undoubtedly increased the pulling-power of many average-to-good films. Considering, too, the public's notorious fickleness (it could never, for instance, be induced to flock to Deanna Durbin movies after the *Christmas Holiday* fiasco), it is not surprising that so much studio effort and star ego went into ensuring that those stars above us would continue to govern our conditions.

Few actors fought harder to attain and maintain stardom than Bette Davis. In 1964 she told her own story as she chose to present it in *The Lonely Life*; as Charles Higham tells it now in *Bette*, the lady's own account seems to have offered just a carefully preserved public persona of brisk New Englander, dispensing crisp honesty and common sense. Higham erodes this image by describing her as self-dramatising, obsessively ambitious and, 'a woman whose brilliance and aggression prevented her from achieving fulfilment in a relationship.' The one great, positive attribute she persistently reveals is energy, but that is certainly made unattractive by the ruthlessness, egoism and egotism that accompany it. This energy seems to have worn out the men in her life though there were brief periods of happiness with husbands 2 and 4 (Arthur Farnsworth and Gary Merrill).

It stood her in good stead for her protracted fighting with Warner Bros, with the result that she got more than her fair share of juicy roles and the power to dictate in what conditions she would perform and how her public would therefore view her. Her worst enemy (competition for the title would be stiff, even with Joan Crawford and Miriam Hopkins now gone) would no doubt grant her energy and courage. There was courage at the time in choosing roles like Mildred in *Of Human Bondage*, or Leslie Crosbie in *The Letter*, or Baby Jane, as well as the perception to assess their potential in terms of her capacities to act them and make the public accept her in them.

Higham's account, as slickly professional and anonymous as others from his assembly line (*Kate*, *Marlene*, *Audrey*), at least does justice to the films and makes something compulsive of the way Davis's energies worked towards making so many of them memorable. He is quite astute at identifying the highlights – *Jezebel*, *Now Voyager*, *All About Eve*, among others – even if his assessments of them are unilluminating. There is surely more to *Now Voyager* than '... of course, a camp classic, a masterpiece of schmaltz'. Higham (and Joel Greenberg) did better with classic Hollywood in their 1970 book *Hollywood in the 40s*. However, he often has interesting comments on the conditions surrounding the making of the films and, discussing *Now Voyager*, he claims: 'Scripts in those days were explicitly tailored for stars, and [Casey] Robinson included many touches that suggested Bette's New England background.' These 'touches' are then considered in relation to several scenes.

The book is full of nasty side-swipes at Davis' consorts and colleagues: at Farnsworth, with his 'aura of fake self-confidence, masculine security, strength that disguised a fawning servile weakness'; at Paul Muni – 'withdrawn, haughty, never a mixer'; at John Farrow, 'a boorish, drunken lecher with a foul mouth'; at George Brent who was 'mean- spirited, tough, and handicapped by a wickedly vicious tongue'; and at that 'small, pot-bellied and balding' great lover, Charles Boyer. In fact, Davis seems to have liked very few men and fought with most of her male co-stars. Her closest friends were younger actresses like Jane Bryan and Geraldine Fitzgerald, whose careers she encouraged, and some of her best performances were opposite strong actresses like Joan Crawford, Mary Astor and Anne Baxter. In fact, as her star rose, say to 1941, she was less and less likely to have a leading man who could draw her full fire – either on-screen or off.

Possibly a terrible woman, Davis was indubitably a great star. She frequently took unpromising scripts, saw something playable in them, grabbed them by the scruff of the neck, belted them and everyone concerned into shape, and as a result she has survived as a star for 50 years. Despite ill-temper, unco-operativeness, little affection or respect for most of her colleagues, she continues to command public respect and attention. Knowing about the woman, as Higham's handsomely-published volume insists we must, adds nothing to the star image. On the other hand, though, the private dirt can't diminish the power with which that image has often worked on us, in the guise of, variously, Mildred, Regina Giddons or Margo Channing.

While Bette Davis was ruling the roost at Warners (known affectionately as San Quentin), Tyrone Power was keeping Twentieth Century-Fox solvent and Darryl F. Zanuck rich. Hector Arce's 'coast-to-coast bestseller'. *The Secret Life of Tyrone Power*,[11] despite its salacious packaging which draws attention to Power's sexual ambidexterity, is in fact a surprisingly humane account of the man and a sometimes shrewd appraisal of the career. If Power's sexual life caused him a good deal of torment, his star career was rarely satisfying in the way that he wanted. Coming from several generations of acting Powers, he always seemed to be after a success which eluded him – that is, as a serious actor on stage and screen.

Power established quickly a potent romantic image in his pre-World War 2 films, films like *Lloyds of London*, *Suez* and *In Old Chicago* opposite beauties like Madeleine Carroll, Loretta Young and Alice Faye. More than usually amenable in his dealings with studio chiefs, he was used by Fox to help launch aspiring stars like Jean Peters, Linda Darnell and Anne Baxter who all profited by exposure in films with Power. He, however, longed for more demanding roles and, as Arce points out, found real critical success only once in his 25-year career. That was in Edmund Goulding's authentically nasty little *film noir*, *Nightmare Alley* (1947), in which he played a shoddy opportunist very well indeed. His earlier, more prestigious film for Goulding, *The Razor's Edge*, had sought to extend his range. 'His long speeches', Arce writes, 'about eventual redemption had to be delivered with a genuine sense of inspiration, since the camera held him mercilessly in its close-up gaze.' But for all his efforts in this role, and for all the film's seductive patina, Power came to fear it was 'pretentious, simplistic claptrap'.

There is something touching in the story of this agreeable-sounding man whose private life was bedevilled by dangerous liaisons and whose public life hardly ever satisfied him, even when it was satisfying millions of cinemagoers. Tyrone Power has not worn well and, 30 or so years after, he rarely looks convincing. Apart from *Nightmare Alley*, he probably wears best in the swashbucklers he grew so tired of, worst in his more high-minded pieces (*vide* his display of tortured conscience in Anatole Litvak's *This Above All*). Hector Arce neither wishes to spare us the more sensational passages of Power's life nor does he wallow in them.

'And the stars are shining bright' (Shelley)

Stars, answering who knows what urge towards the setting up of idols, are essentially a phenomenon of 1930s and '40s Hollywood. Brando and Monroe had their hour but those that shone longest and brightest began their blaze in those decades now sentimentally known as the Golden Years. It is hard to imagine anyone as modestly talented as Tyrone Power getting started in the mid-70s and holding on to star status till the end of the century. But, with the backing of a shrewd and grateful studio who pushed him – not that he resisted – through 25 films in seven years (1936–42), he became a household word in a way that is scarcely possible now that the studios are gone, and households, perhaps, not what they were.

Power died in 1958, just at the stage when the maintenance of a star career was getting tougher as the studios crumbled under threats from television, anti-trust legislation, and possibly a more sophisticated public awareness. But if the studios carefully nurtured their valuable star properties, the latter often seemed to have little sense of creative direction when they left – or were turned loose by – the studios which controlled not only the publicity but which parts the contractees would play.'

Henry Fonda, who had his first successes at roughly the same time as Power, with whom he co-starred in *Jesse James* (1939), retained his star status until his death a quarter of a century after Power's, clinching it with his 1981 Oscar for *On Golden Pond*. It is hard to believe Power could have retained his position that long had he lived. It is not just that Fonda was a 'better' actor – i.e., more complex, more resonant, more eloquent – than Power ever was, and he established this on the stage too. As well, as Howard Teichmann records it, and as the filmography bears out, he was never firmly held in the stranglehold of a long-term contract with any one studio, and he insisted on retaining the right to appear on stage.

Teichmann, a man of the theatre, tends to stress the plays – *Mr Roberts* particularly. *The 'Caine' Mutiny Court Martial, Darrow* – while skimping on the films, but he makes clear that Fonda understood the difference between the two media. He quotes Fonda: 'I just pulled it [i.e., voice] right back to reality because that lens and that microphone are doing all the projection you need. No sense in using too much voice, and you don't need any more expression on your face than you'd use in everyday life.' And Teichmann adds: 'In almost a hundred films the technique Fonda employs has not varied. Some say he underplays, some say he's not even acting. Quiet, calm, even in anger or desperation, whether comedy or drama Fonda uses as little facial mobility as possible. Whatever he does he makes you see inside the character he plays.' Very early on 'Fonda fell easily into the rhythm of film-making', believing it to be largely a director's medium, with actors as 'two-dimensional figures to be used in the exposing of raw stock to its best advantage'.

Considering how much more perceptive Teichmann is about acting than most of the stars' biographers, it is disappointing that he doesn't give more detail about Fonda's film performances. The early meetings with John Ford and the making of *Young Mr Lincoln* and *The Grapes of Wrath* rate about four pages altogether, while *My Darling Clementine*, a time-secured masterwork, gets no more than a passing mention. Other notable films like *The Wrong Man* and *Fort Apache* are skimmed over, while *The Best Man* is not there at all; there is a little more on Sidney Lumet's *12 Angry Men*, which Fonda also produced. 'I don't think if you took a stick and beat him he could do anything false, he's incapable. As a performer, as a man, he's pure', Sidney Lumet claimed, and if it sounds an extravagant claim it is perhaps not far from the public's view of Fonda. He has always seemed like one's ideal of the American liberal; according to Teichmann, there is more than a little correspondence between the screen persona and the real man, though the latter emerges as more ascetic, more rigorous, more egoistic, harder to know and harder still to live with. There is honesty in his approach to some of life's major issues; and in some of his chief relationships a stubborn integrity emerges, not unbecoming Tom Joad, Wyatt Earp and Barney Greenwald.

If Henry Fonda made a career out of persuading us to take him seriously, whether in a humid jury room or bringing order to the wild West, that other wild West – Mae – appeared on screen to take nothing seriously – especially not sex or men, and especially not any of the virtues held dear by middle America. Fergus Cashin's slim volume (a happy change from the never-mind-the-quality-feel-the-length approach) may not intend to cut Mae West down to size, but it does. 'She had spent most of the twentieth century inventing herself', Cashin writes, and, if she did not invent sex, 'She … saw the humour in it and probably no one before or since has had more fun on what she called the linen battlefield'.

And yet, if Cashin is to be trusted, the real-life truth is a good deal less amusing and less glittering than her brief, dazzling star career might have suggested. In fact, *Mae West* is a somewhat sad story of a creature who purveyed lubricity in public, first on stage and then on screen, and perhaps never knew anything about sex, let alone love, in private life. The off-screen facts are shrouded in mystery, starting with date of birth (1893 or 1888? – not that it can have mattered to anyone in over half a century), including the marriage (or was it?) to Frank Wallace in 1911, whether or not, if it happened, it was ever consummated, and indeed most of her private life.

West's 1930s films are now camp classics, a status that has nothing to do with their quality, which, apart from the choice one-liners, is generally atrocious. However, in the '30s the one-liners came thick and fast, many of them Mae's own invention we are told, and she quickly secured a powerful position at Paramount. Her first screen line, in reply to the hat-check girl's 'Goodness, what beautiful diamonds', was the immortal, 'Goodness had nothing to do with it, dearie.' From that moment, Cashin tells us somewhat fulsomely, 'she walked slowly, majestically up the stairs into motion picture history'. The next two, *She Done Him Wrong* and *I'm No Angel*, both with the young Cary Grant, established her as a major star.

If none of the remaining six films she did in the '30s was as good as these, they were good enough to keep her public and Paramount more than happy. The 1940 teaming with W. C. Fields in *My Little Chickadee* was not a happy occasion ('They were, in turn, suspicious of each other, hostile, then indifferent', says Cashin) and this shows in the resulting film. Their comic styles – lewd innuendo from her, misogynistic mutterings from him – prove curiously immiscible.

It was, however, a triumph of subtlety, wit and taste, compared with the last two films of her career: Mike Sarne's *Myra Breckinridge* (1970), a Hollywood sex farce from below the bottom of the barrel, and Ken Hughes' bizarre *Sextette* (1978), in which she plays the bride of a young English aristocrat. But it is absurd to talk of Sarne or Hughes as if they were the authors of those films which defined new nadirs. Mae West was invincibly the author of her own films, as she was of the trashy, funny, finally mysterious drama of her life. There was probably much less, in several senses, than met the eye. The best is there in those '30s gags ('Between two evils, I always pick the one I never tried before') and Cashin does well to quote a good number of them. For the rest, he is left with an enigma: a star who became the target of a ferocious purity campaign, a woman whose private life would almost certainly have undermined the public image.

Another star who scarcely seemed to be taking sex seriously was Dorothy Lamour. By the end of the 1930s, in films like *Jungle Princess*, Ford's *The Hurricane* and *Her Jungle Love*, she had made the sarong and herself famous, but her most prolific period of stardom was in the next decade when she made 29 films. In these she established herself not merely as shapely but as blessed with a nicely deflating sense of humour that worked to best effect in the six *Road* films (1939–52). Her career and her not-very-remarkable private life are now presented for inspection in a volume of artless maunderings entitled *My Side of the Road*, 'as told to Dick Mclnnes'.[12]

One doesn't doubt that Dorothy Lamour was a cheerful, pleasant woman but there just aren't 200 pages in her life. It is almost as if she is aware of this too as she tries conscientiously to whip up a spurious narrative interest: 'Being practical, my first thought [grammar is not her major strength] was how could I get to Hollywood on my limited funds. Why bother? I asked myself; I knew I could never make it in films anyway.' (Actually, this points to one of the weaknesses of all these books: we *know* they all made it, so that suspense is at a premium. This being so, most of them need more unusual – or better-observed – lives to offset the daunting lack of narrative interest.) Dorothy – it would seem unfriendly to call her Lamour – is bent on adhering to the maxim: 'If you can't say something nice about a person ...' She has some trouble accommodating Joan Collins to this principle when Collins gets the lead in *The Road to Hong Kong*; (1961), but elsewhere she is uniformly generous to her colleagues. She insists that life on the *Road* sets was overwhelmingly wholesome and jolly, and that Bob and Bing were endlessly engaged in japes that kept everyone in stitches.

Dorothy Lamour's was not a major career but it provided a good deal of innocent pleasure. To give her – or McInnes? – her due, she does seem to remember who did what in her films. She has either a good memory or has been careful in checking the credits for the films, so that the book is not littered with those unnecessary errors that disfigure so many of the genre. She is genuinely interested in talking about the films, even if this remains on a pretty simple level. Her private life, once over her early marriage to Herbie Kaye, was a model of happy domesticity with William Howard, 'the most beautiful man [she] had ever seen, in or out of motion pictures.' From Howard Hughes she merely received roses; nice girl that she was, she turned down his dinner invitations.

'A nice girl' is probably not the phrase that leaps to mind in relation to Susan Hayward but, as Christopher P. Anderson tells her story, she lived her life, if not endearingly, at least consistently. From the poverty-stricken Brooklyn girlhood onward (much more real hardship than Lamour can muster by way of drama), she was a real fighter – tough, demanding, humourless, loving sparely but intensely, genuinely courageous in her final struggle with cancer. When it was over in 1975, her doctor marvelled, 'Nothing in the medical literature resembles it. It was amazing to live that long with this type of cancer. She was one of the great fighters. I've never seen anything like it'.

It sounds like any number of the characters she played in the heady days of her stardom in the 1940s and '50s: the woman destroyed by drink in *Smash-Up* (1947); the girl who 'loved not wisely but too well' – there was a lot of that about in the '40s – in *My Foolish Heart* (1949); Jane Froman, overcoming disability to entertain troops in a walking machine, in *With a Song in My Heart* (1952); beating the booze again in *I'll Cry Tomorrow* (1955): 'Sip by sip, slip by slip, Lillian Roth hit the bottom of the bottle! Filmed on location – inside a woman's soul!' the posters tempted us; and Barbara Graham, perhaps wrongly convicted of murder and executed in *I Want to Live* (1958). The latter, after four previous nominations, for the films named above, brought her the Oscar at last, with the attendant irony that 'now that she indeed had what she had been striving for all those years, she no longer needed it'.

She no longer needed it, partly because she was now – had been since the late 1940s – a true star and was now unimaginable as anything else, partly because her second marriage, to Eaton Chalkley, brought her the sort of peace that had hitherto eluded her. It eluded her in a big way during her marriage to minor actor Jess Barker, a stormy liaison even by Hollywood standards, a schism growing mainly out of her professional superiority and leading to a scandalous and acrimonious divorce. Anderson quotes transcripts of Hayward's story in response to her attorney's questioning: with no further gloss, the record has the elements of high '40s melodrama, though more explicit in some details than '40s cinema would have allowed.

Despite the more sensational aspects of her life – merely being chased nude round the neighbourhood by Barker but discovered in bed with Don 'Red' Barry (an actor so minor he makes Barker look like Olivier) – and despite her chilling aloofness to most colleagues, in the end, Susan Hayward emerges from Anderson's biography earning our respect. Respect, that is, for the way she worked at her career, for unremitting vigour and professionalism in dealing with the often-ludicrous junk she was handed, and for an unillusioned approach to the Hollywood machine.

Her name and fame were made in more or less lurid roles but I have a special affection for some quieter achievements: for Lucy Overmire, wavering between admirers (not at all a 'frontier spitfire' as Anderson characterises her), in Jacques Tourneur's beautiful western *Canyon Passage*; for the clergyman's wife in Henry King's *I'd Climb the Highest Mountain* (not a 'technicolour blockbuster' as Anderson wrongly claims, but a modestly charming rural romance); and the sorely-tried wife in Nicholas Ray's *The Lusty Men*. But whatever the role, quiet or flamboyant, powerful or inane, she worked like a dog to give it conviction.

Anderson's book pays discriminating tribute to what was best in her difficult life, and that means perhaps a dozen of the 60-odd films she made. Her last appearance – at the Oscar ceremony in 1974 –

epitomises that best: very ill, but exercising the determination that marked her whole career and exhibiting the star power she had acquired over the years, she was unexpectedly and unsentimentally moving.

Hayward's co-star on two occasions was Gregory Peck, who, without ever being especially interesting, has remained a star for just on 40 years in 50 films. Perhaps those figures are significant: in 16 of the years, beginning with *Days of Glory* in 1943, he appeared in only one film, in 14 years he appeared in two and in only four of those years did he appear in three films. Stars who began in the '30s, in the heyday of the studio, received much more rapid exposure (e.g., Bette Davis had four releases in 1931, eight in 1932, five in 1933, six in 1934 and so on). The pace must have been killing but the variety of roles pushed at them gave them a chance to find their métier and prove their mettle. Peck's career is altogether more stately as befits his very earnest persona. It gives the impression of being very carefully moulded around a limited range of responses as he moves from one prestige production to another, doing time opposite the two biggest women stars of the day – Greer Garson in *Valley of Decision* and Ingrid Bergman in *Spellbound*.

Peck is a star of the same kind as John Wayne, James Stewart, Cary Grant and (above all) Henry Fonda, but he is not really of the same calibre. Like them, he is essentially a 'small effects man' (unlike, say, such potential scenery-chewers as Rod Steiger, George C. Scott, etc.); but unlike them he doesn't suggest reserves of dangerousness, anger, wit and sinewy integrity respectively. With Peck, what you get is what you see. Michael Freedland's biography posits a real-life figure that corresponds quite closely to the usual screen persona of a liberal American – and the resulting book is a bit dull, like its subject.

As Freedland presents him, he has unexceptionable political and social views: he stuck to his guns during the HUAC squalors, but he can't help sounding rather a pill from time to time. For example, in his advice to Tony Curtis to 'Stop knocking everything – Hollywood, the Academy', he sounds like one's boring uncle.

The career is all there in Freedland's book but the films are mostly dealt with skimpily, with a few exceptions like *A Gentleman's Agreement*, *The Gunfighter*, *Twelve O'Clock High* and *To Kill a Mockingbird*. Those are all good films and Peck is handsomely intelligent in all of them, perhaps above all in *The Gunfighter*, which is well-treated in the book. According to Freedland, Peck yearned to play comedy. It is hard to see why: he is charming enough for William Wyler in *Roman Holiday* but his is scarcely a comic performance, and in his only other certifiable comedies – Ronald Neame's *The Million Pound Note* and Vincente Minnelli's *Designing Woman* – he shows as much comic flair as Lassie.

In spite of this, there is more variety in his career than one might have recalled – lewd Lewt in *Duel in the Sun*, for instance, as distinct from Father Chisholm in *Keys of the Kingdom* – but somehow it is all suffused in a rather monotonous haze of decency. The roles may have varied but Peck hardly seemed to, and this adequately written account by a reverent hack hardly persuades one otherwise.

Most of the major stars created in the 1950s either are dead, like Marilyn Monroe or James Dean or Grace Kelly, or else film so sporadically, like Brando, as to be no longer powerful at the box-office. Elizabeth Taylor began her career as a child in the 1940s and to that extent overlaps with Gregory Peck, but her real stardom belongs to the '50s – that is, give or take *National Velvet*, which remains her one indisputable star performance. For the curious thing about Taylor is that, though she has been the nominal star of all her films since 1950, she has never really felt like a star; she seems not quite able to take charge of the screen with that effortlessness that characterises great stars, even when they are not necessarily great actors.

As a teenager, from *National Velvet* (1945), through adolescent fluff like *Cynthia* (1947) and *A Date with Judy* (1948) to *Father of the Bride* (1950), she never looked less than smashing and at the time this seemed enough. The apotheosis of her beauty came with George Stevens' still moving *A Place in the Sun* (1951). As Kitty Kelley claims in her biography of Taylor: 'Spilling over with sex appeal, she was indeed the kind of girl American boys dreamed of marrying. She had the kind of beauty that would bring all a man ever dreamed of – wealth, fame, position. George Stevens knew that, with Elizabeth Taylor as his star, the audience would understand why George Eastman [Montgomery Clift] would kill for a place in the sun with her'[13].

Stevens, that is, seems to have understood what could be done with Taylor and that breathtaking beauty, even if *she* scarcely seemed aware of what was going on.

Kelley has a sure grasp of the high-spots of Taylor's career: *Velvet, Sun, Giant* (1956) and *Who's Afraid of Virginia Woolf?* (1966), since which it has been more or less downhill all the way. Increasingly she has thrown herself into the messy saga of her off-screen life, and Kelley records with a nicely sardonic edge how 'The perilous melodrama of dying and coming back to life became one of her most prized roles'. She became, in fact, a bore about her health and, indeed, about most things. Back in 1950 she 'often asked [Stanley] Donen why he thought Nicky [Hilton] ignored her and found her boring'. The answer is not hard to find: apart from a certain generosity and cheery vulgarity, there is nothing to her except her sexual appetite and that, of course, is a matter for restricted circulation – well, fairly restricted. Beating by two Chaucer's Wife of Bath who had five 'Housbondes at chirche dore [not that Taylor bothered too much about the church door] … Withouten oother compaignege in youthe' (no problems here for Taylor), her sexual adventures comprise a sickening chronicle. Husbands and lovers alike are a sorry lot, though she is perennially gushy and hopeful about them, even about Eddie Fisher, whose just published memoirs I have promised myself as a special treat not to read.

Kelley's book is subtitled 'The Last Star'. Surely not the last in any sense – others have certainly followed her so that she was neither the most recent nor the last in a line. Is she even, one wonders, a star? As the looks that made her famous began to bloat, she perhaps took more pains with acting though even at her best the *effort* shows. The book ends with her trying her luck on stage in *The Little Foxes* to mixed reviews. At the end of Kelley's account one feels an unwarranted tolerance for Taylor, based on a certain likeability and survivorship. But perhaps such tolerance should be suppressed in the light of other truths: that she seems really foul-mouthed, dumb-headed, ignorant, mindlessly extravagant and self- indulgent.

Elizabeth Taylor's career is poised between the great star-making era of the 1930s and '40s, when she might have been made a real star instead of just a famous commodity, and the '70s when she looked merely archaic. Shelley Winters, spanning the same period, has weathered the changing cinematic climate better. After a brief starlethood at Columbia, she was thoroughly noticed in Cukor's *A Double Life* (1948) as the doomed waitress. She then starred in half a dozen Universal features before reaching certifiable stardom in Stevens's *A Place in the Sun* (1951).

In this she was very touching as factory hand Alice Tripp who, pregnant, gets in the way of George Eastman's (Clift) ambitions. Thereafter, she was rarely less than entertaining, especially fine for Charles Laughton in *The Night of the Hunter*, for Stanley Kubrick in *Lolita*, and for Paul Mazursky in *Next Stop, Greenwich Village*. But I digress. Winters believes enough interesting things had happened to her up to 1954 to bring her unappetising life-story to a halt with Robert Rossen's *Mambo*, opposite one of her early husbands, Vittorio Gassman. A threatening note is struck on page 497 with an epilogue headed, 'To be continued, I hope …'

What is there to be said for Shelley – *Also Known as Shirley*, except that it is a wholly unworthy account of (half of) a lively career? She offers an egomaniacal wallow throughout – from the picturesque deprivations of youth, through the Hollywood bombshell phase, through the Yearning-To-Act phase – omitting none of her star-studded (if you'll excuse the term) promiscuities with the likes of William Holden, Burt Lancaster, Errol Flynn, Marlon Brando and so on. Her approach to sexual relationships is relentlessly vulgar, each new adventure cutting at the crucial moment to 'A fire roaring in the fireplace, Waves pounding a beach, Fireworks exploding' or some other cliché for cinematic orgasm. In the name of love-of-life, she reveals a shoddy set of values in language of unengaging coarseness. Her ego leads her – and she has this in common with most star autobiographers – to gloss over her deficiencies, to excuse her most unattractive behaviour.

As for the career, she has some sense of where the high spots were (*A Double Life*, *A Place in the Sun*), but the telling is so riddled with errors as to undermine all confidence in the reader. In the epilogue, she writes: 'In this life journey, perhaps I'm sometimes vague about what took place in which year …': this disclaimer is presumably meant to excuse those mistakes that derive from a lazy failure to check her information as well as those that derive from a wilful blurring of time in her first 20 years. Attributable to the latter are bits like how she was 'about 21' when she made *A Place in the Sun* ('about 21' in the sense, that is, of being 29) or the blithe absurdity of 'The roles I could have done were given to Jean Arthur' whose contract with Columbia ended in 1944, almost coinciding with Winters' arrival there to play bit parts. Her sense of her own importance in 1945 leads her to record how her then-husband was mistakenly addressed as Captain Winter. In 1945? I don't believe it.

As for the other sorts of errors, they are legion: she recalls the earlier version of *An American Tragedy* in 'the late twenties' (i.e., 1932) which 'Eisenstein had written and directed'; she claims she co-starred in *The Raging Tide* with Richard Conte (true) and Joan Caulfield (false); she has Marilyn Monroe 'waiting in line behind Betty Grable and Alice Faye for some kind of a decent part' in 1951, just six years after Faye's retirement; and later she has Monroe cast as a schoolteacher in *River of No Return*; and so on.

Interspersed among all this sloppiness are numbing moments of self-appraisal ('What was I doing with my life? I didn't really want to be a movie star; I wanted to be a fine actress, a responsible citizen and a mother') and dim sententiae along the lines of, 'I have come to know that at any given moment in life one has to do what one has to.' Gosh, how true.

Cinema Papers, December 1982. This article was concluded in the next issue.

Notes

1 Stewart Granger, *Sparks Fly Upward*, Granada Publishing, 1981.
2 James Mason, *Before I Forget*, Hamish Hamilton, 1981.
3 Shelley Winters, *Shelley – Also Known as Shirley*, Granada Publishing Ltd, 1981.
4 Michael Freedland, *Gregory Peck*, W. H. Allen, 1980, p. 59.
5 Charles Higham, *Bette: A Biography of Bette Davis*, New English Library, 1981, p. 160.
6 Kenneth Barrow, *Flora, Heinemann*, 1981
7 Fergus Cashin, *Mae West*, W. H. Allen, 1981.
8 Henry Fonda, (as told to Howard Teichmann), *Fonda: My Life*, W. H. Allen, 1982, p. x.
9 Christopher P. Anderson, *A Star, Is a Star, Is a Star! The Life and Loves of Susan Hayward*, Robson Books, 1982.
10 Claire Bloom, *Limelight and After*, Weidenfeld and Nicolson, 1982.
11 Hector Arce, *The Secret Life of Tyrone Power*, Bantam Books, 1980.
12 Dorothy Lamour (as told to Dick Mclnnes), *My Side of the Road*, Robson Books, 1981.
13 Kitty Kelley, *Elizabeth Taylor: The Last Star*, Michael Joseph, 1981.

40

LOCAL/GLOBAL

The Bank and *Lantana*

'Oh ye! who have your eye-balls vex'd and tir'd', wrote Keats in 1817, clearly having in mind future filmgoers. If you have reeled from cinemas, dazzled with the special effects of, say, *Harry Potter* – and I do apologise for mentioning a film that adults may well wish never to hear of again – you may be grateful for two Australian films that provide respite. In their disparate ways, *The Bank* and *Lantana* are a wonderful antidote to films that are overhyped, overelaborate and over here, and that will make the box-office killings for which they were designed. These two, in their more modest ways, have done well enough financially; they have been critically acclaimed; and they are both made with grown-ups in mind. They are, in a word, winners.

They also raise recurring issues of how other English-speaking cultures cope with the dominance of Hollywood, how they create an identifiable national cinema. In an interview in the *Sunday Age* (11 November 2001), Nik Powell, 1960s hippy-turned-producer, claimed that: 'Neither Britain nor Australia should be aiming for the cinema mainstream. Because neither of our industries can afford to make $100m films and that is what you need to compete in world-wide distribution. We are feeding niche markets, and niche markets are generally upmarket.'

There is an element of self-consolation here, of course: if we are not making hugely expensive films to fill the multiplexes, we are more likely to be appealing to discriminating audiences. But there is also some real truth in the notion of finding ways to meet audiences not satisfied by, say, *Mission: Impossible 2*. Both *The Bank* and *Lantana* are 'upmarket' in the sense that they have won almost uniformly golden opinions for their craftsmanship, but it is also true that both have been around for several months across a spread of cinemas, having amply found the 'niches' they need.

Not that they have much else in common apart from being successful, Australian, and both starring Anthony LaPaglia. They represent different approaches to meeting the challenge of Hollywood. *The Bank* is a genre thriller in a big-business setting, which at various points recalls Jimmy Stewart taking on Lionel Barrymore's corporation in *It's a Wonderful Life* (1947) or the sodbusters refusing to give way to the cattle baron in *Shane* (1953), as well as other thrillers about sharp young men dealing lethally with large-scale corruption. In other words, *The Bank* has clearly recognisable genre affiliations. *Lantana* represents a more usual sort of oppositional cinema: the arthouse piece that has taken off and found more niches than might have been expected. Winning seven AFI awards in its first few weeks of screening did nothing to hinder its prospects. 'Arthouse' has become, in some circles, a dirty word, but when it works, as it so triumphantly does here, it can give us access to a higher order of cinema – and it can also be lucrative, without necessarily rivalling *Titanic*, though it didn't cost as much either. Whatever international resonances these films call up, both are wholly Australian in flavour without being in the least parochial.

Much of Hollywood's unrivalled grip on the market has been the result of its command of genre film-making. It made Westerns and musicals when the public wanted these, or romantic comedies or, more recently, high-tech science-fiction as public taste changed (or was changed). Genre film, an accepted aspect of commercial cinema, was often a way of addressing key elements in the national psyche without seeming preachy. There is, for instance, a whole slew of post-war romantic melodramas about women uncertain of their husbands and their roles in marriage and society that clearly tapped into contemporary anxieties. New Australian cinema (that is, from the seventies revival on) has not been especially or regularly concerned with genre film-making, though some of its biggest box-office successes can be so categorised – *The Man from Snowy River* (1982), a species of Western, and *Crocodile Dundee* (1986), a romantic comedy – but the general trend has been away from readily classifiable genres.

The Bank is a very nifty piece of commercial cinema, with the strengths that implies, but it is a modest genre product. It shows that you don't have to spend squillions to make a film that gratifies genre expectations. It is not a film that depends on fabulous (and often wearying) special effects: it shows that Australian films can succeed in genre terms if they choose the sort of genre that can be made on budgets less-than-obscene. Its opening shot of a rural school with kids droning their 'times tables' momentarily recalls those seventies coming-of-age films, but *The Bank* is not going to saunter along as they did. In its tightly edited narrative, it swiftly establishes a young mathematical whiz kid who grows into Jim Doyle (David Wenham), who, for reasons kept hidden for most of the film, plans to destroy

Centabank, under the guise of helping it to predict stock-market lunges. There is a parallel narrative thread about a young couple, Di and Wayne Davis, whose son is drowned and who lose their rural boat-hire business to Centabank as a result of their not having been clearly informed about their loan's link to fluctuating overseas currency exchange rates. In the tradition of classic Hollywood narrative, these two strands come together – in a court scene, and, on another level, in the thematic link established finally by the shot of Jim's father hanging from a tree. Alan John's musical score, with an insistence both unmissable and unobtrusive, provides a solemn, requiem-like accompaniment to this moment and to the finding of the Davises' drowned son.

As in the best Hollywood genre product, everything is accounted for; everything matters; it all moves to very satisfying closure, with loose ends tied up, with director Robert Connolly maintaining a firm mastery of rhythm and tension. Its theme may be the revenge of little guys against faceless modern corporations, specifically against inhumane modern banking, but this is articulated through an emphasis on individuals. Its use of parallelism – sometimes for comparison, sometimes for contrast – is absolutely in line with the overriding urge of classic Hollywood narrative towards clarity, and this is reinforced at every turn by the film's patterns of alternation. It cuts from the chill blue beauty of its cityscapes to the idyllic lakeside setting of the Davises' tragedy, from intimate moments to scenes of ruthless corporate dealings, from the sleekness of suited bankers to leather-jacketed, laid-back Jim (he takes to suits later, but that's another matter). And it uses its stars as stars: it is perhaps not exaggerating to say that this taut thriller, with every excellence of scripting, scoring, cinematography and *mise-en-scène*, hangs together with such power because of the potency of contrast set up by the casting of Wenham as the maths genius with a secret and LaPaglia as the ruthless CEO of Centabank whose idea of motivating his staff is for them to feel 'my foot against the back of your neck'. The kind of contrast they embody is very much part of the melodramatic power that this genre work generates through its play of oppositions.

And speaking of LaPaglia, when one turns to *Lantana* one feels the difference. Here he is not so much a star as part of an ensemble. Not that he, Geoffrey Rush or Barbara Hershey or the others couldn't handle genre star requirements but that this film is less interested in the charismatic protagonists who dominate the action than in a network of interrelated lives. It is not that US films never work in this way: films as various as *No Down Payment* (1959) through *Nashville* (1975) to *Magnolia* (1999) have had something in common with it. Unlike the classic Hollywood model, it does not privilege one individual star over the others, and one is left not with the gratifying spectacle of the star clash of *The Bank* but with the rewards of a remarkable cast at the service of a screenplay unusually profound and complex.

It begins like a genre thriller. Over a black screen cricket sounds are heard, then gradually the foliage and flowers of the eponymous shrub (pretty but, in new South Wales at least, classified as a noxious weed) emerge; to the accompaniment of a buzz of flies, the camera discovers a leg with a laddered stocking and tracks up the body, which is lying – anonymously – face down. With no further explanation as to who or where it is, the film cuts arbitrarily to a couple, police officer Leon (LaPaglia) and Jane (Rachael Blake) engaged in enthusiastic coitus. The body in the lantana will eventually be explained, but the explanation will have little to do with what has happened in the film or to the extraordinarily engrossing and subtly drawn relationships that have constituted its 'plot'. Plot, in fact, sounds too contrived for the fluxions of feeling that have been at the heart of this film. Ray Lawrence, directing his first feature since the overblown and undernourished *Bliss* (1985), maintains absolutely that right sense of measured, reflective tempo that makes us feel we need the time to grasp at the threads of the characters' emotional lives, so as to have some understanding of scenarios that seem often as chaotic as real life.

This curious sense of not everything's necessarily having a reason or leading to an important effect is a major distinction between *Lantana* and *The Bank* (or its ancestors in classic Hollywood). Early in the film, Leon goes jogging, stops because of chest pains, and an old man watering his garden observes but takes no further notice; much later, on his 'second' one-night stand with Jane, the pain recurs. Nothing, though, is made of this pain: in a traditional genre film, it would probably provide some kind of dramatic climax, but here it is just something that happens, something that signifies perhaps a certain vulnerability in Leon. With similar arbitrariness, two joggers, Leon and an unknown man (he will become only slightly less unknown by the end of the film) collide as they approach a corner from different directions. The other man collapses weeping on Leon's chest, again without explanation, and Leon fails to explain to his wife Sonja (Kerry Armstrong) why he is blood-spattered after jogging. It is as good a symbol as any of the way *Lantana* resists the conventional causal chain of commercial cinema.

The film is full of things people can't/don't say to each other. One of its informing ironies is that two of its characters are seeing the psychiatrist, Valerie Somers (Barbara Hershey), who in turn is unable to talk to her husband (Geoffrey Rush), nor he to her. Their child has been murdered and, far from their having been made closer by this tragedy, distance has opened between them (often signified by keeping them in separate frames), so that they rarely talk on any but the most mundane level. She tries, but fails, to push him into saying what he feels, but the most intense interest he can show – and it's not much – is about an academic colleague who is coasting along, not publishing enough. 'I didn't need to write a book about it,' he throws at Valerie, who has exorcised her grief in just this way. What she doesn't know is that he regularly drives to the alley where the child was murdered to leave flowers as a token of the grief he can't speak. The two clients we see with Valerie are Sonja, who wants her marriage to be 'passionate and challenging and honest', whereas 'it feels as if we're just going through the motions', and the gay Patrick (Peter Phelps), who is having an affair with a married man, who may or may not have told his wife. It is not clear why but Valerie, the therapist, needles and is needled by Patrick; when she tells her husband about the difficulty she is having with him, he can only say 'refer him on.' Psychiatrist-shrink-thyself film plots go back at least as far as *Mine Own Executioner* (1947), but, again, the ways in which Valerie responds to Sonja and Patrick have roots that lie deeper than plots, that lie in the way people are.

In a film full of small and large betrayals, the working-class couple, Nik and Paula (Vince Colosimo, Daniela Farinacci), truly and messily love each other and their kids, but they are threatened in small and large ways by some of the others. They live next door to Jane, who has had the guts to walk out of a marriage because she was no longer in love, and Nik meets Valerie in the random way that keeps making one judge and analyse the film in terms of how like life it is. It is of course far from random in its construction; its brilliance lies partly in how it contrives to give a sense of how lives connect, without our wanting to accuse it of using coincidence to push the business on. Whereas the editing in *The Bank* works to establish a thrusting narrative eagerness, to insist on our keeping tabs on this or that because we'll need it later, *Lantana* will often close a segment on a fade that seems to invite us to consider what we make of what we have just seen. Here is a film that constantly interrogates the nature and possibility of relationships (and in the early days of the Australian film revival I recall complaining how rarely it showed an adult interest in these). *Lantana* accepts that they will be disfigured by pain and dishonesty but, equally, that they may transcend such limitations and inhibitions, and sometimes, against all the odds, work. If it is not precisely a work *sui generis*, it succeeds wholly on its own terms, requiring audiences to adjust their expectations.

Whatever their international affiliations, both films feel resolutely Australian in the resonances they set up. *The Bank* may echo classic Hollywood and its genre tradition and *Lantana* European arthouse cinema, but they both bring real, indigenous freshness to bear on their material. If one needs to discriminate between two such different excellences, it is possible to say that *The Bank* is as superbly crafted a genre piece as Australia has produced, but that *Lantana* may be touched with greatness. Equally, though, it is important to add that a sturdy film industry needs both kinds.

Meanjin, Vol. 61, No. 1, 2002.

41

MOTHERS

Some Kids do 'ave 'em

Mothers, generally, have done all right out of the movies. For every monstress like Gladys Cooper who put Bette Davis into unbecoming spectacles and what look like surgical stockings in *Now Voyager* (1942), there is an Olivia De Havilland giving up All for the sake of her 'nameless' son, in *To Each His Own* (1946), rewarded only in the last line with 'Our dance I think, mother.'

Self-sacrifice was what mothers were into in those benighted, pre-feminist times. Think of *Stella Dallas* (1937), with Barbara Stanwyck striding into the night, moved on by a policeman as she watches from the rain-drenched streets as her daughter makes a socially advantageous marriage. (And think how silly this scenario seemed when Bette Midler tried it in the 1990 remake, *Stella*.) Or think of Irene Dunne in *I Remember Mama* (1948 – can anyone remember Papa? It was Philip Dorn, actually), or wise-strong Beulah Bondi trying to point James Stewart in the right direction in *It's a Wonderful Life* (1947). And there were mothers-inspirational, like Jane Darwell, who famously intoned 'We the people' in *The Grapes of Wrath* (1939).

In British films, there was less idealisation but a fair share of the monstrous. To remind us of Victorian stereotypes, Mary Merrall had been only a shadowy defender of her daughters against their tyrannical father in *Pink String and Sealing Wax* (1946), and no match for some of the tough old birds who followed. 'What curious names some of these people have,' says Ambrosine Phillpotts, relaying a phone message to her besought daughter in *Room at the Top* (1959), thus trying to keep an unsuitable suitor at bay. Dora Bryan walks out on pregnant daughter Rita Tushingham in *A Taste of Honey* (1961) when it seems Rita's baby may be black. Thora Hird epitomises lower-middle-class aspiration and vicious prudery when Alan Bates fecklessly gets her daughter pregnant in *A Kind of Loving* (1962). But no-one was ever quite as monstrous as Diana Rigg in the chilling TV mini-series *Mother Love* (1990): with love like hers, hate was irrelevant.

There are a few smart, sassy mothers, like Jessie Royce Landis in *North by North-West* (1959), and see how critic Peter Wollen makes psychoanalytic mincemeat of her in his analysis of that famous Hitchcock representation of motherhood,[1] or, to come right up to date, Frances Fisher in *Laws of Attraction* (2004). But they aren't much help to their offspring. They are too busy being smart and sassy.

It is probably true to say that Sophocles, Shakespeare and Freud knew it all. Oedipus married someone old enough to be his mother but attractive enough for him to want to sleep with; and Hamlet, who should have read his Sophocles at Wittenberg, is surely not serious about Ophelia, at least not until he has given his mother a bad time in the Closet Scene. And 'Closet' is of course where all these forbidden desires are hidden. Mothers are not supposed to have desires of their own, and most of them didn't; for them, as Hamlet tells Gertrude, 'the heyday in the blood is tame'. Where, one wonders, would Freud have been without all this background? And where would we, and film-makers, have been without the very complex he invented out of the original family romance of Oedipus and Jocasta?

The spirit of Sophocles hangs ominously over *The Life and Death of Peter Sellers*. Its psychoanalytic underpinning is in Peter Sellers' relations with his adoring and possessive mum, Peg (Miriam Margolyes), who has elbowed his gentle-mannered father out of the way. When Peg asks him at his second marriage – to Britt Ekland (Charlize Theron) – 'Why are you making the same mistake all over again?' he replies, as if joking, 'Because they won't let me marry you.' But it's no joke really. Peg lays it on the line when Sellers (Geoffrey Rush) comes home dispirited from an early encounter with an agent who turns him down. She won't let him be defeated so easily and challenges him with: 'Do you want to be a failure like your father?' And later on, the father, commenting on Sellers' progress, ineffectually blames Peg for pushing their son too much, claiming that 'Good enough was never what his mother had in mind.' Peg not merely dotes; she is living through her son's achievements the success that has eluded her, and doesn't see his crucial failures in human matters.

In dealing with his own son, Peter shows all the effects of being so indulged and idolised. In one of the film's most disturbing scenes, he smashes his small son's train set in retribution for the child's painting a white stripe on his flash new car. Along with the philandering streak that success enables him to enjoy, there is still an element of the wilful child in him, causing him to see his son as a competitor, not as someone who should look to him for guidance. This childish response is reinforced when, trying to win over his angry wife Ann (Emily Watson), he shuts himself in a cupboard, saying, with what he hopes is ingratiating little-boy charm, 'I've been bad.' Incapable of adult discussion, on personal matters at least, and echoing his earlier destructive outburst, he wrecks their posh new apartment when he finds that Ann, exhausted with his self-absorption, is having an affair with their decorator. Then, without much subtlety (though perhaps as much as is needed), the film cuts to him at home with Peg.

They are cuddling on the bed, as she croons, 'You're all right. You're with Peg now.' Peg's continuing influence depends on Peter's not moving into a fully adult role: instead of encouraging him to face up to his responsibilities, she persuades him to accept the fact that 'She left you. Just let her go. Don't you worry, my little boy. The future's ours now.' Now, that is, that tedious wives are out of the way. When his father dies and she is more preoccupied with Peter's *Pink Panther* hit, she reminds him that 'The reporters will want some remarks.' That is her measure of his success, just as later she murmurs with satisfaction 'Both channels', when news of Sellers' heart condition breaks. The oleaginous clairvoyant, Maurice (Stephen Fry), becomes a sort of surrogate for Peg, and, definitively, Sellers himself will stand in for Peg in a moment of awareness of how she has shaped his life. Margolyes' Peg makes *Hamlet*'s Gertrude seem a model of maternal understanding. Sellers has a kind of revenge when he doesn't go to her deathbed: 'Your boy's needed, Peg. I'm a star now.'

There is of course more to the film than this relationship, but it is the dominating interest. The *Goon Show* associates and the early British film successes with the Boulting brothers, notably as Kite the shop steward in *I'm All Right, Jack*, are glossed over, in the hurry to get to Kubrick and *Dr Strangelove* (oddly omitting *Lolita*), Blake Edwards and the 'Panther' films, and the international career. This is probably understandable in box-office terms, but, despite Rush's superb impersonations of Sellers' impersonations in these roles, they don't carry much resonance. Rush's is a magisterial diagnosis of a man who believes 'I don't really have any personality of my own', who comes to dazzling life only in the roles he plays, and who, in a poignant scene near the end, is watching home movies as if in search of his elusive self. Director Stephen Hopkins keeps the film moving fluently between such reality as Sellers can muster and the fantasy worlds in which something more 'real' is revealed about him, and neither he nor Rush seeks to sentimentalise this brilliant, deeply dislikable man.

By coincidence, the shadowy Sellers father is played by the same gifted character actor, Peter Vaughan, who plays the quickly disposed-of Toots, husband of *The Mother*. This film opens on two elderly people in bed and moves through an austere little montage sequence as they get up, she helps him dress, and they make their way by train to London. The series of fades separating these early glimpses of their lives enacts a sense of modest, possibly arid ritual. They stay with their son Bobby (Steven Mackintosh) and his shrewish wife Helen (Anna Wilson-Jones) and their largely indifferent children. The whole family later has dinner with their daughter Paula (Cathryn Bradshaw), an occasion bathed in what will prove to be an ironically warm glow, with Toots, very touchingly, saying 'You know the thing I'm most proud of – my family', and toasting them with 'Long life'. He dies in the night, and the film's real drama begins. What is to become of Mother? She has a name, May, but until now it's the role that has defined her.

Until this point, it has been unclear what May is making of her life. She seems patient with Toots, but also bored with his perhaps overeager pleasure in the family, as if it's not something she can throw herself into unequivocally. And neither can son or daughter reciprocate, as becomes apparent after Toots's death. Bobby can scarcely conceal his impatience with her and tells her she can't stay there, and Mackintosh's tense, slightly twitchy persona works very cleverly here; while all that Paula suggests is that May, or Mother, could 'mind Jack [small son] some time'. What they haven't counted on is that in May the heyday in the blood is not tame. It may have been subdued into quiescence but when Bobby's hunky young carpenter Darren (Daniel Craig), who is also Paula's boyfriend, responds to her invitation, 'Would you come with me to the spare room?', she knows that she still has a sexual self that wants satisfying.

May is significantly not a 'smart' 70-year-old. Her clothes are post-menopausal in cut and colour and neither director Roger Michell nor screenwriter Hanif Kureishi makes the mistake of having her bloom in obvious ways. It is mainly by noting what happens to the eyes and around the mouth of the actress that one is alerted to the inner liberation that has taken place. Paula is always yapping about 'liberation' and how it is her due; May has quietly undergone it. In films, there is still something shocking about an older woman taking a lover several decades her junior, but the casting of TV actress Anne Reid triumphantly carries the scenario through.[2] Yes, there *is* something shocking: apart from anything else, Darren is involved with daughter Paula, but it is the explicitly stated sexual desire of the elderly woman that is even now rare in films. Most of those strong mothers referred to above, whether dominant or self-sacrificial, are deemed to be past such desire.

In its quiet way, and *The Mother* is quiet in the way that so many of the best British films have often been (think of *Brief Encounter*, resonant here for other reasons, too), the film forces us to think about life's priorities. Personal gratification is only one of these – but it *is one*. Michell, Kureishi and Reid bring a quiet insistence to this story of a woman who refuses to settle into being a little old lady. She doesn't want to become invisible in the city, and she is not prepared just to be at her daughter's beck and call, or to be an irritant in her son's fraught home. However, if there are glimmerings of Sirk's *All that Heaven Allows* or Fassbinder's *Fear Eats the Soul* about May's involvement with Darren, the film-makers have sedulously avoided imbuing it and them with a sentimentally romantic glow.

There's no suggestion even that May has been a particularly good mother. Perhaps she has always been bored with having to fulfil the limited and limiting demands of the role. The tensions between her and her children are thrown into sharp relief when the Mother becomes the Widow. Paula, who is regarded as an inspirational creative-writing teacher, blames her mother for her own low self- esteem. 'You hardly touched me,' accuses Paula, and this line is echoed later when May tells Darren gratefully, 'I thought no one would ever touch me again, apart from the undertaker.' Bobby, perhaps in reaction to his parents' marriage, seems unable to find contentment with his forceful wife.

May is simply 'not ready for old age'. She submits to the sexual huffing and puffing of writing-class widower Bruce (Oliver Ford Davies), but she wants serious physical passion. She may or may not find this, post-Darren, but as she leaves her own provincial home, with sketch-pad, ticket and passport, the camera, in a rigorously held long take, watches her from inside the house, through the leaded windows, and the implication is that this is what she has escaped. There may be no certainty ahead, but there was no future behind.

These two films – *The Mother* and *The Life and Death of Peter Sellers* – offer, *inter alia*, the spectacle of children who haven't fully grown up. Blaming parents for where one is in middle age is a convenient alibi, but it tends not to take much account of the needs of the parents. Feminists may find the psychologising in *Sellers* simplistic but they are almost certain, and rightly so, to approve of the Mother who finally insists that she is a woman first.

Meanjin, Vol. 63, No. 4, 2004.

Notes

1 Peter Wollen, '*North by North-West*: A Morphological Analysis', *Film Form* 1, 1976, pp. 20–34.

2 The casting of Reid, known to television followers of *Dinnerladies* and *Dalziel and Pascoe*), was one of the last inspirations of Mary Selway, doyenne of UK casting directors who died earlier in 2004.

42

PORTRAITS IN CELLULOID

Back in 1945, in the famous toshfest *A Song to Remember*, novelist Madame George Sand (Merle Oberon) had whisked her protégé-boyfriend, composer Frédéric Chopin (Cornel Wilde), away from Paris, promising: 'You could make miracles of music in Majorca.' Well, he doesn't, and she is forced to berate him one wet morning with: 'Stop this polonaise jangle you've been working on for weeks', and order him to breakfast. At the end, she is having her portrait painted when Chopin's old teacher dodders in to say the dying Chopin wants to see her. Not missing a beat, the imperious profile superbly in evidence, Madame Merle says: 'Frédéric was wrong to ask for me. Pray continue, Monsieur Delacroix'.

With that final felicitous touch of verisimilitude – novelist and composer now joined by painter – what a swathe the film cuts through the cultural life of nineteenth- century Europe! I won't say it wasn't fun when I first saw it; it was even still quite fun to watch on video in the mid-1980s; but it must be said that recent cinematic attempts to offer us portraits of the artist as young men and women have gone about their work with loftier intentions. Not for them the lush idiocies of old-time Hollywood biopics. In the 1940s alone, and just to single out composers, Schumann, Brahms, Schubert, Tchaikovsky,

Rimsky-Korsakov, Jerome Kern, Cole Porter, George Gershwin, Rogers and Hart and others were done over, generally kitted out with anodyne romances, shown briefly in moments of creative inspiration, confronted with a few obstacles, and then set on the path to triumph and renown. There would be a routine montage of place and performance, with leaves falling from calendars and trees, speeding trains, iconic architectural features to indicate a European progress, and most memorably in *A Song to Remember* ending with the plop of Chopin's blood on the keyboard.

In recent months, filmgoers have been made privy to the privacies and privations of painter Vermeer (*Girl with a Pearl Earring*), poet Sylvia Plath (*Sylvia*), composer Porter, again (*De-Lovely*), architect Louis Khan (*My Architect*), actor Edward Kynaston (*Stage Beauty*) and playwright James Barrie (*Finding Neverland*). If none of these offers the banalities of *A Song to Remember*, they are not without their own moments of cliché and sentimentality. Writers are perhaps the most difficult of all to render in cinematically interesting form as they go about their art. Joseph Strick's brave 1977 version of James Joyce's *A Portrait of the Artist as a Young Man* avoided the stereotypical shots of the author looking glum or obsessed over his quill or typewriter or computer (think of Jason Robards smoking himself silly as Dashiell Hammett as he typed away in *Julia*, 1977) by focusing, as Joyce does, on the formative influences that will shape the potential artist. He allows protagonist Stephen Dedalus to talk at length about how he must use and/or put behind him the experiences of his first twenty years, and the film stops at his neophyte steps as author.

More often sources of the artist's genesis and development are rather cursorily dealt with. How did a nice American girl like Sylvia Plath end up writing tormented verse in rainy England prior to killing herself? What has brought the marriage of J.M. Barrie to the pass seen at the start of *Neverland*? How important was Porter's ambivalent sexuality to his growth as man and artist? How does Edward Kynaston's sexuality inform his pre-eminence as a portrayer of women on the Restoration stage? All right, none of these films is offered as a full-scale life of the artist, and given the scope of a two- to three-hour film as compared with, say, a 400-page biography, it would be unreasonable to expect a like concern for the minutiae that we expect of a written work. Nevertheless, sometimes it would add depth to the biopic to be given more sense of where the creative inspiration and activity have come from.

Paradoxically, though, these films have sometimes seemed more interested in the private lives of the artists, not so much in formative influences as in matters romantic. It might well be a matter of intense interest to explore the rest of the artist's life, apart from just the art, if we are to understand the kind of art she or he has produced. In the past, however, there was frequently little attempt to offer a convincing sense of other pressures at work in making the artist's life a particularly challenging one. It may well be true, as MGM would have us believe in *Till the Clouds Roll By* (1946), that Jerome Kern lived a life of blameless hard work (not, actually, all *that* hard) and enjoyed an idyllic romance and marriage, but it certainly doesn't make for any kind of productive tension between the private and the professional life as represented in the film.

Irwin Winkler's *De-Lovely* (2004, USA/Lux./UK) has been widely lauded as a major advance on the sort of composer's biopic I've just mentioned, and especially in relation to *Night and Day*, Warner Bros' 1945 version of the life of Cole Porter. The new film is none too kind in its reference to the latter, which starred Cary Grant, who might have made a definitive Porter in a more honest film. Kevin Kline does a carefully restrained Porter in *De-Lovely*, too watchful, too self-aware for real openness; and this performance admirably serves the treatment of Porter's sexual ambivalence in the new film. It is in this respect that it chiefly marks an advance on Michael Curtis's 1945 sentimentalisation: Porter's preference for handsome young men is now made plain, but there is also something undeniably touching in the obvious devotion – the *intimacy*, as he says – between Porter and his wife, the divorcee Linda Lee.

Film-making convention still has its influence, however, as it did in 1945. Whereas the real Linda Lee Porter was known to be considerably older than her husband, in 1945 Alexis Smith's gracious Linda was then clearly younger than Porter (Smith was in fact seventeen years younger than Grant), and Ashley Judd, who plays the new Linda with warmth and grace, is again depicted as much younger (she is actually twenty-two years younger than Kline). The point of labouring this is to suggest that, fifty years on, a mainstream movie about an artist, while it may now be able to deal more honestly with his homosexual preferences, still can't come at the notion of a leading lady's being older than her male opposite – not even in the interests of real-life veracity or psychological interest. (What might Freud have made of this attachment to an older woman?)

In the new film a sort of heavenly impresario, Gabe (Jonathan Pryce), guides the elderly Porter, as they sit in a drab rehearsal hall, through a procession of scenes from his life as composer, lover, husband and friend. Figures from his past and his shows come and go, and the film maintains a fluid mobility between life and performances, between different periods of the life, and between other places and this rehearsal hall. It's a more sophisticated format than the old biopics used, but the film is really still too long and shapeless. A lot of it is attractive to look at and the songs would in any case save it if it weren't, but it's not really all that daring and it still notably privileges the marriage over the lovers.

Composers have the advantage in biopics in that their work *can* be performed, but they are not all that much better off when it comes to the business of showing the creative processes in action. For instance, is Kline sitting at the piano, jotting down notes as he composes 'So in Love', less banal than Grant responding to the pitter-patter of raindrops as he concocts 'Night and Day'? Painters in action have a more assured avenue to visual appeal: in *Pollock* (2002) we can watch Ed Harris in the title role slosh paint over a large area of canvas, and catch some sense of the creative spark and visceral energies involved in the execution of a work such as *Blue Poles*. More subtly Peter Webber's *Girl with a Pearl Earring* (2004) makes us aware of Vermeer's oeuvre, not just by letting us see the emergence of the eponymous girl but also by allowing cinematographer Eduardo Serra's lighting and Ben Van Os's production design miraculously to evoke the Dutch painter's world as it is known to us through his works.

Girl with a Pearl Earring copes well with two of the problems that films about artists must solve: the need to convince us that this person is or could be an artist and the decision of what to do about the art itself. Here Colin Firth is a glum but persuasively driven Vermeer, making us believe that his art matters more to him than anything else – more than his (chronically pregnant) wife, his children, or even the growing sense of erotic tension between him and Griet, the family's maid and the model for the 'girl' in the painting. This painting hangs over the whole film, both in Scarlett Johansson's watchful, minimalist performance as Griet and of course in the emerging portrait itself. The film maintains a sense of how the art of the artist's life is related to but also in conflict with the details of his everyday life. Unlike its source in Tracy Chevalier's novel, already spare enough, Webber and his screenwriter Olivia Hetreed have honed the narrative to concentrate almost wholly on Griet's time in Vermeer's house, thereby stressing the domestic claustrophobia of the drama. It is a physically cramped space reeking of strong emotional conflicts. Vermeer is under pressure from his wife and her dominating mother to produce the kind of work his patron wants and which will bring in money, yet he is the kind of artist who can only do what his creative impulses and perceptions insist on.

Actors, indeed performers of any kind, offer less intransigent obstacles to the film-maker when it comes to showing them at work. Whether it is Moira Shearer dancing her way through the ballet of *The Red Shoes* (1948) – and off a balcony when the conflict with private life becomes too oppressive – or Larry Parks miming to Al Jolson's voice in *The Jolson Story* (1946), there is something to see; there is a performance from which the audience arrives at an assessment of the artistic talent on display. Richard Eyre's fascinating *Stage Beauty* (2004) is adapted by Jeffrey Hatcher from his own play, *Compleat Female Stage Beauty*, in turn based on a crucial period in the life of the Restoration actor Edward 'Ned' Kynaston, famous for playing women's roles in a theatre from which women were excluded. This film provides explicit comments on the nature of art and what it means for the artist and the way it can stain his entire life.

With the enactment of the law allowing women to perform on the stage, Ned's life takes both professional and personal nosedives and, in chronicling these vicissitudes, the film exhibits a persistently intelligent pressure of ideas. 'Why do you act?' he is asked. 'When you act you can be seen', he replies early in the film before his world has come crashing round his ears. At the end, when his former dresser Maria (Claire Danes) has made her debut as Desdemona to his Othello, and the new realism of the performance has left the audience unsettled, she asks him: 'Who are you now?' All he can reply is: 'I don't know.' It is an aptly uncertain note for the film to end on. (As a matter of historical accuracy, Kynaston never played Othello, but there are more important issues at stake here than this kind of scholarly detail.)

Between these two exchanges, Hatcher's screenplay keeps prodding away at the concept of the stage artist. Ned's answer to the first question is a long way from the romantic 'I-act-because-I-must' idea; equally, though, it eschews the anomie of Peter Sellers' bleak self-knowledge when he says 'I don't really have any personality of my own' in *The Life and Death of Peter Sellers*. It is Maria who comes nearest to expressing the artist's yearning when she says to Ned (Billy Crudup): 'I just wanted to act. I just wanted to do what you do', and in the film's opening sequence we see her standing in the wings mouthing Desdemona's words. Her passion to act is urgent enough to send her to perform in a disreputable, unlicensed pub theatre, and she will later tell Samuel Pepys (Hugh Bonneville) that, unlike the writer who can write for himself, 'I cannot do it for myself alone.' As Ned has said earlier, an actor needs to be *seen*; and a little obliquely, 'A part doesn't belong to an actor. An actor belongs to the part.' Perhaps because of its origins in a play, in the screenwriter's own play, the film's dialogue is made to bear a considerable burden in directing our attention to what it may mean to be this sort of artist.

But there is more to Ned's story than his displacement by women actors in women's roles. His personal life is intricately tangled with his life as an artist. As he makes his way home through designer Jim Clay's imaginatively wrought London streets, he is propositioned by a gross nobleman (Richard Griffiths) in search of a whore. At his lodgings though, he is awaited in bed by Villiers, Duke of Buckingham (Ben Chaplin), who wants him to put on a woman's wig before getting down to business: 'I like to see a golden flow when I die in you' ('die' in the seventeenth-century sense of 'orgasm'). Just as he is in his professional life, Ned will be a victim of gender confusions and ambivalence in his private affairs. Villiers later tells Ned he is marrying and, when Ned taunts him, says: 'I always thought of you as a woman?' Villiers may be justifying himself, but his words may also be the sad truth about Ned: 'I don't know who you are now. I doubt *you* do.' Acting is thus presented as a way of both drawing on self in the interests of art, and of obscuring that self beneath an overlay of art.

Like the *Sellers* film, *Stage Beauty* does attempt to take us into the mind of one kind of artist: the kind who expresses himself by pretending to be someone else. If his art has previously been founded on his exquisite representation of women, the rest of his life will have to take a new impulse, an impulse towards greater 'realism' in the theatre, a starting point for which will be the assigning of roles to actors on more obvious gender lines. The film no doubt elides a gradual move away from stylisation to naturalism, but it is to its credit that it takes an *interest* in the art that gives meaning to the lives of its central characters. In passing one might note that, while the sexes are conventionally sorted in *Stage Beauty*, nationality is another matter: like umpteen British films of the last few years, it relies on the importation of US stars Danes and Crudup to play the leading roles. Another sort of disguise is necessary for the film to get

Americans into cinemas to watch a very English tale about English actors.

Architects have been less common film protagonists than composers or actors. There was Joel McCrea struggling to maintain his integrity as architect and lover in William Wyler's *Dead End* (1937); Gary Cooper mixing phallic buildings with sexual passion in the Warners' version of Ayn Rand's best-seller, *The Fountainhead* (1948); Eiji Okada as the Japanese architect who finds love with Jeanne Moreau in *Hiroshima Mon Amour* (1958); Richard Moir as an architect who runs up against militant opposition to the development he has designed in the Australian *Heatwave* (1981); and Brian Denehy, who revealed *The Belly of an Architect* (1987, UK/Italy) for Peter Greenaway. Other examples could be invoked, but in nearly all instances the profession has been subsidiary to the plot, and the plot has often been dominated by sexual passion, as if this were the usual corollary to the life of the architect as artist and the responsibility for huge building projects required a more-urgent-than-usual libido.

Nathaniel Khan's film *My Architect*, at once a search for a father and an exploration of his architectural triumphs, takes the breath away with some of its shots of what Louis Khan achieved. The son sets out to interview colleagues of the father he scarcely knew, finds siblings he has never met, and discovers buildings that, as much as great music or painting, exhibit the human spirit in soaring mode. What most distinguishes the film is the way it memorialises Khan's art. Architecture is, in this respect, a film-maker's dream. The products of the artist's vision are there for anyone to see, and for a film-maker to represent in dazzling images. For me, among the great film images of 2004 are those of the gorgeously shot Salk Institute for Biological Studies at La Jolla, California, where the camera imbues grey concrete blocks on either side of a concourse with something like a spiritual dimension; or of the Kimbell Art Museum, Texas, when there is a sudden burst on the soundtrack of Beethoven's 'Ode to Joy' – another art form being used to intensify the sense of wonder enjoined by the architect's creation.

Khan may be a prime example of the artist who, in creating sublime art, inevitably fails in the day-to-day business of family living. If this was true for Khan, it was also true for Vermeer and Barrie, not to speak of Gaugin who, as the old Hollywood version (1942) of Somerset Maugham's *The Moon and Sixpence* tells us, forsook wife and children for the lure of the golden bodies of the South Pacific, merely making great art in the process.

Finding Neverland, in its dealings with author and the fiction–reality interface of his life, invites comparison with Gavin Millar's *Dreamchild* (1985), that beautiful and poignant reflection on the life of Lewis Carroll/Charles Dodgson, his most famous work, *Alice in Wonderland*, and the real-life Alice Liddell for whom he wrote the stories. As Carroll, Ian Holm (who, incidentally, also played J.M. Barrie in the BBC-TV drama *The Lost Boys*, 1979) offers a more complex insight into the author's mind and his relationship with his young friend than Johnny Depp's much praised rendering of Barrie in *Finding Neverland*. There is charm and sweetness in Depp's interpretation of the playwright at a crucial time of his life, but not much complexity. While I'd agree that in *Pirates of the Caribbean* he showed a hitherto unsuspected flair for a free-wheeling campy humour, Depp has always seemed to me a graduate of the Mt Rushmore school of acting, as if too much thought would spoil the physical perfection.

In *Finding Neverland*, Barrie has just had a theatrical failure and his marriage to social-climbing Mary (touchingly played by Australian

Radha Mitchell) is chilly. It grows still chillier when he meets Sylvia Llewellyn-Davies (Kate Winslet), a widow with young children who provide the inspiration for the Darling family in *Peter Pan*. The film takes liberties with the facts of Barrie's life and with the family that provided the prototype for the Darlings – for example, Sylvia was not a widow when Barrie met her and she lived for several years after the opening night of *Peter Pan*. But *Finding Neverland* also manages an impressive sense of the connection between the art and the rest of the artist's life, and in the film's terms this is more important than strict adherence to the details of the lives. On the day after his failed first night he goes to the park but Mary declines to accompany him: 'You'll be working', she explains, and so, of course, he proves to be when he meets the Llewellyn-Davies family. The children are playing an imaginative game and he talks to the little boy about working on his 'imagination', the camera demonstrating what he means when the dog he is dancing with turns into a bear. There are lots of moments like this, notably that in which the hand of Sylvia's disapproving mother Mrs du Maurier (played with scene-stealing imperiousness by Julie Christie) turns into a hook as she reprimands the Peter-to-be. This isn't especially subtle, but it encapsulates the connection between the real and the fictionalised – in a word, the moment of inspiration. One of the film's recurring pleasures and strengths is this objectification of the imaginative leap.

The film is generous in the end to the two women who, not understanding his art, fear Barrie's involvement with the children. Mary is allowed finally to say to him that she had hoped he would 'take me with you' to the world he has created; and Mrs du Maurier, in a *coup de cinéma*, leads the clapping that signals the belief in fairies central to that intermingling of the real world and the world of the imagination that is at the heart of *Peter Pan* – and of the life of the artist Barrie. These two women, each with grounds for suspecting Barrie, acknowledge the special nature of an artist's vision, and they also stand for the world in which artists must move but which may not necessarily be sympathetic to the peculiarities of their gifts and needs. In Barrie's case, the delicacy of his relationship with the children, whose easy access to the world of the imagination matches his own, leads his friend Conan Doyle (Ian Hart) to warn him that there is gossip about 'how you spend your time with those boys and why'. Doyle goes on to generalise: 'When you get a bit of notoriety, people ... look for ways to take you down'.

This issue of 'notoriety' or 'celebrity' is crucial to the study of artists, and the artists represented in the foregoing films react to it with varying degrees of aplomb. As Ned Kynaston finds, celebrity is a fickle mistress, likely to withdraw her favours when a new allurement appears. Celebrity belongs to the artist's professional life; it may take an exceptional human being to balance its claims against those of the other people who are important in his or her personal life. How – and how far – this balance is maintained may well be the most rewarding aspect of these cinematic portraits of the artist.

Meanjin, 2005, Vol. 64, Nos. 1–2.

43

SHOOTING MINDS

The movies have not generally been concerned with beautiful minds; beautiful bodies have been much more in their line. Even in one of the most obvious exceptions to this rule, the film called *A Beautiful Mind* (2001), the conjunction of its star Russell Crowe and its title can seem risibly oxymoronic, despite the intensity of Crowe's performance. It's hard to put entirely from one's own mind (however beautiful) the press reports of Russell's throwing telephones at hotel receptionists or punching people who truncate his poems, when one is asked to contemplate on screen the beauties of the mind he is meant to be representing.

I'm narrowing my concern here to films that show a concern with the life of the mind. 'Beautiful' minds aren't of course the prerogative of intellectuals, much less of academics, if one extends the definition to include the saintly or even just the good. Here though, I plan to concentrate chiefly on films that have, in one way or other, depicted the intellectual life of those connected with academic institutions or schools. I am interested in how far films seek to grapple with ideas, as distinct from their more usual concern with dramatic – and, very commonly, physical – action. The cerebrations of the engaged mind are not usually susceptible to the visual priorities of film.

The idea of teachers instilling a love of learning in their pupils has given rise to a number of distinguished films – and to quite a few very sentimental ones. There is the potent melodramatic ending of Peter Weir's *Dead Poets' Society* (1989), in which English teacher Robin Williams inspires a class with a love of poetry and they repay him as he leaves by standing on their desks to intone Whitman's 'O captain! My captain!' as a tribute to what he has done for them. Forty-odd years earlier in *The Corn is Green* (1945), Bette Davis had recognised and encouraged a love of the word in a Welsh boy destined for the coalmines and seen him off to Oxford. In 1968, Maggie Smith gathered a coven of teenage girls around her to benefit from *The Prime of Miss Jean Brodie* in an Edinburgh school, before her adoration of Mussolini proved her undoing. And most famously, without actually doing anything very specific for the beautifying of youthful minds, Robert Donat made schoolmastering seem a lovable profession in *Goodbye Mr Chips* (1939). Even the desiccated classics master Crocker-Harris is capable of inspiring respect from one of his pupils in *The Browning Version* (1951; remake, 1994).

More often than not, 'school films' were less concerned with actual learning than with 'problems' associated with, say, unruly students, as in *The Blackboard Jungle* (1955) or the pallid British riposte to this, *Spare the Rod* (1961), or the more interesting British *Clockwork Mice* (1995) in which a teacher tackles head-on the challenges of disturbed kids in a special school. *The Children's Hour* (1961; a remake of *These Three*, 1933), which is set in an expensive girls' school, is really about the harmful effects of malicious gossip rather than the education of youthful minds. Sidney Poitier conquers thuggery and racism by sheer charisma in *To Sir with Love* (1967); and more recently, and more seriously, Pedro Almodóvar has made engrossing drama from the teacher's abuse of trust in *Bad Education* (2004). In virtually all of these scattered instances, attention is focused not on the training of young minds, as if that wouldn't be drama enough, but on some of the kinds of conflicts that develop between children and those whose task is supposedly to nurture what gifts they may have.

Films about the intellectual life are indeed few. Are there any film-makers as concerned with this matter as such novelists as David Lodge or Malcolm Bradbury? And I've deliberately chosen examples of popular writers whose appeal is by no stretch of the imagination arcane. Does this suggest that the readership of novels concerning themselves with ideas, and with lives professionally devoted to their articulation, is more extensive than the cinema audience would be for films comparably rooted? In such films as address the intellectual aspects of living, it is very rare to find academics rendered sympathetically or the academic vocation as offering a sustaining approach to life's vicissitudes. In a recent film, My *House in Umbria* (2005, UK/Germany/Italy), in which an orphaned child's future hangs in the balance after a terrorist attack on an Italian train, the narrative settles happily for leaving the child in Italy with a dipsomaniac author (Maggie Smith again) rather than relinquish her to her American uncle, a chilly academic (Chris Cooper). The implication here, as is often the case, is that his very profession ensures his being out of touch with the affections or the quotidian realities. When not suggesting that those engaged in intellectual activity are totally removed from the hurly-burly of everyday living, movies are likely to depict academe as a hotbed of sexual activity. John Curran's new film, *We Don't Live Here Any More* (Canada/US), recalls in its depiction of two couples living in a college town that archetypal film of campus couples locked in dangerous game-playing, *Who's Afraid of Virginia Woolf?* (1966). Jack (Mark Ruffalo) is a literature academic married to Kerry (Laura Dern), who tells him they should behave more like a married couple and accuses him of making opportunities to be with Edith (Naomi Watts) who is married to creative writing lecturer Hank (Peter Krause). Jack accuses Kerry of being 'horny' for Hank, who has told her he doesn't love Edith. Hank, on the other hand, can't resist making overtures to his students, and a creative-writing instructor may be more susceptibly placed in this regard than most academics, since his students are always likely to be exposing aspects of themselves and their lives in a way that, say, economics students may be less moved to do.

Based on André Dubus' screenplay from his own short stories, *We Don't Live Here Any More* is essentially a drama of tangled adulteries among more-than-usually articulate people. It is less centrally concerned with the minds of its putative intellectuals. In one sequence, Jack is trying to mark essays (with reference to Al Alvarez, not – to the film's credit – the most obvious cultural marker) while Kerry, teetering on the edge of alcoholism, is letting the household fall apart around her. In another sequence, Hank talks about love, and 'fucking without the need to love', and prides himself on his academic's supercool habits of mind – of being able to 'sort all this stuff intellectually'. We see one of his students hanging on his words as he uses his academic position and careless, practised charm to move on her. He has a story turned down and burns it – he seems to be the sort of writer who teaches writing more successfully than he does it, who is distracted rather than stimulated by everyday life – though later he has a poem accepted by the *New Yorker*. ('You're being published. It doesn't get much better than that.' What doesn't get 'much better'? Life?)

The film doesn't pay much more overt attention to the intellectual business of these men's lives, but the mess they make of these seems to point to the film's sense of its certainly not equipping them for the emotional aspects of living. Curran (abetted by his brilliant editor, Alexandre de Franceschi) maintains a rigorous control over the play of intersecting lives, of betrayals and the lies behind the talk, moving with effortless and mutually revealing fluidity between the couples. There is nothing attractive about the glimpses of academe the film offers, and the two adulterous males at its centre, both superbly played by Ruffalo and Krause, seem to derive little delight from the exercise of their intellectual capacities. In this respect, they differ from the academics whose lives and friendship were so warmly and affectingly chronicled in last year's *The Barbarian Invasions* (2003, Canada/France). This latter is a film both seriously interested in ideas and drawn to what might make their pursuit a life-enhancing vocation. These men are as messy in their sexual *affaires* as those in Curran's films, but, without recourse to sentimentality, director Denys Arcand places these *affaires* in a larger context of generous living. There is a sense of real affection as the friends gather round their dying colleague, first in his Montreal hospital and then in a tranquil lakeside retreat, where Chekhovian echoes are poignantly struck.

Arcand does not suggest that these are remarkable minds but that they have been receptive to ideas: 'We've been everything. Separatists, independantists, sovereigntists, sovereignty-associationists ... We were structuralists. Situationists. Feminists. Deconstructionists. Is there any "ism" we haven't worshipped?' (My computer's spell-checker rejects several of these.) But, though it maintains a healthy cynicism along with respect towards its characters, *The Barbarian Invasions* accepts that those who devote their lives to such explorations (when not wandering off into sexual adventuring – it's actually reassuring to know that academics are thought of in this raffish way) may just be capable of real affection and of better-than-average tolerance for the otherness of others. They are also represented as people with a serious interest in what is going on in the larger world, in the 'invasions' that the barbarians have launched in diverse ways against the bulwarks of civilisation.

More recently the film version of Ian McEwan's masterly novel *Enduring Love* enacts the limitations of an academic approach to the arbitrary tragedies of everyday life. Few films can boast a more gut-wrenching opening sequence. Joe (Daniel Craig), a rationalist and academic (not a freelance, popularising journalist as in the novel), and his partner Claire (Samantha Morton), a sculptor (not a literary academic and Keats specialist as McEwan draws her), are enjoying a picnic in a scene of pastoral tranquillity in the Chiltern Hills, and he is about to propose, when suddenly a hot-air balloon crashes to the ground. Joe and three other men race to the rescue of the child in the balloon but a sudden gust of wind lifts it and one man hangs on as the others drop to safety. One of the latter, Jed (Rhys Ifans), begins to stalk Joe, claiming to 'love' him and the title accretes disturbing ambiguities. Does it mean 'love that endures' or does it suggest what it takes to 'endure love', to live with the knowledge of it, to watch it seem to erode as in the case of Claire or to be appalled with its obsessive potential as in the case of Jed? Whatever it means, it increasingly proves to be beyond Joe's attempts to make an academic's sense of the world *enough*.

The nature of love will be the film's major preoccupation. In his university class, Joe, a conscientious academic and concerned to be a decent man, asks his students: 'What is love? Is it just a trick played by nature to make us fuck?' Not just the obsessive Jed comes to haunt his mind and imagination but also the fate of the Oxford doctor who did not let go and who later fell to his death. This leads Joe to visit this man's widow (the brilliant Helen McCrory) who says of her late husband: 'He was bound to die rescuing somebody.' Another, more wide-ranging kind of love? Or was this act the product of a different, more ordinary kind of love: 'He wouldn't have taken a risk unless he was showing off', says his widow, who angrily believes he was having an affair. This is a rare film that grapples with ideas: 'Everything happens for a reason', Joe tries, in his rationalist way, to believe.

The film changes the novel's penultimate sequence, but I do not think it diminishes its intellectual pressure. Perhaps the overwhelming majority of films are about love in one form or other but not many are prepared to take it on board *as a concept* as director Roger Michell and screenwriter Joe Penhall have done. The director of an adaptation of Jane Austen's *Persuasion* (1995), of the popular romance *Notting Hill* (1999), and of that exploration of a relationship between an older woman and a younger man, *The Mother* (2004), Michell has repeatedly shown himself alert to the wayward ways of love and their capacity to disrupt lives. He is blessed here with a cast of more than usually compelling players. Daniel Craig, who was also the younger man in *The Mother*, is one of the few stars around at the moment whose commanding physical presence is matched by intimations of an inner life. (One hopes, despite casting rumours going around, that he will not sell his birthright for a mess of Bondage.) Rhys Ifans's mild-eyed zealot complements Craig with a very unsettling character study. The film's essential drama and tension are the product of what goes on between these two. But, above all, the film's power derives from the too-cerebral Joe's incapacity to articulate the terrors within himself and he comes near to losing everything as a result. What happens on the glorious summer day that opens the film calls into question Joe's intellectual grasp of his life and the alarming events towards the end are, in my view, less a matter of melodrama's taking over than of dramatising ways in which the arbitrary and unexpected can totally alter the course of lives. *Enduring Love* is gripping on every level: as a study in the twists and turns of relationships; as a story with a bizarre starting point and how this impinges on more or less smooth- running lives; and as a study of the gap between what is theoretically understood and the sudden actualities that play havoc with this.

The cinema's academics, then, don't commonly have the command over their private lives that they have over their intellectual activities. Derek Jarman's very imaginative, minimalist treatment of the life of the philosopher *Wittgenstein* (1993) – with a screenplay by guru–academic Terry Eagleton – certainly offers some critique of the over-intellectualising of all life's experiences, but it is genuinely concerned with understanding how a philosopher's mind functions, and in Karl Johnson's bony face the tormented scholar's mind finds an apt reflecting mirror. Unlike the situation in Robert Benton's *The Human Stain* (2003), where the protagonist is a classics professor but the dramatic interest lies in a long-suppressed secret that has nothing to do with Ancient Greek or Latin, *Wittgenstein* is quite unusually focused on a mind of rare distinction. This, along with its austere, non-realist mode, may help to account for its reaching only an art-house coterie audience.

Among recent films, Alejandro Amenábar's *The Sea Inside* (a Spanish/ French/Italian coproduction) is the one that most gives insight into the workings of a 'beautiful mind'. It is based on the real life of the Spanish former merchant marine (and poet) Ramón

Sampedro who, following a diving accident, spends twenty-seven years on his back, paralysed and tended by a devoted family. Ramón (played by Javier Bardem) has had time to reflect on his life and life in general – and wants to finish his. The film is thematically an argued plea for the concept of voluntary euthanasia. Ramón maintains a composure one can believe: this is a man who has come to terms with a dreadful limitation in his life, knows that he wants to finish it, and must then seek help to do so. Bardem's facial acting is minimalist and totally in character, and he makes the man intelligent and humorous, using a screenplay that doesn't settle for smart one-liners and doesn't make the mistake of becoming a purely didactic piece in which the various points of view are carefully – or simplistically – spelt out. Responses to the issue of euthanasia are as a rule lived in the actors' understanding of their roles and grow out of their characters.

What emerges in the central character is a man who knows his own mind very thoroughly and the film benefits immensely from an actor who can persuade us that the operations of this mind have not lost their clarity with the atrophying of the body but have indeed become more sharply focused. And not just about himself. His strength of purpose influences those around him, particularly the lawyer, Julia, who takes up his cause, and Rosa, a local single mother, who tries to persuade Ramón to live but is in the end persuaded by *him* to accept that he is ready to relinquish life and will help him to do so. There are brief exhilarating moments when the camera tracks swiftly across the countryside outside Ramón's window, but these are not just empty pictorialism: they are metonyms for his still-active imaginative life; they are not objectively observed panoramas but the products of intense subjectivity making what sorties it still can into the outside world. *The Sea Inside* is a triumph for director–producer–composer –writer Amenábar. This is film-making that knows how to take on ideas and to render them dramatically and visually, that engages eye, mind and heart; and if the mind it reflects through Bardem's eloquent face is 'beautiful' it is because it has achieved the most basic knowledge of utterly knowing itself.

We Don't Live Here Any More, an exemplary film of its chamber kind, is ultimately less interested in what makes Jack and Hank tick as men engaged in intellectual pursuits, than in what propels them to rip the fabric of their family lives in the interest of sexual gratification. Films such as *Enduring Love* and *The Sea Inside*, on the other hand, are unusual in their direct confrontation of ideas, of the swirling processes of the mind, but without surrendering the dramatic to the merely didactic.

Meanjin, Vol. 64, No. 3, 2005.

44

SIZE DOESN'T MATTER

Big Stupid Films

The title for this essay might have been extended by adding 'and, for that matter, small stupid films'. It's easy to express dissatisfaction with the big spectacular jobs which are my main subject here. But, in the interests of fairness, it is important to recall such appalling, comparatively small films of recent times as *Blackball* or *Raising Helen* or *Plots with a View*. These are films so keen on being winsomely small-scale that they excite curmudgeonly resistance to being won over.

But in recent times it's the big films that have caused most complaint. And what exactly do I mean by 'big'? Two terms that sometimes seem to overlap in writing about cinema are 'blockbuster' and 'epic'. They are certainly not the same, though they are sometimes used as if they were. The *American Heritage Dictionary* defines a blockbuster as: '1. a bomb capable of destroying a city block'. Well, 'bomb' (= flop) is the very last thing on the minds of blockbuster aspirants in the film world. The one indispensable characteristic of the film blockbuster is that it should cause an explosion at the world's box-offices, and everything that promotion can do to bring this about will be allowed for in budgeting. The same dictionary gives, as a secondary meaning of the term, 'anything of devastating effect', and perhaps this is where the overlap with epic may be seen to occur. The epic, in film terms, is above all a big-scale affair, often concerned with 'devastating effect[s]' as part of its plotline, even if the result from a critical standpoint is all too often considerably less than devastating. Epics have been around in film history since the teens when D.W. Griffith was making *The Birth of a Nation* (1915) and *Intolerance* (1916), films embracing a central action of major significance in human affairs, on a scale that remains impressive as much for intellectual grasp as for cinematic genius. A film epic is one that not merely makes money, as any common or garden blockbuster might, but one that grapples with a conception of real magnitude and invokes the resources of the cinema with precision and imaginative power.

And how often does that happen? In recent times, such films could be counted on the fingers of a damaged hand. In case this seems unduly severe, I should make clear what has informed my thinking about epics. In literary terms, the idea of the epic poem can be traced back to classical Greece and the oral tradition, and did director Wolfgang Petersen (of *Troy*, 2004) or his screenwriter David Benioff really go back to Homer, to the world of *The Odyssey* and *The Iliad*? That is to say, to a world that so magnificently meshes the quotidian with the spiritual? Meshes the world of men, recognisably heroic and ordinary, with the world of the gods, arbitrary and omnipotent? To jump a couple of millennia, Milton's *Paradise Lost* has no less an aim than to 'assert eternal Providence, and justify the ways of God to man'. Whether or not you think he achieves this aim, it is undeniable that this (enthralling) work never lets up on its argument – in verse of surpassing grandeur and, when apt, poignancy. Homer ranges over much of the known world in his exploration of man's place in it, and of man's relation to the metaphysical. Milton imagines no less than heaven, hell and the legendary first dwelling-place of man. In drama, the great Shakespearean 'second tetralogy' – *Richard II*, *Henry IV Parts I* and *2* and *Henry V* – seems to require the word 'epic' to encompass its massively comprehensive sense of a nation in uneasy peace and triumphant war, a nation at a stage when it might almost be said to be defining itself. (In passing, it is worth noting how many film epics have 'borrowed' from Olivier's wartime version of *Henry V*, [1944], with its poetic rain of arrows on the ranks of the perfidious French.) Orson Welles's sublime Swiss/Spanish co-production, *Chimes at Midnight* (1966), inventively drawing on the tetralogy, probably came as near to truly epic stature as any film has, understanding that it was not just a matter of battles and verse but of rendering the passing of one age into another.

In the twentieth century, Bertolt Brecht redefined the term 'epic' by describing the sorts of responses his plays were intended to achieve as 'epic theatre'. The essence of his argument was that audiences should be prevented from such emotional involvement in the action of the drama as would preclude their rational, objective, critical reactions to the social conditions that comprised its context. Not even Brecht himself really pulled this off: try watching, say, *Mother Courage* or *The Caucasian Chalk Circle* without feeling emotional commitment. Nevertheless, there is a serious notion of what constitutes the epic here, and it is my contention that filmmakers for the most part have never got beyond a sort of blockbuster attitude to it. It's as though their thinking is along the lines of 'this will cost a fortune to make. How, therefore, do we go about getting back an even bigger fortune?'

Lest anyone think I'm being nostalgic for the great days (whenever they were) of the Hollywood epic, let me say at once that, apart from the Griffith films named, so-called epics were almost always overblown and under-brained. *Troy* and *King Arthur* and *Alexander* don't represent the decline of the American film epic: it was almost always a dud. Having recently viewed/reviewed such elderly exemplars of the genre as *The Robe* (Henry Koster, 1953), *King of Kings* (Nicholas Ray) and *El Cid* (Anthony Mann) – the latter two released within a month of each other in the UK in 1961, so the recent rash of titles in Melbourne is nothing new – and with memories of others such as *Quo Vadis?* (Mervyn Leroy, 1951), *The Ten Commandments* (Cecil B. DeMille, 1956) and *Ben Hur* (William Wyler, 1959), all three of which had appeared in earlier versions, I'd say that this was always a doomed genre. With its blockbuster needs in mind, it was never going to be able to concentrate on those aspects of the great literary epics that made them timeless works of art. Rather, it would need to focus on spectacle, action and stars. The films seem hardly to have a thought in their heads beyond, say, getting Charlton Heston heroically lit.

Watching and re-watching those older films in the light of the recent rush of epics (and the term is now routinely used for a certain kind of big-budget spectacular), it was instructive to note some of the characteristics they have in common, reinforcing the notion that genre is always empirically and retrospectively defined. 'Defined' is of course scarcely the word to embrace a loose set of conventions and recurring traits, but it will do for the moment. To start with, epics are of course immensely expensive (even disgustingly so when you think to what serious uses those megabucks might have been put), and where the money goes helps the process of description. For instance, they are almost invariably over-cast with costly stars who should have known better and a lot of distinguished British supporting actors imported in the vain hope of giving some sort of classic sheen to the enterprise. Vain, that is, because the characterisation is generally so thin that there is little for these eclectically chosen players to get their teeth into.

This heterogeneous casting accounts for a lot of the budget and often for the small artistic return; so too does the location shooting, which is *de rigueur* for such films. At various times, Hollywood producers have looked to Britain, Ireland, Spain, Czechoslovakia and New Zealand in search of appropriate backgrounds (and backgrounds are mostly all they are in these films, rarely part of the film's meaning) and cheaper labour costs. The films invariably run to an inordinate length, as if to numb us into acquiescence, rarely coming within a bull's roar of earning this length, as if they think size and magnitude were entirely synonymous. In matters of style, contact with the genre can reduce otherwise admirable craftsmen like Anthony Mann and Nicholas Ray to fawning acolytes. By this, I mean such matters as the inevitable solemn voice-over to introduce the epic tone, as Orson Welles does in *King of Kings*, and/or to comment on the action intermittently to make sure we are not missing the significance. When they touch on religious themes, as they often do, they naively trust in solemnity to distract attention from the absence of any real interest in the spiritual life. Wit, humour, irony, delicacy and grace are abandoned (or were never even considered) in favour of an insistent high portentousness, usually bolstered with a bombastic music score and extravagant production values.

What matters most to film epics are the action sequences, and sometimes they feel like musicals with battles taking the place of song-and-dance numbers. and of course these sequences are well-staged, at least in terms of composition, even if it is quite often unclear in, say, battle scenes just who is doing what harm to whom. It is no longer much of a recommendation to praise the action episodes, especially in these days of computer-enhanced imagery that can fill the screen with armadas or barbarous hordes at the touch of a keyboard. But even in the older films I found myself asking, as the cohorts gleamed in the desert sun or whatever, 'Who are these people? Was the ancient world really so populous? Is there anyone at home minding not just the store but the women and children?' This is not a sexist remark: the only women one ever sees are either highly-placed temptresses or waxen-looking Madonnas. At least, though, in the days of, say, *Ben Hur*, the crowds were played by real-life extras, so that economic justification in terms of jobs could be advanced. Perhaps, if no one had ever told me about CGI, I wouldn't have become so sceptical as I watched the hordes readying for battle in *Troy*.

By now those still reading will be willing to accuse me of prejudice – and they would be right, up to a point. I resent the sheer mad waste of these films. I resent how little there is to show for all the time and effort as well as money that has gone into them. I resent the way they take on big themes and vulgarise and emaciate them in their search for the huge audiences they need and, I fear, often find. Is there anything to be said for the genre, which is now enjoying one of its major boom periods? About some of the science-fiction sub-category – films like Kubrick's masterly *2001: A Space Odyssey* (1968), the first *Star Wars* (1977) – or Kubrick's *Spartacus* (1960), which was given some sense of contemporary political relevance, or the *Lord of the Rings* trilogy, which grapples with the conflict of good and evil on a vast scale, there is a sense of the grandeur of concept which I'd regard as crucial to epic. Too often, though, 'grandeur of concept' translates merely as ponderousness of execution.

Obviously such a film as *King of Kings* is trying hard to be serious about the life of Jesus. But, whatever the filmmaker's underlying intentions, spiritually or intellectually (and without such intentions it seems hardly worth persevering), the result is vitiated in so many ways. There is an excruciating use of heavenly choir to introduce the undertaking, giving way to the usual pompous orchestral lead-up to the opening action; the solemn voice-over narration is full of locutions beginning 'It is written that …', at once high-sounding and banal; there is the usual bizarre mix of accents, including an Irish Mary (Siobhan McKenna) and an American Christ (Jeffrey Hunter); and there is a rapid run-through of key events in the early life of Jesus (slaughter of the innocents, flight into Egypt, etc).

El Cid, which has admirers, including David Thomson, who found it 'an astonishing departure [for director Anthony Mann] and a total success',[1] but scarcely supports this hyperbole, suffers from most of the recurring negatives of the genre. It has the usual bombastic score, dialogue that predictably mixes the florid and the commonplace, long, boring battle scenes with the odd inserted close-up to remind us of key cast members (the usual League of Nations round-up), and statuesque compositions involving arches and crenellations, with carefully posed actors but no real sense of drama or poetry. 'And thus the Cid rode out of the gates of history and into legend' the solemn voice-over informs us at the end as organ music swells up. As for Charlton Heston as the Cid and Sophia Loren as Chimène (he with a quiff, she with a coif), it is hard to imagine a pairing less resonant: beautiful in their various ways but with that kind of surface beauty that looks as if thought would disrupt it. Again, the original concept, of the clash of Moorish and Christian cultures in Spain, may have seemed the stuff of epic aspiration, and so may the Cid's conflict of honour, as Corneille (unacknowledged as a source here) found in his famous tragedy. Again, the concept is largely defeated by the genre's confusion of size and significance.

The same sorts of criticisms could be adduced of *The Robe*, based on Lloyd Douglas's best-selling 'religious' novel, and the first CinemaScope film, directed by Henry Koster, who had made his name directing Deanna Durbin musicals. Such a useful training for the high solemnity of *The Robe*, which parades what were to become the hallmarks of the genre. There is a truly egregious heavenly chorus at key moments; the film's accommodation with the production period in matters of hairstyle and dialogue is even more fatuous than usual ('I want to apologise for last night', says Richard Burton to Dawn Addams); in those pre-CGI days, the painted backcloth is in evidence; and the turgid voice-over narration attempts to force our attention on to the significance of the material. Again, the idea of Rome coming to terms with a religion spawned in a part of the world under its military occupation is not trivial, but almost everything about its treatment is. It makes one almost grateful for the real earnestness of purpose that led Mel Gibson to put us through such physical excoriation in *The Passion of the Christ* (2004).

All this is by way of an intemperate approach to the recent spate of would-be epics, which led me to wonder if the genre, especially in its pseudo-religious, pseudo-historical incarnations, ever had much going for it. Does the genuinely epic require a rigour and complexity of thought which will usually be at odds with the blockbuster goals of these bloated films? In recent months I've limited myself to just three – enough to confirm my feelings about the genre, and in the interests of self-preservation. The three I've seen are *King Arthur*, *Troy* and *Alexander*. It has to be said that, in their dealings with some of the great stories of the Western cultural heritage, their achievement has been to reduce and vulgarise – and I don't mean even the sort of hearty vulgarity that might have kept one amused during their inordinate length. Of the three, *Alexander*, the most recent, has more going for it than the other two, which strike me as little short of inane in their dealings with their great sources.

There is nothing intrinsically stupid in the sort of deconstructive approach taken by director Antoine Fuqua and screenwriter David Franzoni in *King Arthur*. Producer Jerry Bruckheimer for Touchstone Pictures confidently asserted: '*King Arthur* is the definitive story of the leader and warrior who emerged to lead the Britons against the Saxons.'[2] He goes on to insist that Arthur's period was considerably earlier than is usually accepted and that Arthur, half-Roman, half-British, and his knights ('the Wild Bunch', said Franzoni) were the last Roman forces in Britain, charged with one more mission before returning to Rome. It is a point of view, and so is the deliberately unromantic playing down of the chivalric Round Table ideal of the Arthurian legend that we are more familiar with in the works of everyone from Thomas Malory on, through Tennyson and earlier films such as Richard Thorpe's *Knights of the Round Table* (1952), Joshua Logan's *Camelot* (1967) or John Boorman's *Excalibur* (1981). Arguably, there has never been a great film based on the Arthurian legends, though the three I've named all have good things going for them; certainly, none has plumbed the depths of *King Arthur*.

The stories of Arthur are part of the English-speaking cultural heritage, linking Christianity with medieval chivalry, the real world of righteous fighting with the magic of Merlin, the purity of true love and virtue with the temptations of lust and the quest for power. Every schoolchild once knew about the finding of the sword Excalibur, the search for the Holy Grail (no, not the Dan Brown version), the knights Galahad, Lancelot and Bedivere, the beauteous Guinevere, the wicked Modred and so on. Probably one can't take this knowledge for granted any more, and there's no reason why there shouldn't be a deconstructed Arthur that seeks to account for him and the phenomenon of the Round Table in historical terms, but Fuqua's film fails on almost every count. It makes no sense as history or drama and simply jettisons the legend in the interests of a foolish, scruffy realism (that is, they all look unwashed), though Guinevere, here a doughty Briton lass with feminist leanings, is improbably dressed for the northern winter in hipster pants, bare midriff and some sort of bustier. Just the thing for a battle on ice-floes which unwisely courts comparison with *Alexander Nevsky* (Sergei Eisenstein, 1938) – now there's an epic for you.

There's almost nothing to be salvaged from this farrago. Clive Owen, so good in *Croupier* (1998, released 2000) or *Closer* (2005), is expressionless and curiously modern as Arthur. This would matter less if he weren't given such preposterously olde-worlde declamatory dialogue. Ioan Grufford keeps suggesting he could do something with the role of Lancelot, no longer Guinevere's lover but a seasoned soldier and killer, if the script would only give him a break. Only the battle scenes and the look of the film are worth noting and of what films can one not say that these days? And how little it means, and how little it compensates for the lack of any engagement with character or ideas.

Empire magazine lists *Troy* as a 'Big-Budget Disappointment'[3] because it only made US$133m. Two things shock me about this:

first, that any film has to make more than that to be a success – that is, that any film should cost that sort of obscene money; and, second, that so many people went to see this deplorable film as to get the takings up to even this 'disappointing' level.

Just as *King Arthur* demystifies the Arthurian legends and their world in which the spiritual and the magical play such influential roles, and offers no compensating textural enrichment, so too *Troy* does without the gods. Without this dimension, what we are left with is a tiresomely inflated series of action episodes interspersed with 'personal' moments of jaw-dropping insipidity. Paris's abduction of Helen, and how this precipitates a war in which motive is lost as it drags on, founders on totally uninteresting performances. Orlando Bloom is a pretty, callow Paris, but he seems like Laurence Olivier compared with the stunning vacuity of Diane Kruger as Helen. I kept thinking of Sir Cedric Hardwicke as Priam in Robert Wise's 1955 bore, *Helen of Troy*, as he looked at Rosanna Podesta's Helen and said incredulously: 'Is *this* the face that launched a thousand ships?' Helen may be a silly flighty girl, but that needs to be made a compelling reason for what follows. Mind you, there's not much even more practised actors could have done with dialogue exchanges like this: Helen says to Paris, 'You shouldn't be here.' Paris: 'That's not what you said last night.' Helen: 'Last night was a mistake.' Elsewhere he tells her that he'll hunt rabbits; 'We'll live off the land,' he says unconvincingly. Their lives, one feels, would be Spartan indeed.

Director Petersen takes one of the greatest stories in Western mythology and makes it the occasion for a display of technology. There are digitally summoned fleets and armies which may initially be breathtaking until two niggling worries set in: oh, it's CGI again and so what; and who are all these people? (At least they were real extras in the days of, say, *El Cid.*) Irrelevant concerns, you might say, but if one were really swept away by the drama they probably wouldn't surface. Petersen's direction is banal in the extreme. He keeps things more or less in motion, but resorts to the crudest contrasts for effect. He cuts from 'intimate scenes' (e.g., Brad Pitt's Achilles nudely having his way with vestal virgin Briseis, played by Rose Byrne in one of the film's better performances) to vast panoramas of massed forces on the move. He can't control the risible mix of accents and acting styles (those who come off best – Eric Bana, Julie Christie and Peter O'Toole – seem to be working in a vacuum); and he hadn't the taste to forbid the hideously sugary song on the soundtrack at the end. 'They'll be talking about this war in a thousand years' time,' someone intones. So they might, but not about this film they won't – not, I predict, in even one year's time.

Critics rarely give these 'epics' an easy ride but nothing seems to stop the public from flocking to them. Some have been singled out for praise for particular elements, as *Ben Hur* (which won eleven Oscars – not that that proves anything serious) was for its brilliantly filmed chariot race, though much of the rest was a high-minded drag. Nevertheless, their blockbuster status points to filmgoers' insatiable hunger for these long, shapeless examples of creative elephantiasis. There's not the slightest hope that Oliver Stone's *Alexander* will be the last in the line that threatens, like Macbeth's fears, to 'stretch out to the crack of doom'. It is really no worse than any of the others; indeed, in some respects it is better. At least it is telling a story grounded in earthly achievement, so one doesn't feel that it has ripped the metaphysical heart out of a great story. And Oliver Stone is a considerable director of a certain kind, with a track record of high-powered biopics (e.g., *JFK*, 1991; *Nixon*, 1995), battle-zone reconstructions (e.g., *Salvador*, 1986; *Heaven & Earth*, 1993) and, combining both of these, *Born on the Fourth of July* (1988). You don't have to like all of them to acknowledge that they are not negligible.

Alexander, though, is the least of them, and this may well be because, unlike Stone's earlier 'big' films, it belongs to the epic genre and (increasingly, I think) this is the kiss of death to a director's best intentions, supposing he starts out with the best intentions. *Alexander* is portentous from the word go, with titles in ancient Greek, heavy music backing vast, slow-changing images, ending with a species of mosaic map which homes in on Babylon. Old Ptolemy (Anthony Hopkins – talk about selling your birthright for a mess of Hollywood potage) shuffles about the set telling us that Alexander was a god, that 'he was Prometheus, he changed the world … In his presence, by the light of Apollo, we were better than ourselves.'

The personal story in *Alexander* is more interesting than in the other films. *Alexander* has, you might say, an unhappy home life. His mother, Olympia (Angelina Jolie), has a penchant for snakes which she indulges as she cuddles little Alexander, who watches when his boorish father Philip of Macedonia (Val Kilmer) bursts in and berates her – and Alexander will later disown her. Eight years later, our boy is seen with his wrestling trainer (Brian Blessed) and then at his lessons with Aristotle (Christopher Plummer), who counsels Greek restraint as a way of dealing with the 'barbarity' of Orientals. Well, that's certainly not very useful advice for a film epic: whoever heard of audiences flocking to watch control and moderation? About now, Ptolemy intones on the soundtrack that 'It was said later that Alexander was never defeated, except by Hephaistion's thighs', and Alexander himself talks of 'how men lie together when virtue and knowledge is passed between them'. Stone and his screenwriter are determined to provide a psychoanalytic account of Alexander's bisexuality. It's all pretty much the Golden Books version of Oedipus, but at least there's some move towards – some sense of a need for – a psychology of the hero.

Colin Farrell, unwisely one would think, has publicly belittled the film, and certainly the film doesn't seem likely to advance his career. He is too scruffily modern, too sulkily commonplace, to deal coherently with so giant a figure as Alexander. Bleached blond, he simply hasn't shaken off his image of stubbly badboy, of Irishman-on-the-tear in Hollywood, and the scenes between him and Jared Leto's Hephaistion are more or less ludicrous, full of charged oglings and discreet fondlings, as if Stone feels he is being both very daring and very tasteful. At least, though, and simplistic as it is, he does permit his hero to say to his lover: 'I've missed you. I need you. It's you I love Hephaistion, no other.'

As always, what strengths there are in such a film are to be found in the spaciousness of the action, and there are some genuinely magnificent transactions with the varied terrains in which the armies find themselves – Persia, India, Macedonia, etc. As a forest of lances appears over the brow of a hill, there is momentarily generated a sense of awe and threat, but Stone can't resist repeating the effect. When Alexander's horse Bucephalus rears up against a charge of elephants, Alexander is thrown to the ground and the screen is flooded in red in a wonderfully conceived rendering of personal pain and the broader mayhem of war. Not a film without its moments, but moments really aren't enough return for an investment of three hours, and who knows how many millions of dollars.

Virginia Mayo died recently and this melancholy event made me think I'd like to watch Wyler's *The Best Years of Our Lives* (1946) again, all three hours of it. In this case, I didn't begrudge a minute of it: this film has about it a feel of the genuinely epic. Through its study of three ex-servicemen returning to the same American city, Wyler has contrived to make us feel something of the vast significance of a whole nation shaking itself into post-war readjustment. It is about something, something widely important, and treats its subject with seriousness, though not solemnity; it is long without feeling bloated; and it has images that stop the heart with their understanding of human beings in the most intense moments of their lives. None of the films referred to above does anything like this: is this because the screen has so rarely grasped what an epic truly is? Or because, taking on the kinds of subjects they do, they are unable to investigate them with the subtlety and complexity they need if they are to seem more than merely the occasion for conspicuous expenditure? Consider carefully before you next give up three precious hours to one of these big fat duds.

Metro, No. 144, 2005.

Notes

1 *The New Biographical Dictionary of Film*, David Thompson, Knopf, 2004.
2 *King Arthur* production notes, p.11.
3 Gabriel Snyder, 'Box-office sinners & Winners', *Empire*, February 2005.

45

COUNTRY TOWNS IN AUSTRALIAN FILMS

Trap or Comfort Zone?

It was watching *Strange Bedfellows* (Dean Murphy, 2004) last year, with its patronising view of country-town life, that set me to wonder about how Australian cinema has viewed these buffers between the metropolis and the bush, about what kinds of narratives it has spun around and inside them.

Several films of the last couple of years foregrounded, for me at least, the perception that the country town is neither one thing nor the other, and that it has rarely been subject to the scrutiny afforded the demographic extremes. What follows is more in the nature of reflection and speculation than orderly survey. To turn to Hollywood, glitzy capital of the filmmaking world, one finds paradoxically that small-town Americana was practically a narrative staple, that there was almost a genre of films which took seriously what such towns had to offer.

Genre, though, is perhaps not the best word, as it suggests more similarity than these films are apt to exhibit. Think of Frank Capra's *It's a Wonderful Life* (1947), which so resonantly explores George Bailey's feeling of entrapment in Bedford Falls and, then, his gratitude for the support it offers him at the lowest point of his life. Or of

Sam Wood's version of *Our Town* (1940), from playwright Thornton Wilder's critical celebration of the mores of small-town living. Or the darker uses to which such a setting is put in Hitchcock's *Shadow of a Doubt* (1943), where the comfortable mundane round of daily life is disrupted by the arrival of a killer in the guise of a loved family member, or in Wood's magisterial small-town melodrama, *King's Row* (1942), in which the confines of the town can barely contain the play of psycho-sexual perversities. These four major titles all come from the classic period of the 1940s, but the vogue for affectionate recreation of the life of small-town America persisted much longer, and in comparably diverse circumstances: from, say, Henry King's romance, *Wait 'Til the Sun Shines, Nellie* (1952) to Richard Fleischer's melodrama *Violent Saturday* (1955), in which a quiet town is invaded by a gang of bank robbers. As recently as *Garden State* (Zach Braff, 2004) the sub-genre still surfaces, in this narrative of the return, after a decade, of a TV actor to his hometown on the occasion of his mother's death.

In other English- speaking cinemas, the incidence of such films is not so marked. In British cinema, settings are most apt to be London, provincial cities like Brighton or Oxford, or picturesque villages. Lance Comfort undermined the pastoral calm of agreeably-set small towns in such films as *Great Day* (1945) and *Daughter of Darkness* (1947) by exposing their capacities for constriction and cruelty; and Cy Endfield's *Impulse* (1954) removes its hero from the quotidian predictability of his solicitor's office to the temptations of the city and a dangerous woman; while films such as Jack Clayton's *Room at the Top* (1959) and Ken Loach's *Kes* (1969) relocate class, family and other tensions to industrial northern towns. In Canada, whose films we more rarely see, there is a trickle of films which situate their dramas in provincial towns: films as varied as Alan Bridges' drama of conflicting values, *The Age of Innocence* (1977, Can/ UK), Ousama Rawi's relocation of a Ruth Rendell thriller, *Judgement in Stone* (1986), and Australian John Curran's drama of academic adulteries, *We Don't Live Here Any More* (2005, Can/US). From New Zealand, there have been films about people leaving (like Gaylene Preston's *Perfect Strangers*, [2003], in which the heroine is actually kidnapped from her country town) or returning, as in Brad McGann's compelling drama *In My Father's Den* (2004) in which the revenant uncovers family secrets.

On turning to Australian cinema, since the revival of the 1970s one finds a thin but steady stream of films set in country towns over the next three decades or so, from *Country Town* (Peter Maxwell, 1971) and *Wake in Fright* (Ted Kotcheff, 1971) on. These films have never really constituted a sub-genre, as was the case in the US; more often it has been just a matter of setting – but not always, as we shall see.

As one who was brought up in a country town, who later worked in one with great enjoyment and satisfaction, and who has since gone regularly to yet others for pleasure, I may claim that my response to how they are represented in Australian films is based on some direct experience. This experience has too often had the effect of irritating me about the general tendency to cliché and condescension in how the life of such towns is rendered in our films. There is not much awareness of the vibrant interaction possible in such communities, of the thriving culture that is at work in them, of the support networks they can offer, or even of their no longer in fact being all that separate from metropolitan centres, modern communication modes and processes being what they are. Too often, the townspeople are depicted as essentially out of touch with the mainstream of contemporary life or, in the style of some antipodean sub-Ealing venture, seen as being, in their sly, simple way, actually sharper than city folks. Both views seem to me, in their apparent opposition, to be equally patronising; both seem equally remote from treating the inhabitants of country towns as individuals who are as worthy of sustained attention as bush heroes or city sophisticates.

Do filmmakers actually know anything about the country towns in which they situate their stories, or do they just arrive there on locations with all their pre-conceived notions and prejudices intact? Do they think that because they're not making documentaries it doesn't matter whether their representations have any connection with reality? To test whether I was letting my irritation run away with me after seeing what *Strange Bedfellows* does for Yackandandah, I checked out the Lonely Planet guide *Victoria* to see what it had to say about Victorian country towns. It makes clear that there are dozens of country towns with a sort of life going on that never gets into our films: there are numerous towns that have art galleries or museums or historical societies, some with all three; they take environmental issues seriously and some have institutionalised this concern; they have restaurants worth eating at; they have groups interested in film, books and drama – and if all else fails they have internet cafes. The internet and email mean, anyway, that isolation is a thing of the past, but you'd hardly guess it from the movies which care so little about the dynamics of how such places work, in terms, say, of class, occupations or leisure. I'm not suggesting that we need Pathé Pictorial-type accounts of life of such towns; only that the films set in them would be texturally richer if their *mise-en-scène* evinced more awareness on the filmmakers' part that they have a complex life of their own.

Compared with other forms of representation, such as poetry, drama, painting, or TV, how does the cinema emerge in its dealings with this halfway-house between the city and the bush? These latter two spaces have been easily accommodated by films across a wide genre range. The bush has acquired historic significance as the crucible in which admirable national characteristics have been forged (hardihood, endurance, mateship etc.). The city has often been seen as the site of exciting and/or corrupt possibilities, of potential dangers, except when you move to the suburbs, which in film lore are uniformly dull and conformist. I want now to look briefly at several recent films set at least partly in country towns and to see how they are used and depicted, what kinds of stories are situated in them, which values are celebrated, which mocked. Essentially, I want to see how country towns have been used in Australian cinema.

Disturbances of the peace

Well, what kinds of themes and treatments have shaped the images of the country town in recent Australian cinema? There have been several examples of the small community reacting to a stranger in its midst (*The Oyster Farmer* [Anna Reeves, 2005], *Somersault* [Cate Shortland, 2004], *Love's Brother* [Jan Sardi, 2004], or, going back further, *Love Serenade* [Shirley Barrett, 1996], *Hotel Sorrento* [Richard Franklin, 1995], *Shame* [Steve Jodrell, 1987]). *Mullet*, on the other hand dramatised the case of the local returning home disruptively, but there has been nothing in this paradigm to rival the power of *In My Father's Den*. There are people straining under the constraints of the purely local, wanting larger horizons, as in *Peaches* (Craig Monahan, 2005); and, in generic terms, there have been comedies (*The Honourable Wally Norman* [Ted Emery, 2003], *Strange Bedfellows*, *The Road to Nhill* [Sue Brooks, 1997]) and darker dramas (*The Umbrella Woman* [Ken Cameron, 1987], *The Cars that Ate Paris* [Peter Weir, 1974]), with a sprinkling of films that highlight socially significant matters (*Strikebound* [Richard Lowenstein, 1984], *Black and White* [Craig Lahiff, 2002], *The Fringe Dwellers* [Bruce Beresford, 1986], *Dead Heart* [Nick Parsons, 1996]). Of course, the categories are not necessarily as clear-cut as this suggests, and never were: an earlier film like *Break of Day* (Ken Hannam, 1977) makes its drama from both the revenant soldier finding it hard to resettle in his home town and from the disruptions caused by outsiders arriving, with different priorities.

It is beyond the scope of this essay to do a full survey, so I'll concentrate on more recent films, with reference to just a few notable early examples that might have pointed to fuller treatment of the life of the country town. By my count, over fifty films since 1970 have been at least partially set in or concerned with country town life, but only rarely in the interest of either making good drama or serious investigation of how such places might work. As Neil Rattigan noted, 'The new Australian cinema practically began with a country town film, Ted Kotcheff's *Wake in Fright*'[1] and it was in production at about the same time as *Country Town*, based on the long-running TV serial *Bellbird*, which had been running since 1967. *Country Town* was an affectionate cross-sectional account of its eponym, inevitably more stereotyped than in the serial, where actors had more time to develop their characters. *Wake in Fright*, though, a much more accomplished film, offered glimpses of how ugly a remote town might be.

Thirty-odd years on, its images of boozy male camaraderie in some of its more repulsive manifestations stay vividly in the mind.

In 1974, there were two very significant films set in country towns, in very different generic and thematic modes. Michael Thornhill's *Between Wars* was a romantic drama of a World War One veteran, Trembow (Corin Redgrave), a former army doctor with some advanced (Freudian) ideas, who settles in a small town (Gulgong, NSW, was the location) where he becomes embroiled in the clash of conservative and radical ideas and ideals. The film may now seem somewhat lumbering in its narrative structures, but it was important in its context and is still more adventurous than most Australian films in its insights into the political dynamics of a country town. There is pessimism in Trembow's giving up the struggle on behalf of the Farmers' Co-op and returning to the city, but it is hard to think of many other films which even tackle the left/right conflicts adumbrated here. And in the setting of a country town, such oppositions perhaps emerge more starkly than they might in the diversity of a metropolitan centre.

The other significant 1974 title was Peter Weir's *The Cars That Ate Paris*. Watching this 31-year-old film again recently, I was struck by its formal daring in the way it crosses horror flick with black comedy as it goes about its unsettling business. It offers still the darkest vision of country-town life in Australian cinema. When Arthur (Terry Camilleri) tries to leave the little hill-set town of Paris, the Mayor (John Meillon), all avuncular bonhomie, turns serious and tells him: 'No one leaves Paris' and, as in 'all close families, we don't talk to outsiders'. This vile little town lures motorists into accidents, then lives on the proceeds; the prettiness of the town's setting and the ugliness of its livelihood create a powerful signifier for the deceptiveness of surfaces. At every level, what one expects is undercut by the anarchic imagination at work, as we watch, say, an old lady polishing a hubcap, yahoos driving a spiked VW through the town, or the town's hospital full of 'vegies'. The film remains an alarming exposure of hypocrisies and assorted malevolences at work in the apparently peaceful setting.

These two films, early in the revival, might have heralded new Australian cinema's coming to terms with various aspects of the national life, including the country towns in which a good percentage of the population lived. In the 1970s there were several other films with insights into such places: Carl Schultz's *Blue Fin* (1978) made the life of a small supportive South Australian coastal community the attractive context for its main drama of father, son and a boat; released in the same year, Tom Jeffrey's *Weekend of Shadows* is, by contrast at least in part, an indictment of small-town narrowness; while John Duigan's *Dimboola* (1979) makes a sorry, overstated mess of Jack Hibberd's popular Pram Factory comedy of a Wimmera small-town wedding where everything goes very wrong, and the locals generally are made to look ridiculous.

The incidence of such films tapered off in the eighties, but there were still several memorable ones: Richard Lowenstein's *Strikebound*, Bruce Beresford's *The Fringe Dwellers*, John Duigan's *The Year My Voice Broke* (1987) and best of all Steve Jodrell's *Shame*. All these take serious subjects and deal with them intelligently against diverse backgrounds of country towns. *Strikebound* never found substantial audiences but remains a rare example in Australian cinema of a film centred on the deprivations of a class, rather than, in the Hollywood narrative tradition, an individual. Focusing on the miners' strike in

South Gippsland (where the film was shot) in the 1930s, it gave a sympathetic, realist account of the sort of solidarity the small town was able to muster against ruthless employers. *The Fringe Dwellers*, from Nene Gare's 1960 novel, dramatised the situation of an Aboriginal family relocated from a shack on the edge of a country town (location-shot in Queensland) to a Housing Commission home, and the social problems they encounter in the community. Duigan resisted the usual nostalgia factor in the rites-of-passage drama, *The Year My Voice Broke*, in which the conflicts of adolescence are intensified by the constraints of the New South Wales country town (for which Braidwood stood in) in which the film is set. The result was a toughly affecting drama in which the three young protagonists 'are outsiders, estranged from their society in miniature'.[2]

Still one of the most compelling studies of the workings of a small town, *Shame* built the country-town ambience into something more than mere setting, viewing its class and gender structures as integral elements in its genre narrative of the stranger-in-town paradigm. Given that the stranger was a woman, and a highly placed barrister at that, the scene was set for the shaking up of this ugly little Western Australian town (Toojay standing in for Ginborak), ugly in the ways in which its patriarchal culture has colluded in a culture of gang rape, among other manifestations of masculinist domination. Only a consonant away from the classic western, *Shane* (1952), whose structure it recalls, the stranger-in-town Asta Cadell (Deborra Lee-Furness) can't pull off quite the triumphal victory that Shane did, but she has exposed the cruelties at the heart of the town's class system and its misogyny – and perhaps planted some seeds of rebellion in the more ordinary minds of the townswomen.

I want to break free

To jump to the new century means skimming past Richard Franklin's thoughtful *Hotel Sorrento* (1995), in which two siblings return from abroad to their father's home for a round of guilts and griefs that resurface in the reunion in the idyllic eponymous coastal town. And it means a brusque sentence for Shirley Barrett's romance *Love Serenade*, in which two sisters in a listless Riverina township compete for the favours of a DJ from Brisbane who's come to run the local radio station, and Sue Brooks' *The Road to Nhill*. The latter, with its cast of distinguished veterans (Patricia Kennedy, Bill Hunter, Monica Maughan and others), is a quiet, uneventful rendering of the solidarity of a small community when four lady bowlers are involved in a car accident; and solidarity has not, generally, been a key narrative element in these films, except for the politically motivated *Strikebound*.

Curiously, it is the more recent films which have seemed locked into a sort of time warp where country towns are concerned. *Strange Bedfellows* is the most extreme – and, not to put too fine a point on it, offensive – example. Having previously written about this wretched film at greater length in this journal, I'll restrict myself here to repeating the two central points of my criticism. First, the film is patronising in its view of its country town (Yackandandah), suggesting in plot details and *mise-en-scène* that it has registered nothing in the way of change since the 1950s – just consider its treatment of the climactic firemen's ball. Second, it is internally incoherent: its narrative premiss, relating to a tax break for same-sex couples, is entirely a twenty-first century concept, whereas all the film's other narrative 'information' seems to belong to a period several decades earlier.

Further, for a film that no doubt thinks of itself as being very liberal, it seems at heart seriously homophobic.

Another recent film which I've also written about here is *Love's Brother* (2003), a wet little romance about an Italian bride (Amelia Warner) fetching up at a Victorian country town (Daylesford locations) to marry the plainer of two brothers (Giovanni Ribisi) and falling for the handsome one (Adam Garcia). Writer–director Jan Sardi evokes nostalgically a lot of the surface of 1950s living, but doesn't seem to offer any 2004 purchase on the material. The filming style recalls the syrupy sounds and pictorial longueurs of early CinemaScope films, without anything to suggest that he has any critical perspective on either such aesthetic matters or the cultural mores of the period, and he seems to have fallen for the sentimental notion of Italians as lovable and exuberant in his representation of their impact on this little country town. By chance as I was writing this, I came across English critic Philip French's comment on the new film version of *Oliver Twist*: 'The movie lacks any serious point of view about individuality, society, community.'[3] It seemed wholly apt in reference to *Love's Brother* (and to any number of other Australian country-town films): we are told that distance lends enchantment, but surely it should also lend, well, distance – that is, critical detachment and perspective, as well as emotional involvement.

Mullet (David Caesar, 2001) was made of tougher stuff than Rob Sitch's meandering, likeable *The Dish* released in the same year, not wallowing in nostalgia, as *Love's Brother* does, or the sub-Capra sentimentalising of small-town politics in *The Honourable Wally Norman*. The return of Eddie (Ben Mendelsohn) to his coastal hometown (Gerringong, NSW) is not an occasion for rejoicing either on his part or on anyone else's. His city career hasn't glittered and, if he hasn't exactly come home with his tail between his legs, he certainly doesn't come trailing clouds of glory. His policeman brother Pete (Andrew S. Gilbert) is chary of him; his ex-girlfriend Tully (Susie Porter), now married to Pete, socks him on the chin; his parents (Tony Barry and Kris McQuade) give him a qualified welcome; and the friendly barmaid Kay (Belinda McClory) berates him for sleeping with her without having sex. Eddie leaves at the end, not much wiser, but having exploded to Pete at a cathartic 'barbie': 'You've got everything I ever wanted!'

What we get in *Mullet* is a cross-current of family and other conflicts brought to some kind of head by Eddie's return. Nothing very dramatic happens, or so it seems, but, as in a Chekhov play, tumultuous feelings are stirred under the surface of life in the sleepy fishing town, where football (Eddie's dad coaches the rugby team), drinking and quieter interactions prevail. It's essentially a working-class township, and, apart from a tonally dubious and probably anachronistic bit about the father's pride in the installation of a flush toilet, director–screenwriter David Caesar avoids patronage in the way he creates its ethos. The film acknowledges that this life may not suit everyone and clearly doesn't suit Eddie: Eddie may be nostalgic about aspects of its life but the film is not. It is clear-eyed about the kinds of decency that find fulfilment here, and beautifully exact performances, especially from Gilbert, Porter and McClory, give real poignancy to the choices, rewards and limitations that are available to them. Further, Robert Humphreys' cinematography eschews the merely pictorial in favour of something more affect-drenched: there are moments of spotlit loneliness that suggest he was advised by a combo of Edward Hopper and Russell Drysdale. It is still perhaps the best and most heartfelt Australian film about life in a country town: it is small-scale, not ambitious on the scale of the great US films mentioned above, but by not taking refuge in nostalgia, pictorialism or condescending humour it has a ring of rigorous truth about it.

Apart from the largely contemptible *Strange Bedfellows*, the three most recent Australian films with country-town settings are the multi-AFI-award-winner, *Somersault*, and, this year, Craig Monahan's *Peaches* and Anna Reeves' *The Oyster Farmer*, two superior films, the first of which suggests that a small-town ambience might be stifling and the second that it might provide a sort of liberation from city tensions. The protagonist of *Somersault* is Heidi (Abbie Cornish), a teenage girl who arrives in the picturesque mountain town of Jindabyne, after fecklessly inviting advances from her mother's boyfriend. Director Cate Shortland doesn't succumb to the natural beauties of the place, and what stays in mind a year later is her concentration on Heidi's sexual venturesomeness, and several very acutely drawn relationships with the people of this small community. These include the scion of a local landowning family, Joe (Sam Worthington), whom she meets in the pub, her co-worker Bianca (Holly Andrew), in the local 'server' and, most affectingly, the woman (Lynette Curran) who runs the motel where Heidi stays. There's an unemphatic sense of hierarchy encapsulated in the run-ins Heidi has with these three.

Peaches is set in the Gippsland river town, Swan Reach, though the fruit cannery which looms so large in it was located in Riverland, South Australia, and indeed the other locations were mainly South Australian. Like *The Oyster Farmer*, it is one of those rare films which takes work seriously. The cannery is the centre of the small town's life and all the relationships with which the film is centrally concerned are connected to it. The young girl, Steph (Emma Lung), who leaves at the film's end because she realises there is no future for her in the town, works there briefly as a casual and attracts the attention of the foreman Alan Taylor (Hugo Weaving), once the lover of Steph's foster-mother Jude (Jacqueline McKenzie). Around these three is a complicating network of secrecy, deceits and acrimony, and Steph leaves finally when the past is fully excavated – and when the cannery is to be closed down. The film is less concerned with the town than with the cannery and the present-past nexus which preoccupies Steph, but there is a pervasive feel for the camaraderie of those who work at the threatened factory and a real concern for how, in a very small town, opportunities and relationships might be limited. There is some self-consciously 'lyrical' camera work in relation to the sex scenes and the natural environment, and there is something determinedly art-house about the film's ambitions that settle for some diffuse narrative habits. However, it accretes something to the cinematic representation of the Australian country town as a place where work and the rest of daily living might be seriously difficult to sustain.

In *The Oyster Farmer*, the beauties of the Hawkesbury River terrain are palpable but not allowed to swamp the feel for the life of the place, where oyster farmers have been going about their business for eight generations. A girl in a boat says: 'It's time we had some new blood round here' and the narrative, like so many before it, gets under way with the arrival of newcomer Jack Flange (Alex O'Lachlan) from Sydney. This isn't a documentary about oyster farming, but it wins respect for spending enough time on the job for us to grasp its centrality to the remote community into which Jack comes to work for Brownie (David Field). Jack has a sister in a nearby hospital recovering from a car accident, but he has more on his mind than brotherly duty or a love of oysters. He has executed a robbery at the

Sydney Fish Markets, showing unusual inventiveness in his choice of weapons, and he awaits anxiously the arrival of a package of money he has sent himself. His anxieties lead him to suspect the postal delivery girl and other unlikely locals, and bring him into contact with a Viet vet (Jack Thompson), living in a small, scruffy community upstream from the township which, we assume, wouldn't be easy with their iconoclasm.

The plot is in fact quite well worked out, not settling for obvious thriller complications, but rather for a gradual unfolding of several human dramas. Jack's acceptance into the oyster-farming hamlet, with its precarious dependence on its one industry, is the film's centre, and personable newcomers, Alex O'Lachlan and Dianna Glenn as Jack and Pearl, bring an apt sexual charge to this element of the film. As do Field and Kerry Armstrong as Brownie's estranged wife, who has legendary powers over the spawning habits of oysters. The tentative reconciliation of these two benefits from the sense of experience as actors they bring to the experience of their characters. As with *Peaches*, the personal matters and the work are almost symbiotically intertwined, and one of *The Oyster Farmer*'s points of appeal is in the way Jack's absorption into the community gradually comes to replace his larcenous city-based interests – and the plot's own interest in this latter.

Small towns, big lives

When I began to prepare and even to write this piece, it seemed to me that the Australian country town had been inadequately represented in locally-made films, that such usages of their attractions as had been made remained no more than 'usages', as often as not plagued by either nostalgia or easy, metropolitan-derived contempt. The more

I have (re-)considered the films, the less intemperately I adhere to this point of view. I think it is still true to assert that we do not yet have a film which whole-heartedly takes on the phenomenon: such a film would take us into the ways in which such a town works, across class and gender divides, the kinds of expectations and limitations that fuel its dynamics. We may yet get an Australian film which works as potently as the great American small-town melodramas I mentioned above – or even as wittily and insightfully about small-town class politics as the British comedy, *A Private Function* (Malcolm Mowbray, 1984). In the meantime, if there is as yet no great Australian small-town film, when our filmmakers have broken free from the easy options in dealing with Main Street, Australia, there have been some undeniably rewarding moments. These moments tend to arise from the films' perceptions of why some people find refuge in such towns and why others feel they need to leave them. If that sounds like modest rewards, well, thus far the films that enshrine these perceptions, even at their sharpest, *are* essentially modest, but within those limits they have suggested that there is life – and lives – out there in country towns worthy of further cinematic exploration.

Metro, No.146/147, 2005.

Notes

1 Neil Rattigan, '*Country Towns*', in Brian McFarlane *et al* (eds) *The Oxford Companion to Australian Film*, Oxford University Press, Melbourne, 1999, p.80.

2 Raffaele Caputo, '*The Year My Voice Broke*', in Scott Murray (ed.), *Australian Film 1978–1994*, Oxford University Press, Melbourne, 1995, p.237.

3 *The Observer*, London, 9 October 2005.

46

FROM ROCK OF AGES TO ROCK 'N' ROLL

Just how enduring has been the popularity of films about pop-music idols and trends? Does anyone now ever watch the seminal *Rock Around the Clock* (1956)? It was little more than a 'B' movie in budget and running-time, its title deriving from the hit tune of the previous year when it was introduced in *The Blackboard Jungle*, in which teacher Glenn Ford tamed a class of hooligans. And, it was said, cinema ushers had to tame teenagers who were carried away by the theme song to the point of leaping about in the aisles. As far as I can discover, *Rock Around the Clock* is not available on DVD or video. Even those films that had higher aspirations, featured major names of the day and were big box-office successes in their various decades rarely proved to have a very long shelf-life. Every now and then one will acquire a cult following, as *The Rocky Horror Picture Show* (1975) did: after its initial box-office failure, it became a favourite with late-night movie audiences who responded to its camp references and presumably didn't care much about its qualities as a film. For them, the fun was putting on fishnet stockings and going to the movies at midnight.

Elvis Presley, who got started at about the same time as Johnny Cash, may have legend status but it's quite hard to hire his films. My normally well-stocked video store had only two of his films and apparently gets very few requests, though, at the time of writing, Channel Nine is doggedly screening such items as *Harum Scarum* (1965) in unlikely viewing slots such as Saturday afternoon, when small children may be watching. When the Beatles' black-and-white hit *A Hard Day's Night* (1964) was revived a few years back, it was hard to see what all the fuss had been about. It's no more than a mockumentary of the fab four going from Merseyside to London for a recording session, taking with them Paul's grandpa, a 'very clean old man', and trying to keep him out of trouble. There were fewer songs than I'd remembered, but enough to remind us of what once was the most famous sound in the world. 'I Wanna Be Your Man', 'If I Fell in Love with You': songs that now sound pleasantly simple, tuneful, as if they belong to some innocent bygone age.

And what about those other films of the 1970s and 1980s that cashed in on the latest rock phenomenon? What would the Maysles brothers' documentary *Gimme Shelter* (1970) about the Altamount pop festival in 1969, which featured the Rolling Stones and the Hell's Angels, and ended in murder, look like now? Perhaps it still has the raw power to keep mindless nostalgia at bay. Hollywood took to rock in a big way in the 1970s with films such as *American Graffiti* (1973), set in small-town America in 1962, and the John Travolta hits *Saturday Night Fever* (1977), *Grease* (1978) and *Staying Alive* (1983). There were also *The Buddy Holly Story* (1978), with Gary Busey as Holly, whose life story has some points of contact with Cash's, and the rock musicals *Jesus Christ Superstar* (1973) and *Godspell* (1973) adapted from the stage, the Streisand remake of *A Star is Born* (1976), in which the big number is the love song 'Evergreen'; and Milos Forman's airbrushed version of *Hair* (1979). For all the strenuousness of the Forman film, it was utterly clear that the moment of *Hair* had passed.

I'm not sure if any of these films could be revived today. Their success at the time depended so crucially on the interaction of the political climate, which accounted for what was being reacted against, and the pop culture scene. The heady mixture of sex, drugs and rock' n' roll has perhaps claimed too many victims among their luminaries and the survivors are now grandparents or pompously knighted or both. My own theory about the unwatchability of many of these films has to do with the clothes and hairdos. Could anyone look at Frank Zappa today and keep a straight face? Film history is strewn with forgotten movies, or movies that deserve to be forgotten, about the rock ascendancy. Maybe its real potency could only be experienced in the live-stage environment, when there was always the edgy possibility of everything getting out of hand.

Even a great film such as Robert Altman's *Nashville* (1975), which more overtly than most brings politics and popular music (mainly country, with rock standing in for political savvy) into collision, was never a popular success. It is, however, a film of shining intelligence that manages both to critique and to pay tribute to the music and musicians that make up its many-threaded plot, which ends with an assassination at the Parthenon (Nashville, that is, not Athens). There are authentic notes of loneliness and longing for certainties in the country songs, some of them done for satiric effect, like those of *Laugh-In*'s Henry Gibson as Haven Hamilton, dressed like a sawn-off Roy Rogers without his horse, and others allowed their due of poignancy, like 'Dues' or 'Bluebird', sung by Ronee Blakely, as Barbara Jean, country-music royalty who falls apart in Nashville. The rock trio of Bill and Tom and Mary (Allan Nicholls, Keith Carradine and Cristina Raines) are meant to be more astute politically; that is, they are as Mary points out registered Democrat voters, though

Altman is too generous and clear-headed a film-maker to believe in a straight-down-the-line attribution of virtues according to political affiliation.

The toll on performers of the *facts* of performance and of the celebrity that goes with it, and what it takes not to be destroyed by the concomitant demands and temptations, account for the narrative trajectory of James Mangold's *Walk the Line.* I should come clean at this point: until I first saw this film in January, I knew who Johnny Cash was but had never consciously listened to him. So, I came to the biopic in a state of almost virgin ignorance and was utterly carried away by it, surrendering to its narrative sweep, its affirmation of romantic love and – to my surprise – the range and power of the music. Those who know more about Cash than I did (there can be few who knew less) have quibbled a bit about the film's dealings with this or that aspect of his life, but this is not a documentary: it is a biopic, and as such will of course take liberties with the life (and documentaries don't?), eliding and highlighting in the interests of narrative rhythm and dramatic cohesion. Less narrow in its time-span than *Good Night and Good Luck*, which treats one run-in of Ed Murrow's life, or *Capote*, which focuses entirely on the author's obsession with the Kansas killings that made his name and ruined his life, *Walk the Line* still shares with them and with last year's *Kinsey* an old-fashioned craftsmanship that knows the value of contrasts in emotional tone and visual sheen.

Walk the Line was initiated with the cooperation of Cash and June Carter Cash, which might have been the recipe for a bland hagiopic, but isn't. What emerges is an exhilarating and moving show-business tale of huge success, a spiralling out of control and a final, sustained reclamation. Biopics of performers have to convince us of their stellar capacities. Here, let it be said straight off, Joaquin Phoenix as Johnny Cash and Reece Witherspoon as June achieve this triumphantly. They do their own singing (some have suggested that Witherspoon is actually a 'better' singer than Carter, at least technically) and maybe this helps to account for the really remarkable immersion in their roles they exhibit, especially when on stage.

The film is chiefly taken up with the years between 1952, when Cash is with the air force in West Germany, and 1968, when he proposes on stage to Carter at a concert in Ontario – a moment that might smack of old-time Hollywood if we didn't know that it actually happened. There is a brilliantly concise prologue set on the Cashes' cotton farm in Dyess, Arkansas, in 1944, sketching Johnny's adoration of his older brother Jack who dies following a sawmill accident, and his drunken father's abuse of him: 'Nothing – that's what you are. The devil took the wrong son.' There is no announcement of the eight years passing: the film just cuts to Phoenix's face and dispatches him to Landsberg, West Germany, where, more convincingly than is usually the case in such films, he is seen tentatively composing 'Folsom Prison', with its indelible line 'I shot a man in Reno just to watch him die'.

The first marriage to Vivian (Ginnifer Goodwin), contracted on inadequate knowledge of each other's needs, founders quickly. Viv, who has the look of a 1950s starlet, a Debbie Reynolds *manquée* who will aspire to Jackie Kennedy svelteness in the 1960s, wants him to take up her 'Daddy's' offer of a good safe job. He's clearly no good as a door-to-door salesman and this episode has a shrewdly imagined look of the 1950s, with black boys doing shoe-shine and Johnny in terrible two-tone jackets. While Viv entertains her middle-class friends at afternoon cards, Johnny and his 'band' ('two mechanics who cain't hardly play', says Viv disdainfully) twang out 'I know when Jesus saved me' on the porch.

This whole sequence sets up economically the basis for the failure of the marriage, articulating the oppositions with precision and an impressive fairness. Viv may be profoundly conventional but the film allows that she has a case. Much later, when Cash arrives home from touring and with the feeling for June beginning to take shape in him, Viv will cut him off with: 'I have a casserole in the oven and I don't want to talk about the tour.' 'What do you want from me?' he asks with scarcely warranted exasperation. 'I want *you*.' And the film shows that she, as his wife and the mother of his children, has this kind of right, just as it acknowledges their fundamental incompatibility.

Sequence by sequence, the film works its way with fine discriminations of this kind. At the turning-point audition, Sam Phillips (Dallas Roberts) of Sun Records says 'I don't believe you' when Johnny and the boys try gospel, adding 'It's got to do with believin' in yourself.' The gradual displacement of the boredom on Sam's face with a gradual dawning of a this-is-the-goods discovery as Johnny sings 'Folsom Prison' involves both subtle character playing from Roberts and our introduction to the Cash charisma and vocal power. In the touring episodes that follow, Mangold skilfully builds a tension between, on the one hand, the off-stage problems of disintegrating marriage, descent into drugs and drink, the wariness of the relationship with June, and on the other, the magic of the on-stage performances. At a much later point, June admonishes Cash in the dressing-room: 'The only place you're allowed to speak to me is on stage.' She means here that he is to back off in personal terms, but the audience is free to consider how their most electric communication seems to take place around the microphone.

The concert sequences are superbly staged. Often backlit, Phoenix and Witherspoon incarnate the magical quality that great performers have that enables them to lift an audience out of itself, to have that audience seem to reach across the footlights in a rapture of joy and gratitude. Having since first viewing bought several Cash CDs and the 'Duets' selection of Cash and Carter, I'd say that Phoenix doesn't quite manage the deepest registers of which Cash is capable but that he more than compensates for this by the sheer intensity of his involvement in the character. Witherspoon is something else. She seems to me currently the smartest, sassiest woman in Hollywood and here she sings her heart out as June and is mesmeric in doing so. At Cash's first glimpse of her, backstage in a Texas concert hall in 1955, she is in the opposite wings from him, and she instantly lights up the screen. Her performance as a performer is perhaps the best I've ever seen: she entirely persuades us that her professionalism can overcome anger or anguish and that, while she's on stage she belongs to the audience. When he finally proposes to her on stage, it's like the culmination of a courtship that has been conducted most significantly right there in front of the crowd – and one of the great romantic movie moments in recent years.

Mangold has structured his film with the sort of skill that keeps us anticipating the next gig with excitement, gratifying this anticipation, then making us want to see how the off-stage lives are coping with it all. He hasn't made one of those musical biopics where you wish they'd stop the story and just get on with the numbers. The bulk of the film comprises a long flashback that begins and ends in Folsom Prison. It is introduced by a dazzling montage of feet tramping along prison corridors until Cash is found waiting to perform before the audience of inmates, his hand running along a saw, which initiates the flashback to Arkansas 1944. The flashback ends with the triumphant Folsom performance ('Don't sing songs that'll remind them they're in prison', an official warns him. 'You think they forget?' he replies) and the film then moves to Ontario, the proposal, and a brief lakeside coda between Cash and Carter, her parents in the background and a series of end titles that tell how they stayed married for a further thirty-five years. By the kinds of structuring I've referred to, as well as neat parallels (Cash's composing of 'Folsom Prison' in Germany is later echoed in June's 'Ring of Fire'), by juxtaposing her care for her children with his increasing neglect of his, and her sassiness on stage with Viv's prissy disapproval, Mangold has avoided the biopic trap of offering a mere string of events as a narrative.

In the matter of personal relations, *Walk the Line* both respects the claims of ordinary domesticity and understands the strains that pop-idol celebrity might enjoin on a marriage. In professional matters, it makes us privy to the awfulness of the touring life. Not since *Lolita* (the novel especially) has a film given us such glimpses of the tattiness of American motel life: the temptations of easy lays; the quick gratifications of drugs and drink that might make you forget their nasty downsides; the scruffy, morning-after feel of a misspent night; then trying to get some sleep in a bus not designed for comfort.

Unlike in the case of Sid Vicious and his girlfriend, the subjects of Alex Cox's film *Sid and Nancy* (1986), for Cash and Carter there was to be a long and loving epilogue. In this respect, they were also lucky by comparison with Presley and Jerry Lee Lewis, who both got their start with Sun Records and who are seen hovering around the edges of *Walk the Line*. Mangold's film doesn't spare viewers the unattractive aspects of the Cash persona – the addictions and moral sloppiness – before June finally sorts him out. It does, though, try to understand him. This is more than just a matter of seeing him succumb as so many prime rockers did to the seductions that came with the territory. Cash's career started in gospel, took in rock but remained essentially country in its emphasis, but he shared with the rock greats the sort of temptations that ordinary lives can barely grasp. In Cash's case, the other key influence is surely the violent drunken father who couldn't say more than 'Don't miss your bus' when Cash is heading for Germany, then spits, and who years later scornfully derides his son as a 'rock star'. When Cash asks him what he thinks of the house he's bought, his father (played with an exact, buttoned-down envy and disapproval by Robert Patrick) can only say that it's 'not as big as Jack Benny's'. The film is too intelligent to lay all Cash's failings at the door of an unsympathetic father – or to underestimate the importance of such an influence.

With two dazzling performances at the film's centre, it would be easy but indefensible to overlook the people (and their faces) who surround them. Tyler Hilton's Elvis doesn't amount to much, on stage or off; Waylon Payne's Jerry Lee Lewis has more to work with and does more with it, in a sketch of narcissistic insolence. Robert Patrick and Shelby Lynne, eloquent of face and voice as Mrs Cash, and Sandra Ellis Lafferty and Dan Beene as the cautious and forgiving Carter parents, father Ezra seeing off a drug-dealer threat to June and Johnny's final idyll, are all immaculate in suggesting how parents may not be the best judges of our potential but they're what we all have. And there is a tiny, perfect, uncredited sketch of a self-righteous check-out woman in a supermarket who bitterly abuses June for her divorce. Even the crowds at the concerts have been carefully directed: they convince one of their excitement as a group and as individuals, and they, like the subtly modulated dress and hair styles, change in the degree – and manifestation – of their abandon from the mid-1950s to the late 1960s.

They say that films, like books, can change your life. I wouldn't go quite so far about *Walk the Line*, but the intoxication I felt on first viewing led me to find out more about the Cash–Carter duo so that on second viewing the effect was little short of exhilarating. As a result, life has been much richer (and noisier, say those nearest to me).

Meanjin, Vol. 65, No. 3, 2006.

47

SOFTLY AND TENDERLY ...

> Softly and tenderly Jesus is calling,
> Calling for you and for me;
> See on the portals He's waiting and watching,
> Watching for you and for me.

In two of the most attractive American films of the year, *Junebug* and *A Prairie Home Companion*, this popular hymn by Will Thompson is sung without a trace of affectation or condescension. The surprising incidence of the hymn in films released here within weeks of each other is not, I think, indicative of religious revivalism at work in American cinema. If they have anything broader in common, it is that they are essentially modest treats, films that make one grateful for their kindly but rigorous interest in intersecting lives.

As well as enjoying widespread critical acclaim, *Junebug* has been a surprise commercial hit in Melbourne, suggesting that quality, like blood, will out, and that word of mouth can do the work of the aggressive publicity that accompanies the 'big' films. Despite a title that gives nothing away and may even seem off-putting, it ran for three months or so in several cinemas. As for *A Prairie Home Companion*, everyone seems to like it. Its success is less surprising: it's a Robert Altman film (his last, as it sadly transpires) and it stars Meryl Streep and other well-known people. Together these two films remind one of what a humanist medium the cinema can sometimes be, of how, in among the expensive claptrap that occupies so much screen time, films of humane orientation can still claim our attention.

The informing scenario for *Junebug* is that of the family reunion or the clash of cultures when a newcomer is introduced into the family circle. This template has been a narrative stalwart of films at least from *You Can't Take It with You* (1938), where it was played for hilarious comedy and, finally, sentiment. More recently, it was the subject of the mildly engaging *Meet the Parents* (2000) and its unspeakable sequel *Meet the Fockers* (2004), and the crudely schematic *The Family Stone* (2006). In *Junebug*, elegant, sophisticated English Madeleine (Embeth Davidtz) runs an 'Outsider's Gallery' in Chicago, meets there and falls for the handsome and agreeable George (Alessandro Nivola). They marry fast and happily, without her having met his folks in North Carolina. By chance, she wants to meet a cranky old artist there and suggests they combine this with a visit to his family. The scene is set, we suspect, for a lot of more or less predictable comedy or melodrama but nothing happens as expected. The template keeps sliding.

The family consists of a somewhat dour, dominant mother, Peg (Celia Weston); a peaceable father, Eugene (Scott Wilson of *In Cold Blood* fame); a boorish, sullen younger son, Johnny (Ben MacKenzie), unexcited by his brother's return; and his very pregnant chatterbox wife Ashley (Oscar nominee Amy Adams). The film refuses to patronise these lower-middle-class people and equally it doesn't want to make Madeleine seem patronising. She seriously tries to get along with them. 'I'll be fine,' she's assured George. Tiny moments like the one when, on first meeting, she goes to kiss Peg first on one cheek, then in sophisticated continental style on the other, and Peg is not quite ready for this, thinking they've finished kissing, epitomise the care and subtlety of the film. The merest tremor of Peg's eyes is all that is needed to register that she and Madeleine will have some awkward territory to negotiate together. Ashley thinks she and Madeleine are going to be buddies and they aren't, but again the film doesn't criticise either – Ashley isn't just pushy, she is also genuinely sweet-tempered; Madeleine isn't just reserved, she's a little bewildered at being so far off her usual turf. Again without being an urban tough cookie, Madeleine is shown as willing to compromise her integrity in dealing with the anti-Semitic artist, and we're not invited to condemn her for this.

The film is full of episodes that speak of its humanity and perceptive observation. For instance, the church social where George joins some old friends to sing the Thompson hymn is done with exquisite tact, as Madeleine is stirred to re-view the man she loves and has married. Later, when Ashley has had a miscarriage, there is a beautifully written and acted scene between her and George when he visits her in hospital. And there's the scene at Replacements Ltd where seething Johnny works and where, away from the constraints of home and of imminent fatherhood, he is a quite different person. And at the end what passes for closure is really a matter of signalling continuities. As Madeleine and George drive away, she gently strokes the back of his neck, and one recalls the sensual gropings they engaged in on the drive down south. Distance has been traversed, and director Phil Morrison seems unerringly to know how much 'information' we need and want on all these occasions.

If the narrative impresses by never taking any of the obvious, clichéd paths, the camera on the other hand behaves with the most perfect discretion. Again and again one anticipates its next move, not because it's conventional but because it seems so right. You hope it's going to light on this or that face, or you hope it will stay on this figure who's moving away – like the close-lipped neighbour who is not sure how to respond to Madeleine's graceful wave across the street. And the acting is as near perfect as makes no matter. Davidtz and Nivola convey the sensuality of the newly married couple and are just as convincing at the end when this has been tempered by a gentler understanding. The parents and Johnny are immaculately detailed, drawn with a kind of minimalism that says a great deal about them, and from Amy Adams comes a heartbreaking performance of reckless good nature.

In *A Prairie Home Companion*, Thompson's hymn is sung backstage at the Fitzgerald Theatre, St Paul, Minnesota, by Meryl Streep and Lily Tomlin as Yolanda and Rhonda, the two still-performing members of the Johnson Sisters quartet. What the episode does is to confirm our sense of the bond between these sisters, Streep the simpler and softer of the two, Tomlin more forceful, but united in their loving recollections of their mother and their home and in their devotion to Streep's bespectacled, poetry-inclined daughter Lola (Lindsay Lohan). The occasion for all this is the putative last night of Garrison Keillor's well-loved radio program of the same name as the film. Fiction blurs with reality here: this is a real program on public radio in the United States, broadcast in Australia for a while on ABC Classic FM, and still a going concern. The 'last night' device is presumably there in the film partly to give some shape to the loosely connected moments that constitute its 'plot' as it meanders on and off stage, and, perhaps more important, to underline the elegiac aspect of the film.

This element of elegy works on several levels. For one thing, Robert Altman, just deceased, was already into his eighties when he made the film and for those of us who have loved his films there was a question of how many more he will be able to deliver. For another, the days when radio could muster huge audiences, let alone when audiences would gladly fill a theatre every Saturday night to watch a 'live' radio show, are surely numbered. The film gives off a poignant air of catch-this-while-you-can. It invites our contemplation for the passing of time, for the way things valued are always fleeing and fleeting. At the same time, it enjoins on its viewers the need to value what they have, even as they are aware of the inevitability (and even imminence) of its passing, and not to be fearful of endings. If this sounds solemn, it's not meant to: this is a hugely enjoyable movie that just happens to touch on – well, matters of life and death.

Altman made more ambitious films – think of *Nashville* (1974) or *Buffalo Bill and the Indians* (1976), *A Wedding* (1978), *Short Cuts* (1993) and *Gosford Park* (2002), among others – films that revel in multi-story plotting, taking on big issues such as the anti-war stance of *M.A.S.H.* (1970), or reworking classic genres such as the western in *McCabe and Mrs Miller* (1972) and the 'hardboiled' Raymond Chandler thriller in *The Long Goodbye* (1973). Yet none of his delectable oeuvre is more enchanting than his last offering. The sheer warmth of his affection for the small world on display here is irresistible, and so, mirrored here in the activities of the radio station, is the wonderful sense of collaborativeness that always marked his films. *A Prairie Home Companion* is a mellow joy from an indisputably great director.

Keillor, who plays himself or someone simply called GK, holds his radio show together by an endless capacity for improvisation, important when his assistant stage manager drops all the material in her frantic effort to find the right sheets for him. His is an engagingly low-key persona; he keeps his head, just, while various kinds of crisis are happening backstage. Though backstage isn't just a crisis scene: it is also the place where relationships have been forged (such as that of the food lady and the elderly Chuck, who dies quietly in his dressing-room) or where the Johnson sisters idly and warmly reminisce or where the two dirty-minded 'cowboys' Dusty and Lefty (Woody Harrelson, John C. Reilly) swap anecdotes and jokes.

GK's program, first heard on a car radio travelling somewhere in the Midwest, is an amalgam of country and western songs, comedy and advertising, and it all takes place in front of a frame-house set, before which the actual band from the radio show does its stuff with great panache. Some of the singers are also from the real show: Robin and Linda Williams, who do several country songs in fine style ('Old Plank Road, 'You've Been a Friend to Me' and others); and gospel singer Jearlyn Steele ('The Day is Short'). The others, including Streep, Tomlin, Lohan, Harrelson and Reilly, do their own singing, and very exhilarating it is. Yolanda and Rhonda, in contrast to the tender simplicity of the backstage hymn, give a rousing version of 'Swanee River' with the words somewhat adapted; Lola, casting aside her suicide-dominated poems for the moment, steps in with a vigorous 'Frankie and Johnny'; and the whole cast gathers for 'Red River Valley' and 'In the Sweet By and By' at the film's end. The songs are a potent factor in the film's appeal: whether singers or actors, the cast throw themselves into the numbers as if it matters to them to woo the audience in the imagined theatre, let alone us in the cinema.

Backstage, other things are going on too. The security guard, Guy Noir (Kevin Kline), who has delusions of Chandleresque grandeur though he's as accident- prone as Inspector Clouseau, copes with the routine by living at least partly in his imagination. Who then is the mysterious woman in a white raincoat (played by Virginia Madsen) who wanders into the theatre and seems to have easy access to the circle or to the corridors behind the stage or to the onstage house-set? *Noir*-addicted Guy obviously thinks she's going to prove to be Jane Greer from *Out of the Past* or some other dangerous lady from 1940s Hollywood. Well, she is and she isn't dangerous: she may be the angel of death and she certainly sends the take-over man (Tommy Lee Jones) on his way to a timely accident; but it's not her function to get people scared. 'I used to listen to your program till I died,' she tells Keillor, and she seems almost to be bestowing benison as she moves softly around.

In the film's last scene, set in Micky's Diner opposite the theatre and reminiscent of the diner in that famous Edward Hopper painting, Yolanda and Rhonda, GK and Guy talk about taking the show on the road. The woman in white is still hovering; Lola has become a smart business woman in a suit; but lest you think the film is going to finish on a downbeat note Altman brings the whole cast back to sing again, and with such a robust joy in the act of performing that no mere theatre closure could extinguish. Like *Junebug*, Altman's film, in its way, insists on continuity. If it is an elegy for times passing it is also a gentle celebration of the same.

The third of our modest treats in recent months is *Mrs Palfrey at the Claremont*, adapted from the novel by Elizabeth Taylor (not the diamond collectress). Technically an American film with an American director (Dan Ireland), it is in all other creative aspects about as British as could be: its locations are entirely English and its cast is a roll-call of British character acting. Taylor's novel is a rigorous and unsentimental account of an elderly woman who goes to live in a cut-above-genteel private hotel where everyone dines at

Rattigan-style separate tables. She falls in the street one day and is rescued by a young man struggling to be a writer and an unlikely but touching friendship ensues. Ireland's film follows this outline more or less closely but, at certain points and in certain ways, can't help softening the story's edges.

What is nevertheless impressive is that the film has confidence in the idea of such a relationship as the centre of its narrative. Certainly it has the advantage of a very finely eloquent, subtly understood and felt performance from Joan Plowright as the elderly widow: she has adequate means but is concerned about how to fill her days. Plowright has sometimes in recent years given way to grande-damehood, but not here. The nuances of the woman fetching up among people with whom she has little in common, tentatively feeling her way in her new surroundings, finding an affection for the rescuing Ludo that neither her daughter nor her grandson can excite, dealing with the brusque attentions of the hotel's male guest who invites her to a Masonic Ladies' night: all this is precisely observed and full of the kind of detail that acts as a guarantee of the authenticity of what we are seeing.

Ludo (Rupert Friend), a handsome young man, is kitted out with a much more likeable girlfriend than Taylor had astringently allotted him and this undermines the toughness of the central concept, as if the film is anxious for us to see Ludo as a real charmer. Without in the least yearning for 'fidelity' to the original, I think it would have strengthened the film's core to have retained some of the novel's reservations about both Mrs Palfrey and Ludo – and some of theirs about each other.

The scenes at the hotel, with the other permanent guests eying the newcomer, almost forcing Mrs Palfrey into passing Ludo off as her (neglectful) grandson Desmond and pushing her into unaccustomed deceit, are played for slightly broader comedy than Taylor chose to employ. This, though, is only a minor quibble, and, when one knows that these guests are played by the likes of Anna Massey, Millicent Martin, Georgina Hale and Robert Lang, the quibble is further diminished. It is a film that assumes that what goes on between people is about the most interesting narrative topic to be had.

When you feel most movies are being made for people under twenty-five (and that may be stretching the upper limit), it's heartening to note that there is still a steady stream of films that, often on comparatively small budgets, seem to be made entirely for grown-ups. These are films where you don't have to cut your way through the comic-strip foreground on the off chance that there may be lurking beneath or beyond something adult or 'dark' as critics are fond of saying in justifying these big jobs. In the line of other recent modest treats, such as *Winter Solstice* and *The Squid and the Whale*, *Junebug*, *A Prairie Home Companion* and *Mrs Palfrey at the Claremont* are films that seem adult all through.

Meanjin, Vol. 65, No. 4, 2006.

48

FINDING OURSELVES IN AUSTRALIAN FILMS

Why on earth should Australian filmmakers want to try replicating Hollywood? No one can do Hollywood as well as Hollywood can, and the attempts to emulate it have usually, perhaps inevitably, led to flavourless or otherwise misbegotten enterprises. I know that this is the era of international co-productions, and that where the money comes from is undoubtedly influential, but where the creative personnel come from is surely still more so. I shall want to argue for the cultural significance of the small-scale filmmaking that doesn't depend on US funding and thereby isn't subject to the sorts of compromise that such involvement may entail.

It is always going to be difficult for Anglophone cinemas, whether Australian, New Zealand, British or Canadian, to establish a viable place for themselves in domestic – let alone global – markets in the face of the all-conquering Hollywood product. As someone once remarked, if the US spoke Chinese it would be easier for, say, Australia to maintain a sturdy film industry. For Anglophone films to be truly commercially successful, they need to break into the American market. There's nothing new in that sort of 'wisdom'. But is this the only sort of cinema that can justify itself? Is an Australian film (I use 'Australia' as a metonym for those other English-speaking countries referred to above) only worthwhile if it attracts audiences from Seattle to Dallas to Boston?

The very engaging semi-mockumentary, *Rats and Cats* (2007), allegedly made for three hundred thousand dollars, ended with its scurrilous ex-'celebrity' protagonist addressing the viewers as the final credits unfold. He says: 'A lot of people say they want to see Australian films. But they don't. Not interested. The film ends up sinking 'cos the Australian public won't get off their arses and support Australian films.' For the benefit of the many who, I hope, still plan to seek out this beguiling local film, I won't tell you Darren's succinct reply when asked why this might be so. Especially because it runs counter to my case here.

It nevertheless raises the question of 'What do we want?' of Australian films. And who are 'we'? Perhaps 'we' don't all want the same things. This article has two essential sources: one is the fact of having watched a lot of Australian films lately for a piece on a local subgenre that might be called family-centred, as well as several other low-budget Australian movies in recent years; the other is a sense of rage at an article by playwright Louis Nowra entitled 'Nowhere Near Hollywood: Australian Film' in *The Monthly* (December 2009–January 2010). I'll deal with the latter first.

The general tenor of Nowra's essay seems to be no more than 'there's enough sorrow and unhappiness in the world without having to go to the movies to see more'. He believes that 'Movie-going should be a communal activity of human smells, the eating of food, united laughter and tears.' He saw Australian films in yawningly empty cinemas, and his experiences led him to a great many generalisations about 'the condition of our industry', and about crucial and damaging differences between the local and the Hollywood product. 'In

Hollywood, actors drive the story; in Australia, actors are the vehicle of the story.' What *is* he talking about?

Further, after talking to his friends, he found that 'The general consensus was that Australian films were boring, grim and unsatisfying'. They 'suffer from a surfeit of glumness': when, he seems to be asking, did you last come out of an Australian film and say, 'Laugh! I nearly died!'? Among their other faults, 'the lack of love stories and even sexual intimacy … is unnerving', and above all they don't emulate 'the Hollywood preference for happy endings'.

I trust that I have quoted enough to suggest the level of cerebration at work here, the readiness to rush into easy conclusions without having worked to *establish* any of his vague ideas. Our movies 'lack a second act', 'our storytelling is austere and joyless', and we are confronted with such slabs of critical wisdom as this: 'In the 1960s and 1970s audiences wanted to watch serious movies seriously. But audiences and their expectations have altered, and the era of art films is over …'. Have I missed the statistical survey which led him to this sage discrimination?

So much is wrong with Nowra's article that it would take the rest of this essay to unpack it all, whereas I want to use my remaining space for other purposes. The problem with such articles as Nowra's (and especially when they come attached to so well-known a name) is that they may encourage other wiseacres to leap in with their equally ill-considered jeremiads which can do nothing for 'the industry', that monolithic structure they never actually get around to dissecting. What I wonder is this: is it possible to sustain a steady stream of small-scale filmmaking in Australia, and whether funding can be found (from government or other sources) to help with providing adequate marketing to bring such films to the attention of those who might be interested in seeing them? There may be segmented audiences ready to respond to cheaply but intelligently made films if they know about them and where to find them, and it's to some such films that I want to draw attention. There just may be substantial minority audiences that don't care if they never see *Avatar* or *Australia* or *Twilight*, that have some interest in Australian cinema, and that wonder what kinds of alternatives exist.

How many people, I wonder, knew about Christopher Weekes's 2008 film, *Bitter & Twisted*? This unsentimentally affecting study of a family trying to come to terms with the death of its older son, Liam, is an emotionally rich experience as it makes its unhurried way to – not a 'happy ending' but an ending in which we can believe because it seems to derive from the network of relationships and tentative approaches to a future without the missing son. The father has quit the job he hates and has come to some recognition of his life's priorities, in a quietly heartbreaking moment registering 'the opportunities Liam will never have' and asserting his need and love for his family. The mother, who wants to feel loved and desired, reaches for his hand, and the younger son accepts that, try as he might to emulate Liam and pursue Liam's girlfriend, he must adjust to the realities of his life. This is not a family melodrama that ends with big music or birds in flight to signify liberation or romantic clinches, but it leaves one feeling that what's been on offer has a kind of truth, sometimes painful, that makes both compelling drama and persuasive contact with reality.

There are several others that fall into this sort of category, not straining for size or compromising their integrity in the hope of taking on Hollywood. In their various ways, Pene Patrick's *Playing for Charlie* (2010), Anthony Hayes's *Ten Empty* (2008), Alkinos

Tsilimodos's *Blind Company* (2010), and Michael Joy's excoriating *Men's Group* (2008) all focus on family relationships and tensions and ways of dealing with crises of death and illness. This doesn't mean, however, that they are necessarily depressing films, or that they would be 'better' if they paid attention to Nowra's recommendation that they should heed what makes Hollywood so successful. They are uneven in quality, but they all make serious claims on our attention as they articulate ways in which our closest ties can be put under pressure – and they do so with considerable filmmaking accomplishment.

For instance, look at the ways in which Michael Joy deftly and economically sketches the kinds of dysfunction that have brought his five guys to take part in the eponymous men's group. The story-telling is terse and evocative of whole lives: for instance, the fleeting shot of the mail-boxes of a characterless apartment building immediately signifies the isolation of Alex (Grant Dodwell), the foul-mouthed recruit to the group who has stuffed up his family relationships. Or, in *Ten Empty*, the son's rejection of his father's 'home brew' because he'd prefer 'a red' is enough to signal the tensions that will develop between them. Sylvia Lawson rightly praised such films for their 'courage in pursuing family-centred stories to their real emotional boundaries' in *Inside Story* (4 February 2010).

I am not highlighting these films just because they are 'worthy' in terms of the material they tackle, commendable though that is, but also because they are in all sorts of ways skilfully made. On both grounds they deserve to be heard of and *seen*. These low-key realist appraisals of family life and its off-shoots aren't the only sort of Australian product that warrants notice. There is, for instance, a sharply intelligent trickle of mockumentaries. I have already referred to *Rats and Cats*.

Scarcely less irreverent fun was to be had from *The Magician* (2005), said to be made for $3000. In this, the pre-title sequence in which hitman Ray Shoesmith briskly dispatches his first victim (somewhere up the top end of Bourke Street) then goes on his way sets the mood and tone for the 'documentary' that follows. And the 'plot', such as it is, is also underway: as Ray goes matter-of-factly about his work, it is all being recorded by his old friend and one-time neighbour, Max Totti, who is making a documentary about the daily life of a hitman. And a third in this vein is Darren Ashton's *Razzle Dazzle: A Journey into Dance* (2007), about suburban dance competitions (the colon in the title announces its lethal satiric intentions), and it led London's esteemed critic Philip French to say: 'it's in the same class as the best movies by Christopher Guest's company', the latter famed for its success in the genre.

I want only to suggest that we shouldn't be browbeaten by the likes of Nowra who assumes that filmmakers can have no higher aspiration than to take on Hollywood at its own game. At very least, a country's art forms might be supposed to have something to say about the culture from which they draw their being. If they can rework established genres to give them an antipodean flavour and, more demanding still, they can create their own genres and sub-genres (like the suburban family study) as a way of explaining us to ourselves and others, and doing so with coherence and integrity, they may well be doing their bit towards a national cinema. Being near or far from Hollywood is neither here nor there – certainly not here, anyway.

Australian Book Review, July–August 2010.

49

A CURMUDGEON'S CANON

Random Thoughts on *Summer Heights High*, *The Office* and Other Nasty Pleasures

If you don't want to watch 'reality television' (an oxymoron, if ever I heard one) or crime series in several continents; if you don't feel like being improved with well-meaning documentaries about matters of Grave Importance; if above all you hate having your heart warmed; what's left for you on television? Well, one of the real treats available to you is 'cringe telly', the sort of entertainment that appeals to your inner curmudgeon. This is television that is as excruciating as it is lethally funny, that makes you squirm as you try not to rupture yourself with improper laughter. This essay is dedicated to all those who would rather spend the evening in traction than watch *Australian Idol* or another episode of *Midsomer Murders*.

What is 'cringe' television?

What follows is not a theorisation of the genre at issue, but a tentative go at isolating some of its characteristics – that is, a few of the reasons that make it so attractive a proposition to some viewers. The approach is entirely empirical, growing out of merely watching the stuff and trying to discern recurring patterns across about ten programs that, with some clear variations among them, seem to qualify for inclusion in such a genre. This could raise issues about what constitutes a genre – how many exemplars does it take to consider a genre established? I'm not sure how widely the term 'cringe television' is used; I'm employing it here to cover a range of series that seem to me to have key elements in common, though not necessarily to the same degree.

First, all of these series have about them an air of documentary, as if they were free from the usual expectations and restraints of narrative structuring, from the interrelation of character and event. But there are more positive identifying marks of the documentary mode. There is a pervasive sense that what is being shown has been *caught by*, not staged for, the camera, and of course this is no more true of, say, *The Office* or *Summer Heights High* than it was of many 'legitimate' documentary films, from *Man of Aran* (Robert J. Flaherty, 1934) to David Attenborough. There is always a mélange of the real and the contrived. But the cringe series set out – sometimes subtly, sometimes not – to mock the procedures of classic documentary. I mean, for instance, the function of the on-the-spot interviewer, the direct address to the camera, and the careful awkwardness of the 'non-actors' – the whole faux documentary, or mockumentary, mode.

What sorts of situations are these series set in? Mostly they purport to examine work-places (office, school, etc.), though there are some exceptions to this, as in *We Can Be Heroes*. If there is an underlying seriousness in such programs, it may well be because work is a serious business: it can be, and no doubt often is, the site of major stresses, of jockeying for positions, of doing others in, of control freaks doing their best to live up to their descriptor, of a lot of unrewarding activity.

Most people, in a work situation, will be at the beck and call, if not indeed the mercy, of some higher-up. Relationships can thrive or they can be suspect if there are goals to be aimed at competitively; there is immense scope for self-seeking and self-aggrandisement, as well as for the rewards of friendship and the stimulus of co-operation. The faux documentary approach, trying to look as unscripted as possible, lays these possibilities bare – with brilliant astringency in *The Office* and *Summer Heights High*, comically but more crudely in *Very Small Business* and *Stupid Stupid Man*.

What kinds of people does cringe television have in its sights? The protagonists tend to be monsters of egoism such as David Brent in *The Office* or Mr G. in *Summer Heights High*, characters whose personal vanity and solipsistic view of the world render them almost invulnerable to sullen looks or innuendo or even downright opposition. However, when someone with real authority challenges them, they're stuffed, since their own *amour propre* is based almost wholly, if not only, on their own view of their capacities. For them, other people exist to cater to their needs, to bolster their vanities, their already golden opinions of themselves. An exception to this generality is the unseen Roy Mallard, the innocent, bumbling interviewer in the BBC's *People Like Us*, who is always apologising for the untoward ways in which others have made him look a prat.

One of the recurring reactions cringe television incites in us is a barely suppressed sense of outrage at the way it flies in the face of political correctness. It is perhaps true to say that most of us who pride ourselves on our liberal recoil from sexism, racism, fatism or any of the other -isms so repellent to our generous-spirited consciences are at least passingly excoriated by the appalling offence offered to such high-mindedness. This can happen overtly, as in *The Office* when we instinctively shrivel at the awfulness of David Brent's views, or bumblingly as in Roy Mallard's ever-polite way of going along with what is offered to him as an investigative reporter. One way or another, our carefully monitored liberalism will get a terrible doing-over by the way these series go at it. Sometimes, just to complicate our reactions further, we may feel that the comedy has just pushed the barriers too far; is too near the bone for a sly laugh at political correctness. Am I really suggesting nothing more than a shiver of revulsion at what we may think of as 'bad taste'? Has such a criterion any place in appraising such series?

So, is it all a question of tone? Of what it feels like? If so, how would we characterise this tone? For one thing, and a crucial thing, it is devoid of sentimentality. It is ruthless in going for the egoists' jugulars, whether subtly (by not letting them ever become aware of the awfulness of their me-centred view of the world) or by their sheer incomprehension of the massive ego-puncturing that has been dealt them. But over-weening vanity and ego(t)ism doesn't always get it in the neck, and this may be what affronts us most. It's one thing to be entertained, in our superior way, by those who are so obviously less charming, less insightful, less liberal than ourselves, as long as we can be certain, in the ways to which classic Hollywood has habituated us, that these will be brought to book and, possibly, more nearly to our way of thinking in the end. If we don't respond, appalled, to what they so often seem to be getting away with, this means that our reaction has demanded and met with an awareness of how irony works. If there's no 'placing' character with whom we – nicer we – might align ourselves, and in these series there often isn't, it becomes harder for us to tell where our sympathies are meant to lie. Is this a new viewing situation?

Lineage of cringe

There were apparently some cries of outrage at episodes of *We Can Be Heroes* and *Summer Heights High*, but was the kind of affront to our tender sensibilities really so new? I think back to Jonathan Swift's *A Modest Proposal for Preventing the Children of Poor People in Ireland from Being a Burden to Their Parents or Country, and for Making Them Beneficial to the Public* (1729). This savage tract suggests the fattening of such children to feed the rich, and one reads it open-mouthed with horror, even while registering that Swift is, in the mode of ferocious satire, not seriously proposing a scheme for political economy. He has to rely on our own sense of what is appalling to generate the response he wants, not opting, as so much satire does, for the easier procedure of including a mouthpiece we can trust or, less explicitly, a figure with whom sympathetic alignment is a possibility. Some readers may indeed feel that Swift goes too far, just as some viewers of cringe television will find some of the comedy too near the bone.

To come nearly up to date, surely Barry Humphries, in such incarnations as Dame Edna Everage, with her breathtakingly casual racism and sexism, or the gross Sir Les Patterson, Minister of the Yartz, ensured that the Swiftian spirit was alive and well in the late twentieth century. These two, egoists both in their contrasting styles, enabled Humphries to engage in some wild political incorrectness in the guise of being true to his outrageous personas. Then, in different mode, there was the toe-curling incompetence of interviewer Norman Gunston (Garry McDonald), with his comb-over, shaving nicks and bumbling intrusiveness, conning his way into the presence of nonplussed victims. In the 1990s, the eponymous fictional current affairs show in the ABC's *Frontline* was cleverly satirical in ways that might have caused some red faces among the producers, hosts and reporters of the real thing, drawing attention to some very questionable ethics in their preparation and presentation.

Still, though, the series I'm concerned with have taken things a little further. They strive to look and feel like realism, to give off an air of being unstructured in narrative terms, of on-the-spot locations, and of being willing, with apparent artlessness, to utter the most appalling sentiments. To clarify this distinction, it is instructive to compare the US version of *The Office* with its ground-breaking UK original. The US *Office* is entertaining enough but in an altogether more conventional framework. Sure, there is still the intermittent direct address to the camera, but the plots of the episodes are more obviously structured, not seeming to allow enough scope for what the camera might just pick up (an illusion, of course, in the UK series), and the characters seem too 'acted' for the same reason (in other words, they've lost the air of having just happened to be on the spot as the documentary filmmaker and his camera were passing). Could this be the result of commercial TV's strictures requiring, as it appears to, a steady move to mini-climaxes before the ad breaks? Its jokes are more carefully honed, and it doesn't dare risk quite so unattractive a protagonist (unattractive on all counts, that is) as Ricky Gervais' David Brent. Steve Carell may be no matinee idol, but he's Brad Pitt compared to Gervais. The edge of cringiness has been lost, and as a consequence its pleasures, real enough as they are, have a more readily recognisable sitcom aura. The fun is broader, the 'realism' has been tailored to the demands of narrative, and the excruciation factor has been softened – and the rewards for curmudgeons have been trimmed. In some ways this is also true of the US version of *Kath & Kim*, but it doesn't quite belong in the cringe category as the

UK's *The Office* does. *K & K*, even in its Australian series, didn't espouse the realist look and sound of *The Office*.

The cringe-makers

The great Australian cringe-maker is surely Chris Lilley: in two senses of the word, that is. First, as writer and producer, he is the creator of *Summer Heights High* (2007) and its predecessor, *We Can Be Heroes* (2005); and, second, as an actor he has incarnated their cringe-making protagonists like Ja'mie King (in both), Mr G. (in the former) and Phil Olivetti (in the latter). He has been rightly garlanded with awards and nominations in both creative capacities. What do his characters have in common with Steve Coogan's roving reporter Alan Partridge (*The Day Today* [1994], *Knowing Me, Knowing You with Alan Partridge* [1994–5], *I'm Alan Partridge* [1997–2002]), Gervais's David Brent, Chris Langham's temporising politician Hugh Abbot in *The Thick of It* (2005, 2008), Robyn Butler's Frances O'Brien, aggressive chief of *The Librarians* (2007), or Wayne Hope's shyster entrepreneur in *Very Small Business* (2008) or incompetent editor of COQ men's magazine in *Stupid Stupid Man*? One answer is suggested above: they are all utterly self-serving, unable to conceive of a world-view of which they are not the centre, and are all, as a result, capable of appalling insensitivity to the needs and feelings of others and to any denigration of them. And how po-faced that sort of description sounds in the face of some of the most demanding comedy that television has given us.

If I were considering cinema as well, I would need to take account of Sacha Baron Cohen's *Borat: Cultural Learnings of America for Make Benefit Glorious Nation of Kazakhstan* (Larry Charles, 2006), whose sexist, racist protagonist wreaks havoc across the United States, bewildering scores of the unwitting. Baron Cohen has, of course, a history of outrageous television personas, most notably as Ali G from 1998: he is just too outré for mere comparative consideration here. He is worth having in mind as we think about these other cringe-makers, as he is perhaps as outrageous as any of them, though there is an order of crudity (and I don't just mean of the prurient kind) in the way he is drawn that may have something to do with the need to reach international big-screen audiences.

Lilleys of the field

To some observers, Lilley, 33, is simply the most exciting comic satirist to have emerged in Australia since Barry Humphries, with whom Lilley is now sometimes bracketed (along with the unknowable chameleon Peter Sellers and the prince of excruciatingly confronting humour, Ricky Gervais).

Personally, I'd have no difficulty in accepting either the accolade or the heady comparisons in the above. In *We Can Be Heroes* he creates, as both writer and actor, six disparate characters, five of whom are contending for the title of Australian of the year, and these five have little in common apart from the fixity of their attention on their own affairs and images. From the start, the series exhibits an absolutely straight face. There is a high-minded voice-over from a breathily serious Jennifer Byrne, extolling 'inspirational role models' as the camera pans 'across the country', stopping to take in some clear examples, such as sporting heroes and a group of happy Aboriginal children. Nothing in this introduction to each episode prepares us, except in malicious hindsight, for what follows. 'I wanted to be special up there with your Einsteins and Ian Thorpes' are the opening words of former Queensland policeman Phil Olivetti, who has saved some children from danger when a bouncy castle took off. His entire conversation is about himself, sometimes coloured with mock-modesty (he says he doesn't want people hounding him now that he's become a celebrity; in fact no one is). 'Phil's life is about to change,' interposes narrator Byrne. 'I want to get into the inspirational guest speaker circuit,' he adds hopefully, but his only invitation (and he's manoeuvred this) comes from his son's scout group, which ends in disaster when a small boy is pinned under a fallen tree trunk, as part of Phil's showing his skills in an emergency. And he finally lies his way to Canberra for the Australian of the Year finals, in which he hasn't been included.

The other would-be heroes (all played by Lilley) are Ricky Wong, a Physics PhD student whose father's aspirations for him parody the idea of immigrants and high achievement; a South Australian farm boy, Daniel Sims, who donates an eardrum to his deaf twin brother, and whose every remark ends with 'and shit' ('our teacher's done a banner 'n' shit'); Pat Mullins, a buoyant Perth housewife who has one leg substantially longer than the other, but is determined to roll from Perth to Uluru; and Sydney north Shore schoolgirl Ja'mie (pronounced 'Ja-may'), who's 'basically good at everything' and who sponsors eighty-five starving African children ('If they don't write in three months, I forfeit their payment,' she tells us compassionately).

There isn't space here to indicate the kinds of wicked pleasure to be had from the behaviour of these egoists – as they all are, whatever lofty motives they profess. The political incorrectness is stunning, though you catch yourself wondering how you dare to be laughing at, say, disability (and I think Pat's death from cancer before she can start her epic 'Rock and Roll' tour probably goes too far: even so, the cliché of 'passed away' gets a deserved little shaft of its own) or the idea of Chinese students, all blacked-up and painted, putting on a musical called Indidgeridoo, or the sheer monstrous complacencies of them all, or of the vile Phil trying to bribe Mal, a member of the selection panel, to put in a good word for him, while confiding to him how large his member is. And so on. The series blows a refreshing gust of cliché-rattling wind through its six episodes, and it makes you wonder how the ABC was ever able to continue with its *Australian Story*, which takes seriously the sort of 'issues', as Ja'mie would say, that are given such a doing over in *Heroes*. Unsurprisingly the series won Logies in 2006 for Outstanding Comedy and Outstanding New Talent. But appallingly funny as *Heroes* is, it is really a curtain-raiser to the still more appalling but more substantial *Summer Heights High*.

The three protagonists of *Summer Heights High*, though all are involved in the eponymous secondary school, never meet each other in the whole course of the series. Can this have been intentional on Lilley's part? Not just to avoid the logistical problems of all three being played by the same actor – that is presumably hardly a problem in these technologically advanced days – but as a means of reinforcing the essential solitariness of Ja'mie, Mr G., and Jonah, however populously they surround themselves with admiring sycophants. It's as though they occupy separate semi-worlds in the larger world of the school which director Stuart McDonald and cinematographer Nick Gregoric render with, simultaneously, a documentary-style verisimilitude and a cod-teen-movie genre affiliation via the artfully syrupy theme song and would-be lyrical overhead shots with which each episode starts. This is followed by the solemn titles that read: 'The following programme was filmed on location at a public high school. Three individuals were chosen as subjects. Their daily lives were documented over one school term.' In these titles a Griersonian influence would seem to be at work – and the father of documentary might well rotate in his grave, but was allegedly not always above a little fakery.

Lilley is undeniably brilliant in the three leading roles. A small toss of the head and he catches to the letter Ja'mie's vanity, or her careful use of the phrase 'no offence' before uttering some wholly offensive sentiment; Mr G.'s appealing smile keys us in to his egoism, and his fey but steely concern with promoting his image as an 'inspirer'; and stroppy, break-dancing Polynesian Jonah, rightly described by one reviewer as 'the one character who isn't a monster all the way through, the victim himself of a bullying father',[2] is nevertheless a foul-mouthed bully as well, claiming he only said 'puck off' when he actually said something far worse. The bragging, the racism, the wild incorrectness ('I love disabled people,' Jamie gushes to the principal of the state high school to which she goes on a term's exchange), the sexism and the lewd sexual banter, the tragedy of drug abuse – these and so much more are lightly and intricately woven into Lilley's screenplay and into the texture of his playing.

The body language and diction that so distinguish each of the three, not only from each other but from those around them, amount to comic genius, but one should note as well the importance of 'those around them'. These characters are played by a mix of actors and non-professionals, actual students and staff. A notable example is real-life high school headmistress Elida Brereton, who plays Miss Murray, principal of *Summer Heights High*, and who acts with perfect restraint and straightness of face as she tries to accommodate Mr G.'s vain-glorious ambition. Another is actor David Lennie as Doug Peterson, the student-welfare officer, played with the quiet understatement of a man sorely tried by the unruly Jonah but determined to persist in his 'work with the victim and also the perpetrators [of bullying]'. I'm aware that it is almost impossible to give any idea of how funny these people are while they remain completely documentary-natural.

Beyond the cringe: tricky Ricky and *The Office*

If Ricky Gervais' *The Office* didn't actually introduce the idea of cringe television, it is by now perhaps the program most closely associated with the mode. Steve Coogan's naff reporter Alan Partridge is as wholly self-centred and as unaware as David Brent of the impression he makes on other people; and Chris Langham as Roy Mallard in *People Like Us*, with his roving mic, is terminally and embarrassingly inept. But Partridge is not quite as crudely self-seeking as Gervais's David Brent, and Mallard keeps stumbling over his own efforts to be self-effacing. Australia's Wayne Hope, in his Don Angel persona in *Very Small Business*, has to keep slipping around to maintain some control over his life, and this is probably also the case with his *Stupid Stupid Man* character, Carl Van Dyke, whose sexism is encapsulated in his casual remark to his secretary 'G'day sweetie, make us a cup of coffee, would you, love?' One might make the odd excuse for any of these as they go on their blinkered way, but with Brent it is as painful as it is funny to watch as he puts his foot wrong every time, without ever being aware of it.

A local television reviewer, writing about the American version of *The Office*, noted:

> Like that other US adaptation (you know the one [i.e., *Kath & Kim*]) this is broader, softer and much prettier than the original. But in this case, that's no bad thing. The British original, for all

> its brilliance, was so excruciating you regularly had to leave the room[2]

Well, there's an element of hyperbole in that, but it is true that David Brent is possibly the least likeable protagonist of any television series in living memory – and the one you can least easily take your eyes off. He can't talk on the phone without rolling his eyes to anyone watching, to suggest what a cool dude he is. His casual and inveterate racism reaches its apotheosis in his 'joke' in which he asks, 'What's black and slides down nelson's Column?' My delicate liberal sensitivities forbid my giving you the answer. When it is decided that the Swindon branch of the paper manufacturing company should take over the Slough office where Brent has reigned supreme, he does his best to undermine the process, torn between competing with the incoming Swindon boss, Neil, (even to the point of buying – and badly wearing – the same leather blouson) and bad-mouthing him to the Slough staff, of whose loyalty Brent is fatuously and erroneously sure.

What is so remarkable about *The Office* is the firm grip it has on the documentary technique. It doesn't feel obliged to soften or to conventionalise the narrative impact of the cross-currents of life in the workplace, or in the neighbouring pub. It keeps its eye on the realist exposure of the tensions and aspirations of the office, interspersing Brent's complacent self-regard with the sycophancy of Gareth (assistant to the regional manager, not, as Brent reminds him, assistant regional manager) and the quite touching glances of affection between Tim and the receptionist Dawn. However, the real poignancy is in the aftermath of the excruciation Brent has so repeatedly caused: his total lack of self-knowledge, his unthinking certainty of his own proficiency (as communicator, comedian, all-round fun guy) and of his popularity as a boss can end by freezing our laughter as we contemplate his utter solipsism.

These series are not without an element of pathos, but not of any conventional kind: it is most likely to arise from the fleeting glimpses we get of the protagonists' insecurities, and from our grasp of the solitariness that springs from their inbuilt solipsism. It is this 'pathos potential' that really takes us beyond the cringe. These programs offer us several crucial challenges. We probably have to accept the fact that we are laughing at Brent or the Lilley creations at least partly from a position of our own superiority, a fact that perhaps becomes only apparent to us when we stop to think of where the comedy comes from in this very confronting genre.

Metro, No. 160, 2009.

Notes

1 Thomas Sutcliffe, 'Last night's TV: Class act from a Man of Many Parts', *The Independent*, 25 June 2008.
2 Melinda Houston, 'Critic's Choice', the *Sunday Age*, 'M', 26 October 2008, p.38.

50

HOW WEIRD DOES THIS MOB STILL SEEM?

They're a Weird Mob (1957) by Nino Culotta

They're a Weird Mob (1966) directed by Michael Powell

It's probably a bit shaming for someone who was around at the time, and more or less mature even then, not to have read *They're a Weird Mob* when it first came out more than half a century ago. Like everyone else, I knew about it, of course, and its reference to 'King's Bloody Cross' quickly became iconic, encapsulating a place, a time and an experience.

The book, first published in November 1957, had gone through seventeen impressions by March 1959, according to the edition I'm at last reading. In fact, *They're a Weird Mob* 'was reprinted every year for the next thirty-eight years. It sold the best part of a million copies' and the movie derived from it in 1966 'echoed the novel's success by breaking all box-office records for a local production,' according to Jacinta Tynan in the introduction to this new edition. In other words, Nino Culotta (the pen name of John O'Grady) gave birth to a publishing – and, indeed, a cultural – phenomenon back in the remote 1950s.

Coming to it now, decades later, I wondered how dated it would seem, and in what ways. Perhaps the first thing that struck me was the mildness of its swearing: in a time in which variants on the 'f' word are common linguistic coinage it's hard to remember when 'bloody' or the occasional 'bugger' were the characteristic epithets for expressing outrage. On the matter of language, O'Grady exercises remarkable tonal control over the sloppiness of everyday diction: the endemic use of 'ut' instead of 'it' (as in 'Nothin' to ut, mate'), for instance, or the slurring together of several words into a semi-literate version of those long German words made by the simple adding of shorter ones to each other (as in "Owyergoin?'). But it's not just the language that seems so innocent, so devoid of concern for possible offence; it's also the way Culotta renders the unthinking response to, say, 'New Australians' or 'sheilas.' It seems less a conscious attempt on the part of the working men to diminish those they're referring to than a total imaginative failure to grasp any sense of otherness. 'Innocent' is hardly the word for it, but neither is 'vicious.'

What interests me now is the balance O'Grady maintains between critiquing and celebrating the Australia into which he plunges his narrator. Nino is a north Italian journalist whose editor has sent him on a fact-finding mission to post-war Australia, which has become a goal for Italian migrants. Language is, of course, central to his coming to terms with the experience, and his growing rapport with the builders' labourers derives in part from his gradual grasp of such essentials as the idea of 'shouting' in a pub – both the word and the idiotic practice of being in a drinking school that requires him to have more 'schooners' than he wants or needs. It was a clever notion of O'Grady's to make Nino a journalist because this provides a legitimate narrative device for some reflections on what he is making of his time Down Under (as it was no doubt thought of). For instance:

> I wish I could reproduce the accent, and the close-lipped rapid enunciation. I have thought of using a tape recorder to capture it. But when an Australian is asked to speak for a specific purpose, everything that makes his conversations the delight they are, disappears.

This kind of rumination gives the book a lightly worn seriousness that punctuates but doesn't puncture the sheer good-natured fun of so much of it. The differences in sense of humour – perhaps crucial to any country's sense of itself – also emerge early among the ways in which Nino will come to understand his new country. 'Getting' a joke in a foreign language may well be the best sign of assimilation.

The element of critique, albeit lightly worn, is there in attitudes to xenophobia and racism. There are jokes about 'niggers' (in a comment about *Gone with the Wind*), about 'I-ties' and/or 'bloody Dagoes.' ('Who won the war? We did, didn' we?' one charmer asks rhetorically as he puts down the post-war influx of Italians.) But O'Grady doesn't fall into the trap of crudely attributing such qualities only to ignorant, insular Australians. He avoids this by having Nino record his prejudice against the Meridionali: 'These are Italians from the south of Italy. They are small dark people with black hair and what we considered to be bad habits. We are big fair people with blue eyes and good habits.' He recalls how he had 'drunk a lot of vino, and kept on yelling out "dirty Meridionali" and other things' just before boarding the ship to Australia. O'Grady captures accurately the unthinking attitudes of the complacent era he was writing in *and* makes clear that, however insular we were, we didn't have a monopoly on such prejudices.

Nino's manners appear courtly by comparison with those of the rough-and-ready Australian blokes who are his workmates, and there are a couple of interesting points made by this contrast. First, as with almost everything about his adjustment, Nino's formality is a by-product of linguistic uncertainty in his new environment. Second, when the workmates parody his diction and manners, it makes one wonder if the slapdash ockerism of their everyday speech isn't a conscious assumption of an anti-British vernacular. When foreman Joe's wife, Edie, serving breakfast, wonders aloud 'why he couldn't learn to speak nicely like Nino,' other workmates, Dennis and Pat 'began to imitate my speech in an exaggerated manner':

> 'I say, old chap, would you mind passing me another slice of that excellent toast?'
>
> 'Not at all, old man, I always think toast refreshes one, do not you?'
>
> 'Indubitably. Indubitably. But I must say the coffee is superb.'
>
> 'Superb, my dear fellow, is an understatement. It is elegant. Only the sublime technique of our kindly host could produce such a delectable beverage.'

And so it goes on. 'Stretching credulity' was my first reaction to this, but then it seemed more interesting to wonder if the author wasn't slyly making a point about the everyday locutions of Australian blokes desperate not to be caught seeming old-world or affected in any way. Perhaps their diction was just as much 'put on' as that of the Poms – or, indeed, of any more mannerly types – they are mocking.

O'Grady parades such Aussie rituals as pub-drinking, rabbit-shooting and the local procedures for courtship and marriage. And these are offered with both affection and satirical observation. Nino himself, adjusting seriously to the contemporary mores, decides 'I am going to get married' and applies himself to this project with the same earnestness as he does to acquiring the idiom of his fellows. This decision leads him to The Corso at Manly beach, where he makes the acquaintance of two young women, one of whom, Dixie, is waiting for her fiancé, Charlie, and is trying to eat spaghetti with a spoon. She is not responsive to Nino's advice to use a fork. Her friend Kay replies to Nino's telling them, 'I am looking for someone who is my type, and whom I can marry,' with the terse rejoinder, 'Have you tried the zoo?' In time he will overcome Kay's lack of interest, woo her mother's approval with a bunch of flowers, and overcome her father's resistance ('First bloke that's stood up to me in years,' he tells his daughter approvingly). And in time again, he will have cleared the hurdle of being 'a bloody New Australian,' one of those 'who are still mentally living in their homelands,' and will thank God 'for letting me be an Australian.'

The book ends on a paean of praise to Australia and its egalitarian ways. This can be read as Nino's journalistic summarising of his views, and this function of his profession needs to be kept in mind so that the ending doesn't seem merely to bathe everything in a warm glow. Nino has worked with Australians, lived among them, observed them with a receptive mind and an appraising eye, and married one of them. Even so, his impressions are offered without sentimentality. We don't feel we're headed for a group hug; instead, we are left with a work of charm and good humour that allows a certain degree of critique along with a modicum of satisfaction with the way we are.

Or, in 2012, the way we *were*. Apart from the book's intrinsic values as a piece of imaginative writing – for instance, its tonal control as it moves between situations dramatised in dialogue and journalistic commentary, between Nino's careful diction and the cheerful slipshoddiness of his mates' vernacular – it has acquired almost an historical dimension. In its pages are preserved with verve and shrewd humour all sorts of cultural information about an era that now seems impossibly remote in many ways. It predates the admirable emergence of the idea of multiculturalism that I now associate with the likes of Al Grassby, the vividly suited immigration minister in the Whitlam government. It recalls both the greater innocence preceding the psychedelic explosion of the 1960s and the easy intolerance of so much of our thinking about 'others,' and it does both with energy and grace.

What, I wondered, could have attracted the British director Michael Powell to adapting *They're a Weird Mob* for the screen? At the time, actor-producer John McCallum was the managing director of J.C. Williamson's theatre chain and was keen to see the company embark on film-making again after a long interval. McCallum arranged the deal between 'the firm' and Powell to make the film for $600,000, and the result was a big commercial success in Australia but not elsewhere. Powell needed a hit after the disaster of *Peeping Tom* (1960), now regarded as a masterpiece but then almost universally reviled. It finished Powell's illustrious maverick career in Britain.

Apart from the prosaic reality of Powell's need to kickstart his career, the film does reveal a certain continuity with some of his more prestigious work. The element of cultural difference, treated for comedy in *Weird Mob*, had claimed Powell's fascinated attention in such diverse works as *The Life and Death of Colonel Blimp* (1943), *A Canterbury Tale* (1944), *I Know Where I'm Going!* (1945), *A Matter of Life and Death* (1946) and *Black Narcissus* (1947). There are touches of comedy in how, say, the American sergeant reacts to English habits in *A Canterbury Tale*, though for the most part in these films the matter of cultural difference is embedded in more serious entertainments. The Anglo-American rapprochement of *A Canterbury Tale* and *A Matter of Life and Death* was a serious business in the mid forties, but the first of those films and the Anglo-German amity depicted in *Colonel Blimp* can be seen as studies in friendships and understanding which override differences in language and nationality, while *I Know Where I'm Going!* and *Black Narcissus* offer explorations of women coming to terms with strange physical and/or social environments. I'm not mounting an *auteurist* case for *Weird Mob* as belonging in the director's canonical achievements; I simply want to suggest that it might be less of a departure, in thematic interests at least, than perhaps supposed. The celebration of Australianness is not so far removed, at core, from the magisterial eulogy to Englishness that concludes *A Canterbury Tale*.

In terms of technique, *Weird Mob* doesn't do much to recall the visual splendours of Powell's greatness in the forties, but there are touches that suggest he is using the beauties of Sydney for something more than just postcard pictorialism. Stretches of Bondi beach seem to stand for Nino's natural, unaffected delight in the country's possibilities, and contrast with the building site he works on or with the conventional interiors of pubs or houses that create other contexts for the life he is coming to terms with. There is also a moment of focus-distortion to render Nino's exhaustion that recalls some of the evocative power and precision of Powell's genius, but it would be wrong to make great claims for the film, which is essentially an easy-to-enjoy entertainment put together by a director who could almost have made it in his sleep.

As an adaptation, the film retains the novel's characteristic procedure as a series of more or less discrete episodes – Nino arriving, Nino at the building site, Nino in the pub – but in one major matter it strikes out and acquires a more obvious 'shaping' than is found in the book's narrative procedures. This is to do with the enlargement of the role of Kay, whom Nino marries. Whereas she doesn't appear in the novel until over three-quarters of the way through, the film introduces her in a very early scene at her workplace and we have a sense of her background when she pops up in a not-too-likely coincidence on Bondi beach. When Nino announces 'I think I'm going to get married' we have been prepared for it in a way that costs the film some of the novel's comedy.

But the scene in which Nino meets Kay's father, played by Chips Rafferty in a role that epitomises his brand of authoritative self-made Australianness, builds very satisfactorily both as a comedy confrontation and as a climax to Nino's absorption, without loss of self, into Australian life. One might add that if Rafferty was by then regarded as an Australian 'icon' (that word again), the same might have been said of Walter Chiari, who played Nino, in relation to his native Italy. He'd become internationally famous for co-starring with Ava Gardner, on and off the set of *The Little Hut* (1957), as well as for dozens of Italian films. The film thus ends on a note of mutual acceptance by two matched charismas.

It's good that we no longer talk about 'New Australians,' let alone 'dagoes,' and we'd hope there has been serious progress in the ways that Australian men treat and talk about women. If it didn't sound too solemn, I'd say that O'Grady's book now has historical significance – as well as offering a nostalgic wallow for those simpler times.

Inside Story, 1 May 2012.

51

KATH & KIMDERELLA

From Box to Multiplex

Has there ever been a seriously good film derived from a television series? I ask as one seeking information, not having done the serious research that would enable me to give a definitive answer to this question. When I run my eye over the list compiled for that utterly reliable organ of public information, 'Wikipedia', I am not at all inclined to pursue the issue by submitting myself to viewing the big-screen likes of *The Beverly Hillbillies* just to be sure of my ground.

Adaptation of one kind or another is to me an endlessly provocative issue in filmmaking. There is plenty of incidence of novels, plays, short stories, even poems, being turned into interesting films; there are even some 'based-on-a-true-story' jobs that don't discredit their sources and provide the basis for decent films. So what is it about TV series that seems so endemically to resist the process of adaptation from the small to the big screen? Perhaps it is to do with running-time. Whereas a smartly written half-hour series can run satisfactorily on a single idea, dressed out with shrewdly calculated observation of milieu and the lives fleetingly glimpsed in it, the feature film, by inevitably having to stretch to about 90 minutes (if you're lucky) or (if you're not) two and a half hours, is constrained to go in for much more clotted plotting.

A key example of recent years was *Sex and the City*. A student of mine, correcting me about some wise pronouncement I'd made about the changing roles and status of women in society, laid down a rebuking challenge with: 'You should watch *Sex and the City*.' Well, I took up this gauntlet and found the half-hour programmes to be persistently sharp, perceptive and witty. Nothing in them could have prepared me for the awfulness of the 145-minute film version (2008, Michael Patrick King) with its overcrowded plot and undernourished screenplay, which simply relied on our being willing to spend a lot more time with the four protagonists and not to need to find out anything new about them. Once bitten twice shy, I certainly shied away from the sequel (2010, King again) in which the famous four took themselves away from their natural and formative habitat, Manhattan, to Abu Dhabi. The result, I am reliably informed, was dire, but I am no longer prepared to put it to the test of personal viewing.

There must be exceptions to this depressing rule: I seem to remember *Sweeney!* (1977, David Wickes) managed the transfer with a rewarding share of tough action and tough insights, and Kevin Macdonald's 2009 version of the riveting British series *State of Play* (2003) didn't lose too much in having its investigation of the links between politics and press relocated from London to Washington. But we all know what exceptions can do to rules.

K &K heading for the big-time

All this is by way of giving a pretty comprehensive thumbs-down to *Kath & Kimderella* (2012), directed by Ted Emery, long-time director of the series. The very considerable fun of the series was mostly at the expense of everyday situations in which aspirations of various kinds are made the material of satire. Think of Kath and her courses (she has a diploma for her success in 'Recycling') or her power-walking with second husband Kel; or daughter Kim whose unassailable ego urges her again and again to posit herself as suburban princess in the making, and to assert herself against anything that might be construed as opposition (such as long-suffering husband Brett); or butcher Kel who designates himself as 'purveyor of fine meats'; or hopelessly overweight neighbour Sharon (Kim's 'second-best friend') hopelessly aspiring to various romances and nursing a long-term crush on Shane Warne.

In general, one of these aspirants and his or her latest goal will impel the 'plot' of the episode. How often, for instance, are events set in motion by Kim's entirely solipsistic view of the world? Even at Kath and Kel's wedding, she begins her speech by saying she needs to say something about herself first. And so many episodes observe her egoism at play against Kath's eagerly outgoing nature that can catapult them into enough fun and games for the ensuing half-hour. There may be something patronising in the treatment of these women and their ineffectual but engaging menfolk, but there is also affection for the characters and their lower-middle-class lives as lived in Fountain Lakes. If there is a touch of patronage, or maybe just good-natured critique, in the treatment of this outpost of suburbia, it carries over too to the snooty Prue and Trude (not for nothing are they played by the same actresses who incarnate Kath and Kim), who aspire to be more than just posh-speaking shop assistants.

Simply put, the series was just very funny indeed, with Jane Turner and Gina Riley, as Kath/Prue and Kim/Trude respectively, creating solidly realised characters in a credibly realised setting, and most reliably supported by Magda Szubanski (Sharon), Glenn Robbins

(Kel) and Peter Rowsthorn (Brett). It's a cliché to say that the US doesn't do irony, but some UK series have indeed lost their edge after an Atlantic crossing (e.g., *Till Death Us Do Part* [1967–75], which became *All in the Family* [1970], or *The Office* [2001–03, UK; 2005–12, US]). Similarly, reports suggest that the US version of *Kath & Kim* took itself too seriously in its US version and that the mother-daughter relationship lacked the comic verve of its Australian source. One reviewer blasted it as 'a contender for the worst remake ever', claiming that the first two episodes 'were jaw-dropping in their awfulness.'

The triple-length episode: Kath & Kimderella

Getting started

Trying to keep an open mind about the new film's possibilities in the face of the bleak history of adapting series, one is lulled in the opening minutes to expecting some of the same sort of laughs. The film opens on a close-up of trainer-clad feet which prove to be Kath's as she goes about her power-walking ritual. As she nears her house, a red car pulls in. It has the number plate PRINCEZZ and out steps an overweight Kim with her laundry which she has come home to do. There are shots of Kath's many certificates and diplomas, all lovingly framed on the kitchen wall; there's a flashback to her first husband Gary Poole (Mike Molloy) and his desertion of Kath; neighbour Sharon, almost spherical but talking excitedly about her diet, comes in to use the loo from which she emerges kilos lighter; Kim has announced, for an opening remark, to the marriage counsellor she and Brett are seeing, 'I want a divorce', and she moves back home, to Kath's dismay; and, among all these perfectly acceptable comic capers, the credits have been unfolding with one that reads: 'Introducing Barry Humphries'.

These touches relating to Poole and Humphries seem to augur well for the film's tone. In hindsight at least, it is with the plot-initiating move in which Kath wins an overseas trip to Papilloma, a small kingdom on the 'heel of Italy', that misgivings begin to creep in. Moving this lot out of their native Fountain Lakes may well require some serious adjustments if it's not just to be a matter of innocents abroad. And for a while it looks as if it might work. Kath takes Kim for the trip because Kel doesn't like flying, and Kim has no compunction about leaving little daughter Epponnee-Rae behind with Brett, the husband she wants to divorce. The airport departure scene has plenty of good nasty fun, including the loading-up of Sharon who is tagging along with Kath and Kim, and glimpses of Trude and Prue, who of course are heading off with a much plushier trip in mind.

Getting there – more or less

Predictably the accommodation that comes as part of the prize is extremely scungy and, by means too unlikely to dwell on, Kath, Kim and packhorse Sharon end up at the palace of the King of Papilloma, having made their way there via some vertiginous overhead shots of winding cliff-top roads – and with a side excursion to pursue their mania for shopping. Once installed in the castle the film tends to be overtaken by plot, with just enough small jokes scattered throughout to remind us of why we liked the series so much. But though the film is restrained enough to last only 86 minutes, it still feels like being given five kinds of mustard to go with your meat and veg.

Kath attracts the eye of King Javier (Rob Sitch in a grey mane) whose page tells him that she is 'Just your type … rich and stupid'.

The King is in a bad way financially, and is despotically at odds with the population of his small kingdom, which is baying for his blood, so he makes up to Kath, taking more interest in her share portfolio than in her 'green' impulses. He hopes that she and her 'sister' will enjoy their stay, and good-natured Kath throws herself into things: she admires his shoes ('Are they Rivers?' she asks), and mistakes the torture chamber for a gym, the wheel spinning out of control. The prince, Julio (Erin Mullally), half-masked in phantom-of-the-opera mode, seems to fall for Kim, and, begging for a lock of her hair, catches her swatch as it falls. The unexpected arrival of Kel, who's had a tricky time on the flight, and Brett with Epponnee-Rae, complicates all these essentially idiotic moves. Sharon, nursing a passion for Alain (Richard E. Grant), the King's sinister page, finally settles for a lesbian date. When I add that there are further confusions about who are the real heirs, who is legitimate and so on, and that there is a scheming princess-in-waiting with an eye to bigger things, it should be clear that this is a film wildly overloaded with plot – and plotting.

Modest pleasures

All this is not to say that there is *no* fun to be had from *Kath & Kimderella*, only that, like so many films adapted from TV series, it trades situation for event. There are some good jokes, like the running verbal gag in which the disdainful-looking Alain routinely addresses the King in rhyme: 'As you desire, sire', 'If you require, sire', 'Look, sire. The fire. In the spire', *et al.* And Trude and Prue are allowed several remarks that make clear their political affiliation. 'Who would you go gay for?' asks one, to which the other replies, 'What about Julie Bishop?' Or when they take Javier off at the end, they tell him, 'We could use you in the Liberal Party.' As well, there are echoes of the well-loved series, including the obligatory 'Look at moi, Kim' and Kath's saying 'I'm as gropable as you are about the situation here', as she seeks to reassure the downtrodden proletariat. Kath's tendency to malapropism also produces 'The crème de menthe of Papilloma society will be here tonight'. The royal wedding (of Kim to Julio) is accompanied by headlines and merchandise which offer a satirical slant on recent monarchical celebrations, and – my personal favourite – the way the newspaper is delivered to the castle recalls Kath's running battle with the newsagent back in Fountain Lakes.

Yes, there are jokes sprinkled over the narrative stodge and these assuredly help to make the film meal a little more palatable, but too often they tend to remind us of how much tastier those half-hour segments were. It would be tempting but unfair to dismiss the whole enterprise. It does represent a dumbing-down of the series; it does underline everything the series could simply glance at wittily; the social edge of the series here has to fight to make itself felt in a scenario choked with exaggerated incident. A sign of the film's insecurities may be felt in the number of pointlessly pictorial vistas it succumbs to, as if it were an old 1950s' Fox CinemaScope job. Riley and Turner, credited as co-authors and co-producers as well as stars, have too good a grip on their characters, as do Szubanski, Robbins and Rowsthorn, for us to feel utterly bereft in the face of the inflation of situation into heavy plotting. They can't help giving us some good moments when the original comic inspiration comes through, but even this can be counter-productive. That is, these serve to remind us of how much better-off we were with half-hour helpings than an extended meal that tends to feel bloated and bloating.

A word of warning to whoever feels the need for it: the film ends with Kath and Kim sitting in the garden at home and talking about the possibility of a sequel, 'a bit like the Harry Potter franchise', says Kath. You have been warned.

Metro, No. 175, Summer 2013.

Notes

1 http://en.wikipedia.org/wiki/List_of_films_based_on_television_programs
2 http://www.sfgate.com/news/article/TV-reviews-Kath-Kim-Testees-3266718.php

52

THE VOICE OF A GENERATION

Testament of Youth by Vera Brittain, 1933

Testament of Youth directed by Moira Armstrong *BBC, 1979*

Testament of Youth directed by James Kent BBC Films, 2015

Many decades ago a well-meaning teacher urged me to read a book with the not-too-enticing title of *Testament of Youth* by someone called Vera Brittain. It didn't sound like the sort of stuff I was into at the time. Then, thirty-five years ago, I bought a copy of the book in an edition inspired by the TV series of the late 1970s. Now, in 2015, I've finally read it, and I must say that few books in recent memory have struck me so forcibly with the passion of their response to life's challenges and the wonderful eloquence of the prose in which this is rendered. First published in 1933, *Testament of Youth* remains amazingly acute in its perceptions about both the author's journey through twenty years and what was going on in the larger world during the tumultuous period between 1914 and the mid 1920s.

So, who was Vera Brittain? Before the First World War interrupted her life, as it did for so many of her generation, she was a schoolgirl whose middle-class parents, especially her father, determined that she 'should be turned into an entirely ornamental young lady'. Middle-class they may be, but Brittain describes them as 'robustly low-brow', adding that 'there is no evidence that any of them ever did anything of more than local importance'. By Vera's time, 'local' was first Macclesfield, Cheshire, then, when she was eleven, it became Buxton, Derbyshire, where most of the wives, like her mother, 'kept house' and were clear about who belonged to 'the set'. Vera, aged thirteen in 1906, was sent away to a Surrey boarding school, where many of the girls came from 'country houses of which the name 'Hall' or 'Park' was frequently a part'. From an early age, she became aware of the constrictions of class and gender. Further, her reading turned her from 'an unquestioning if somewhat indifferent church-goer into an anxiously interrogative agnostic'. The ritual of deb dances failed to excite her, and her yearning for higher learning took her to Oxford's Somerville College where she kept a diary, on which the book draws freely, and came to believe that 'the golden hours' of youth were often overrated.

Crucial events were about to complicate the texture of her life. During the Easter school holidays in 1914, her younger brother, Edward, a key figure in her story, introduced into their Buxton home a friend from boarding school, Roland Leighton, who would become the love of Vera's young life. But in that year, 1914, such progress as she had made towards intellectual and social freedom would be 'closed for [her] by a Serbian bomb hurled from the other end of Europe at an Austrian archduke'. Her account recalls Alice Duer Miller's in her famous 1941 verse novella *The White Cliffs*: 'The name of a town in a distant land/Etched on our hearts by a murderer's hand'. Perhaps this was a common reaction: what could this faraway assassination have to do with young women in England?

'Oxford Versus War' is the title of a long chapter, in which Vera comes to find public and private matters inseparable. Her brother and Roland will both be killed in the war, along with others of her friends, and she finds herself renouncing Oxford and taking up nursing, first in London, then at various European sites, finding work a sort of opiate. There is a most moving account of Roland's death in December 1915, and of her coming to terms with this, as she will later have to do with the death of her much-loved brother. Letters to the latter, which do so much to sustain her during the years of chaos, reveal that, for her, patriotism has 'worn very very threadbare'. Here, the words of another famous nurse, Edith Cavell – that 'patriotism is not enough' – come to mind. Vera's maturing feminist views are now strengthened by a tenacious pacifism. She may have hated the horrors of war, but she has contempt for such home-front sufferings as the difficulty of finding reliable servants – or any servants at all. In her role as a VAD (Voluntary Aid Detachment, a nursing unit serving field hospitals at home and abroad) she has seen enough of the rigours and squalor that trailed in the wake of war to ensure a lifetime commitment to the pacifist cause. Neither would she find enough reassurance of a better world in the early days of the peace that ensued.

There is not space here to trawl through the 660 pages of her memoir, tempting as such a project is. I've wanted simply to suggest some of the formative influences on a young life, receptive to both serious thought and strong feeling, and I want to stress how persuasively she writes about both. Her Foreword makes her agenda clear: it is to 'attempt to write history in terms of personal life', to tell her 'own fairly typical story as truthfully as [she] could against the larger background', and the evidence of the memoir is that she has succeeded brilliantly. For instance, the 'eager feminism' of her own prewar girlhood will later inform, and be hugely extended by, her awareness of the fight for women's suffrage, and by her friendship with another burgeoning writer, novelist Winifred Holtby. She will return to Oxford to read History, not English as in her prewar days, and the shift in interest no doubt grows from her war experiences.

What is so impressive is the unclamorous firmness with which she unfolds her gradually life-changing dealings with such issues as class, war, love and the women's movement. How, I wondered, would film-makers deal with all this without succumbing to the risk of talky didacticism? It is the quality of mind behind the prose even more than the chronicle of events that accounts for the inspirational element of *Testament of Youth*. Yes, 'Youth' is in the title, but the book's appeal and significance go well beyond that demographic.

Why should we read Vera Brittain now, nearly a hundred years on? Partly because she is a writer of real accomplishment, of course, but crucially because, as much as anyone, she gives us such an astute, committed insight into the interaction of private and public worlds. And perhaps above all she exposes the hideousness of war and how it smashes up lives – and how post-war peace gives no guarantee of real repair.

Brought to the small screen

In 1979, the BBC and London Films reminded viewers that Brittain's young womanhood, though so clearly a product of her time, still resonated strongly nearly fifty years after the book's appearance. The series was written by Elaine Morgan, who had adapted many novels to the demands of television series, and directed by the comparably prolific Moira Armstrong, and perhaps there was no coincidence in the presence of two very experienced women in these key collaborative roles. But just as Brittain's memoir makes its case for feminism, among other key issues, with clarity and without shrillness, so too this miniseries version commands respect for keeping its eye on crucial matters.

Adapting Brittain's 660-page work to the small screen in five episodes of roughly fifty minutes each must have been a major challenge. Each episode is allotted a year of Vera's experience. Episode 1, 1913, establishes her as being at odds with the stifling conventions of middle-class Buxton society. Vera (Cheryl Campbell) is first seen at the piano she hadn't wanted her father (Emrys James) to buy, wishing instead that he had used the money to send her to university. When brother Edward (Rupert Frazer) comes home, she tells him with some bitterness that *he* will get his own way but she *won't*, as far as their futures are concerned. She wants to go to Oxford but her mother (Jane Wenham) fears this 'might spoil her chances' – that is, for marriage. As well as giving a sense of what Vera is reacting against, this first episode introduces two further key encounters: with Miss Penrose (Rosalie Crutchley), the not very sympathetic principal of Somerville College, Oxford, to which she does eventually win an entrance exhibition; and with Edward's school friend, Roland (Peter Woodward), with whom she can talk about writing and religion, and life at large – and with whom she falls in love.

So, the ground is laid in this first episode for a viewing experience in which our attention will be required not just for incident but also for the interaction of character and idea, and all this against the momentous background of war. Episode 2 (1914) begins with the grandiose statement that 'honour has come back ... and we have come into our heritage'. All Europe is arming, and 'Your country needs you', as the famous Kitchener poster proclaims. Vera's father relents about her going to Oxford, but by the end of the episode she had decided she wants 'to go down for a year' and to become a nurse. 'A waste of talent', says Miss Penrose when Vera announces her plans. Her feminism leads her to reject angrily the notion that women have no useful role to play.

Episode 3 (1915) opens with Vera reading a letter from Roland, whose voice is heard on the soundtrack, and dramatises some of her nursing experiences primarily in English hospitals and, in a finely calculated moment, her learning of Roland's death. In Episode 4 (1917), she applies to go to France where she serves in the nightmare of a military hospital in which she (and the viewer) gets a potent sense of the horror that warfare brings in its wake. The final episode begins with a shot of Big Ben at 11 am, and with crowds cheering and cannon firing to proclaim Armistice Day. Vera will experience 'blind rage' at some of the ensuing peace-time attitudes; she returns to Oxford, to read History now rather than English, the war having changed her priorities, and she will eventually embark on a writing career, as will her postwar friend the novelist Winifred Holtby (Joanna McCallum).

By drawing attention, in a little more detail than usual, to "what happens" in each episode, I have wanted to stress the skill with which the miniseries has been constructed. The overarching trajectory will trace Vera's development from seventeen-year-old girl dissatisfied with the conventional opportunities that seem to be open to her to the young woman who has found her own way through loss and struggle. In pursuit of this narrative agenda, the series' makers have made clear the key stages by which this is achieved. There is plenty of persuasive detail of person, place and period in each episode, but this is essentially at the service of articulating the shifts in Vera's thinking and delineating the world turmoil that has influenced that thinking. So much of the book's compelling interest is in the spectacle of a mind and heart coming to terms with a changing world that I was a bit apprehensive about how the visual medium might render this – or whether it would just settle for incident. I needn't have worried. A great deal is required of the actress playing Vera and Cheryl Campbell meets its every challenge. What she offers is in fact a *tour de force*, as, so often in close-up, she registers Vera's progression from talkative outspokenness to a more reflective turn of mind to a silence that suggests a serious inner life. Campbell has always had a way of hinting at more than she is letting on, and this serves her very well here as she documents a woman who so often moved between the passionate outburst and enforced reticence.

But just as the memoir/autobiography places the protagonist in the context of the wider struggles of war and peace, so too does the television version. Each episode is introduced by black-and-white images that derive from actual footage: at least, these images have the *look* of newsreel material, relating to the horrors of war or to the activities of suffragettes or the graves of the dead. Colour characteristically seeps in on the pensive face of Vera, and this editing strategy is another way of enunciating the book's and the series' preoccupation with the individual caught up, as she must be, in the swirl of life-changing events.

It's not that what happens to Vera is what matters most, but rather that her situation is in many ways emblematic and she is increasingly articulate about this, as when she declares at the end of the war: 'In the last four years, my God, my king and my country have taken everything I value'. The series doesn't exploit the hardship and terrible injuries that war has brought, but these are sufficiently suggested in key images to account for how harrowing and disruptive they have been in Vera's life and those of many others. These images – of, say, a soldier bleeding to death in a military hospital – are contrasted with scenes of civilian life in which the editing often skilfully juxtaposes her mother's ongoing problem with inadequate servants or Miss Penrose's talk of 'waste of talent' with those of real horror. Such images make the effect without resort to didacticism or polemic.

The major issues that preoccupy Brittain in her book – the dissatisfaction with what is available to women, the smugness of class, the displacement of patriotism by pacifism, her growing agnosticism – are appropriately dramatised rather than discussed in the series. Characters age subtly so that we are made aware of the passing of time and of ideological shifts. Moira Armstrong's command of television's resources, and the performances of an accomplished cast, bring Elaine Morgan's screenplay to affecting life. The main stages in Vera's move towards some kind of independence in a changing world are rendered with persuasive admiration for what the human spirit may aspire to.

And now to the big screen

I approached the new film with some trepidation, coming as it does in the wake of my late-arriving admiration for its great literary antecedent and of the compelling TV miniseries. No need to worry: director James Kent's cinema feature is a wholly engrossing experience.

Whereas Vera is the narrator – obviously – in her autobiography, in the film she is inevitably *narrated*. In the book everything is seen through her perceptions; in the film we watch her as she acts and *reacts*. We are above all observing *her* rather than seeing everything through her eyes. Of course there are important point-of-view shots, but there is a good deal else that the film compels us to perceive from a more or less neutral stance.

This is not to dazzle readers with a great theoretical truth: clearly any film derived from an autobiography will tend to work in this way. The point I really want to make is to draw attention to the film's incarnation of Vera in the superb performance of Alicia Vikander. This Swedish actress, last seen here as Kitty in *Anna Karenina*, and with an immaculate English accent, is entirely equal to the camera's and our scrutiny. The director has allowed the camera to linger on her face to register some complex shifts of thought and emotion. From the first almost-androgynous close-up, her face encircled by an unbecoming cap, to the last moment as the camera homes in to reflect her response to a major experience, Vikander reminds one why Brittain's *book* is so powerful, as she creates on screen a Vera whose passion and perception we can respond to and count on.

Mention of the book leads one to ask how a film of just over two hours has chosen to deal with a 660-page memoir of one woman's life against, and taking part in, a wildly shifting panorama of world events. What kind of obligation has the film-maker to the facts of Vera Brittain's life as she has chosen to tell them? We come up against the 'based on a true story' syndrome, which often seems to imply a coherence about 'real life' that is rarely the case, but, when those life events have already been *constructed* into a cogent narrative by the protagonist of their action, the film-maker may perhaps be allowed a certain leeway in the matter of where the emphases of *his* film may fall. Working from a screenplay by Juliette Towhidi, James Kent has exercised an imaginative control over the material that seems to know how long to hold a scene or insert a moment of memory or invoke a voice-over, or how much detail is needed to create, say, the horrors of wartime France or the prejudices of class and gender on the home front. In doing so, he has made a coherent drama of his own.

In structural terms, the film-makers have elected to open with the riotous triumph of Armistice Day, 11 November 1918, in the crowded streets from which Vera, first seen in pensive close-up, extracts herself, and makes her way into a neighbouring church. This opening leads us to wonder what the peace means to this young woman: why has she opted for silent retreat rather than celebration? What has the war meant to her? Has her sense of loss outweighed relief and joy at the end of hostilities? There's an episode towards the film's end that will recall to us this opening episode – and a respect for the skill that has gone into organising the film's structure. It ends with Vera's passionate plea for not harbouring hatred for the defeated enemy, recalling Nurse Cavell's 'Patriotism is not enough'.

Between these memorable opening and closing episodes, the film divides itself into three main 'chapters'. The first of these depicts the end of Vera's girlhood, her reactions against the conventionality of her provincial middle-class upbringing, leading her to Somerville College, Oxford, much as her parents fear the effect of this on her matrimonial chances. Towards the end of this section, she has met and fallen in love with Roland (Kit Harington), school friend of her beloved brother Edward (Taron Egerton). The lives of all three, along with those of so many others, will be irrevocably disrupted by the war, and the large central section of the film will dramatise vividly the nature of this disruption. Vera quits Oxford to become a nurse, and the exposure to the horrors of 'the front', where she nurses 'Huns' as well as British wounded, along with the deaths of those closest to her, alters her forever. In the third section, she returns to Oxford, with all the appalling knowledge of the last four years behind her, and announces a change in her intellectual pursuit, from the comparative safety of Literature to the messier demands of History.

This structure highlights the centrality of the experience of war, not just for Vera as an individual but for her representative function. Virtually everyone's life is disrupted by the war but what Vera's trajectory emphasises is the way such an experience might alter the whole course of the rest of a person's life. Postwar, she will head off in different directions, with new commitments. She has always resented the restrictions placed on her as a woman by parents and others; now, she will have no truck with these. She will go her own way, not out of obduracy but from the honing of perceptions of what matters – and there will be a very brief glimpse (for those in the know, anyway) of the man she will marry.

Director Kent maintains a firm grasp of all this, offering an astute but unhurried account of Vera's metamorphosis (brilliantly incarnated by Alicia Vikander) and of the changing world in which this occurs. That she has changed more than the provincial world in which she has grown up is depicted through its narrow conventionality, which will be shocked and shaken as it wonders what to do with the peace. Her parents are played by Emily Watson and Dominic West (who both seem to get better with every film) with a fine eye for their innate prejudices, and are nicely contrasted by Anna Chancellor as Roland's much more liberated mother and, in a different way, by Miranda Richardson's parade of certainties as the principal of Somerville College. And the two young men, played by Harington and Egerton, movingly enact two kinds of youth whose promise will never be fulfilled.

Kent's film does justice to – *honours* – the great work on which it is based, and earns the right to share the final title, which describes Brittain and her book as: 'The voice of a generation'. It is salutary that this should be heard again.

Inside Story, 1 April 2015.

Part III

Afters – or Just Deserts

The following pieces refer to persons or films that have in various ways influenced a lifetime of filmgoing – and writing about film. They are essentially more personal than critical.

53

A GIFTED, TRENCHANT FRIEND

Lindsay Anderson

'Irascible', 'trenchant', 'iconoclastic', 'difficult', when not indeed 'impossible'. These were some of the words used to describe film and theatre director Lindsay Anderson, who died last week. Up to a point, they were true but they did not reflect the whole truth of Anderson's personality. He was a man who could also inspire affection and great friendships.

Born on 17 April 1923 in Bangalore, India, into an upper-class military family (his father was a Scottish major-general), Lindsay Anderson was educated at Cheltenham College and, after war service, graduated from Oxford. His background was the only conventionally upper-class thing about him. He was already rebellious at Cheltenham and, later at Oxford, he initiated an influential journal of radical film criticism called *Sequence*, whose contributors included Karel Reisz, Gavin Lambert and Penelope Houston. *Sequence* lasted for 14 issues; though the journal asked for contributions 'on any aspect of the cinema, written from any point of view', the editors were 'only interested in publishing what we agreed with'. Already then, Anderson was indulging the luxury of 'saying exactly what

[he] liked', and he went on doing just this for the next 40-odd years. This made him a formidable enemy – and an irresistible friend.

He was savage in his attacks on the shoddiness and social irrelevance, as he saw it, of much 1940s and '50s British film making. 'I think one of the worst things was the restriction in terms of class,' he said. When he began making films in the mid 50s, they were documentaries about ordinary lives, of which the most famous are the Oscar-winning short *Thursday's Children* (1953) and *Every Day Except Christmas* (1957).

With his friends Karel Reisz and Tony Richardson, Anderson set up a season of their short films in 1956, naming it 'Free Cinema', which was seen and praised by critics as a breath of new life. They were all documentaries but Anderson always had a sort of poetic realism; he wanted not merely to inform but also to move and anger.

Karel Reisz had made a great success of his first feature film, *Saturday Night and Sunday Morning* (1960), and was then offered *This Sporting Life* (1963), based on David Storey's novel. Reisz agreed to produce it only if Anderson were director. The film belongs with that group of realist films beginning with *Room at the Top* (1958) and including *Saturday Night* … and *A Kind of Loving* (1962), but it is different from them. It is realistic in its surface treatment of the life of an inarticulate professional footballer (Richard Harris's best performance), but its real power is in its depiction of frustrated emotions. Today it is considered a masterpiece.

But it is Anderson's next British film, *If* … (1968), which was his greatest success, a clarion call to youthful rebellion that makes it still a cult favourite. He uses the public school as a metaphor for a divided Britain; all his life, he detested the class system that he felt was the source of Britain's social ailments.

None of his subsequent films was ever such a commercial success, but they are all notable. *O Lucky Man!* (1973) follows the career of Mick Travis, the young rebel from *If . . .*, played again by Malcolm McDowell, and is an abrasive, Brechtian satire on opportunism and hypocrisies. Anderson's 1982 film *Britannia Hospital* had a sense of Swiftian ferocity. In this, the rundown hospital preparing for a royal visit is presented as an image of a nation in terminal decline – and its commercial failure had almost the same effect on his career.

His other two films include the intensely moving *In Celebration* (1974), a film version of David Storey's play. The film, set almost wholly in the house where three sons visit their aging parents on their 40th wedding anniversary, is not remotely stiff and stagy and boasts a beautiful performance from Bill Owen as the miner father. The other film is the poignantly elegiac *The Whales of August* (1987), made in America and starring Lillian Gish and Bette Davis in roles that honoured two of film's greatest actresses.

As well, there were numerous influential stage productions, notably at the Royal Court in the 1960s and early '70s, the brilliant miniseries, *Glory, Glory* (1989), satirising television evangelism; a telling performance as an acidulous don in *Chariots of Fire* (1981); a touching three-part tribute to the life of his great hero John Ford (1993), about whom he had also written a book in 1981; and, fittingly, last of all, *Is That All There Is?* (1993), a day-in-the-life of himself, one of a series commissioned for British television.

With an oeuvre as impressive as anyone has achieved in British cinema, Anderson was yet too outspoken for popular taste, too uncompressing for the box-office. He gained a reputation that made it difficult for him to find work in later years.

It is none the less clear that he also inspired devotion in a great many people: Sir John Gielgud attributed his induction into the modern theatre to Anderson's direction of him in *Home*. Actors like McDowell, Rachel Roberts, Alan Bates, production designer Jocelyn Herbert, writers Davids Sherwin and Storey, and music director Alan Price worked for him again and again.

He could be, and very often was, generous, courteous and stimulating. Trenchant, too, of course. 'Have you no discrimination of any kind?', he once asked me as I expressed enthusiasm for some ancient British melodrama.

I once asked him whether producers thought of him as primarily a stage director who did some films or a film director with a notable stage record. He said: 'I don't think people think of me at all.' I think he was absolutely wrong about this.

This was written prior to a commemorative screening of *If*... at the Lumière Cinema, Melbourne.

The Age, 10 September 1994.

54

WHO IS LANCE COMFORT?

The answer is not, as a colleague suggested, a porn star, but one of the most-neglected and under-rated of British directors. When I was asked by *Cinema Papers* to write, on this historic occasion, a short piece reflecting 'the author's passion for cinema', the opportunity to trumpet this unsung hero was too much to resist. After my 21 continuous years of hard labour in the *Cinema Papers* vineyard, it seemed like a reward for good behaviour.

Lance Comfort entered movies in 1925, fulfilling such functions as Sound Recordist, Special Effects man and 'Technical Supervisor' on several dozen films before directing his first feature, *Hatter's Castle*, in 1940. This was based on a sadistically downbeat novel of domestic tyranny by A. J. Cronin (does anyone remember him?), with wild-eyed Robert Newton as Brodie, the Scottish hatter with ideas above his station and a family under his thumb. Comfort released the novel from the shackles of its dour and spurious realism, and brought real melodramatic panache to bear on its tableaux of obsessive aspiration and patriarchal cruelty. Brodie browbeats his careworn drudge of a wife; brings his barmaid mistress to live in the 'castle'; and kicks his pregnant daughter out into the snow – and that's only when he's feeling good about life. The youthful James Mason,

Deborah Kerr and Emlyn Williams respectively vivify the doctor hero, the put-upon daughter he rescues, and her slimy seducer; and cinematographer Max Greene's luminous chiaroscuro does justice to James Carter's Gothic production design. I mention these names because, if Comfort was never a candidate for auteur status, at very least he was able to orchestrate some impressive talents.

He was at his most buoyant in the 1940s when he made a series of melodramas that are worth anyone's time and which draw regularly on such rewarding collaborators. *Great Day* (1946) affectingly combines English pastoral (a village prepares for a visit from Mrs Roosevelt) and the melodrama of obsession (a former World War I captain steals a ten-shilling note, and is brought to the brink of suicide). *Bedelia* (1946) is a handsome wicked-woman thriller, with Margaret Lockwood, the decade's archetypal 'Wicked Lady', murdering her way through several husbands and towards handsome insurance pay-outs. The film is sharp about her sexual distaste for men; and this theme is even more potently treated in *Daughter of Darkness* (1948), in which an Irish nymphomaniac servant girl, Emmy Baudine, comes to work on an English farm and seduces and murders her way through the local eligibles. Remarkably for its time, the film retains our sympathy for her 'otherness' at the expense of the clipped vowels which seek to keep her in her sexual and social place.

If there is a continuing preoccupation running through these films it is that of the obsessive personality, and Comfort is not afraid to give some showy actors their enjoyable heads as they render this condition. Not only Newton, who appears for Comfort again in the sombre 1947 Simenon-based thriller, *Temptation Harbour*, but also Lockwood, who narrows her eyes and flares her nostrils to dangerous purpose as Bedelia; the Irish actor Siobhan McKenna, who brings a compelling intensity to the genuinely strange, mad Emmy; and Eric Portman, whose neurotic edge superbly serves the needs of the déclassé captain in *Great Day*. The last of the 1940s obsessives is the parvenu country gent in *Silent Dust* (1949), played to suggest chilling monomania by Stephen Murray, his physical blindness acting as an index of his blinkered dedication to the memory of his wastrel son. And the actors' pyrotechnics in these films are again and again reinforced by full-throttle musical scores and cameramen with more on their minds than pictures of people talking.

Comfort never enjoyed the acclaim accorded those filmmakers who worked in the critically-privileged literary and realist strands of British cinema of the period. Melodrama had a strong commercial innings from 1943 to 1946, with the Gainsborough bodice-rippers, disdained by critics then, but recently and astutely re-evaluated. Comfort's first melodrama was too early for the Gainsborough cycle launched in 1943 with *The Man in Grey* (Leslie Arliss) and, by the time he hit his stride in the later 1940s, the vogue had passed. During the war his films were untouched by the new fashion for 'authenticity' in the fiction film: he made spy thrillers (*Squadron Leader X* [1943], *Escape to Danger* [1943], both for RKO's London operation), a stodgy biopic (*Penn of Pennsylvania*, 1941, which brazenly solicits American solidarity with beleaguered England), a director-proof *Old Mother Riley* farce (1943) and a charming version of Priestley's regional comedy, *When We Are Married* (1943).

Sadly, Comfort never seemed to be doing the right thing at the right time, for either major critical or audience support. As the industry changed in the 1950s, as different kinds of genres commanded popularity, as the studio structures grew more precarious and the audiences less reliable, he found himself confined mainly to making

'B'-movies – that is, supplying the bottom half of the double bill, which was then the standard exhibition mode. However, some of these are very good indeed, including *Bang! You're Dead* (1954), a moody, off-beat piece of post-war malaise; *Eight O'Clock Walk* (1954), a thriller which quite daringly turns on the issue of child molestation; *Touch of Death* (1962), in which robbery is complicated by unsuspected poison; and the gripping kidnap drama, *Tomorrow at Ten* (1962). All these films move smartly, create the right tension, and often look stylish beyond their modest means.

The budgets grew less, but Comfort adapted himself to straitened circumstances, tightened his belt and his plotlines, worked second-string stars to often striking effect, made resourceful use of locations within easy reach of London, and kept his eye on the changing social climate. He had the advantage of a number of recurring collaborators, including cinematographer Basil Emmott, screen-writer Lyn Fairhurst and editor John Trumper. It's encouraging to see what can be achieved in discount filmmaking if the personnel care enough about it. Comfort's is not a solitary case: others such as Vernon Sewell, Lawrence Huntington, Montgomery Tully and Arthur Crabtree are similarly ripe for reappraisal. Lance Comfort, perhaps, hurdled the decades more persuasively than any, until his untimely death in 1967. It's time to give him his due. That's why I'm writing a book about him.

Cinema Papers, No. 129, January 1990.

55

JILL ESMOND OLIVIER

The First Wife

When I was eleven, an Australian schoolboy already besotted with the movies, I saw a film called *My Pal Wolf* (1944) at a kids' holiday matinee in rural Victoria. In it a little girl was left in the charge of a governess, Miss Munn, while her parents were engaged on hush-hush war work in Washington. The strict disciplinarian Miss Munn gave the child and the dog of the title and the folksy servants down in Virginia a bad time of it.

What struck me was the notion that, in real life, I'd have hated Miss Munn and found her nasty, cold and mean, whereas I couldn't take my eyes off her up there on the screen. Jill Esmond played Miss Munn with steely conviction and in doing so taught me an awareness of how different art and life were. I couldn't have put it that way then, but the fact hit home, and I became her life-long fan.

A recent biography of Laurence Olivier, Terry Coleman's *Olivier* (2006), claims to have had access to previously unavailable sources. Yet, among the welter of footnotes in this unappealing 'life', one sentence has stayed in my memory: the recollection of one of his secretaries, an exiled Russian princess, who described Jill Esmond, the first Mrs Olivier, as 'one of the very rare unequivocally nice people [she] had ever met'.

Being 'unequivocally nice' is all very well in its way, but I want to suggest that there was a lot more to Jill Esmond than such a phrase implies. My claim is that she was a fine actress and a woman of character: I base the first half of that claim on what I saw of her on screen, and the second half on having had the privilege of becoming her friend.

Who, then, was this briskly incisive character-actress who could make meanness so compelling on screen? She came from theatrical royalty I subsequently found out: her father was actor-manager H.V. ("Harry") Esmond and her mother was the noted stage actress Eva Moore, and they were buddies with such famous families as the Barrymores and the DuMauriers. She was already an established actress when she met the aspiring Olivier in 1928 when they were both appearing in *Bird in Hand*, and she was instrumental in launching his acting career. She was even responsible for changing his looks, so that his forehead was no longer diminished by low-growing hair.

Married a few months earlier, they both went to New York in 1930 at Noel Coward's invitation to appear with him and Gertrude Lawrence in his *Private Lives* on Broadway, and in the wake of its enormous success they were both beckoned to Hollywood. In all her films of the decade, she looks and sounds, far more than Olivier did then, a natural for the screen. She had already appeared in two British films, *The Chinese Bungalow* (1930), as Jill Esmond-Moore, and for Alfred Hitchcock in *The Skin Game* (1931), in which she played with an ease before the camera not shared by some of her co-stars. She made several films for RKO, holding her own with such stars as John Barrymore in *State's Attorney* (1932) and Irene Dunne and Myrna Loy in *Thirteen Women* (1932). In the latter she brings a crisp and unaffected sympathy to the role of Dunne's commonsensical friend.

Garbo turned Olivier down as a possible leading man for *Queen Christina* (1933), and they left Hollywood at his instigation. Who knows what might have been the effect on her subsequent career if she had played Sydney Fairfield in the Selznick production of *A Bill of Divorcement* (1932)? Years later; she wrote to me: 'I was offered *Bill of Divorcement*, George Cukor directing and John Barrymore playing the father. But I had to sign a 7-year contract, as whoever played it was bound to become a star. Larry rightly didn't want to stay in Hollywood, so I turned it down. Although my marriage broke up, it is a decision I have never regretted. I don't think I was cut out for a film star.'

Well, Katharine Hepburn, who played Sydney, indubitably *did* became a film star, and Jill never did, but she went on to become one of those character players who stamp their scenes with the kind of reality that acts as a guarantee for the truth of what's going on around them. The use of the word 'rightly' in her letter points, too, to the kind of generosity that characterised her: there is no recorded sense of the bitterness that many in like circumstances might have felt.

Back in England, she co-starred with Conrad Veidt in the Gaumont-British/UFA futuristic thriller, *F.P.I.* (1932), and she and Olivier made a film together in 1933, *No Funny Business*, where he seems stilted by comparison. He would of course go on to scale major heights, and, as the world knows, her marriage collapsed with the arrival of Vivien Leigh on the scene, and divorce ensued in January 1940. It is not my intention to trace these unhappy events which have been more than adequately recorded elsewhere. Their son Tarquin was born in 1936 and early in the war Jill took him to America where they stayed for the duration.

It wasn't easy at first to get work and she spoke feelingly of the difference between the experience of being in demand in Hollywood in the early 30s and the wartime return, now a divorced woman with small son who had been seriously ill. She recalled visiting a very grand Greer Garson, to whom Jill and Olivier had been helpful in the pre-war London theatre. Garson's manner was now so condescending, Jill recalled, that 'When my little dog lifted its leg a dozen times around her house, I never dreamt of stopping him'. On the other hand, she had nothing but kindness from Joan Crawford, who alone treated her as if she were still being hailed as a promising new star. In the early '30s, kind-hearted Jill had felt for the under-educated Crawford's sense of being out of things when the rest of the company was playing clever word games.

When I suggested she'd been busy in Hollywood in the war years, she said, 'Not nearly busy enough'. Certainly most of the roles she had were more or less cameos but they are memorable enough to make you suppose they were longer and more numerous than they were. She makes a sharp impression as a cynical wife in the breakfast scene in *Random Harvest* (1942), is shrewdly humane as a nurse dealing with deserting soldier Tyrone Power in *This Above All* (1942), sorts out with persuasive sympathy, Robert Young's problems in getting two orphaned children to the US in *Journey for Margaret* (1942), gives Gladys Cooper a verbal serve in *The White Cliffs of Dover* (1944), and combines crisp professionalism and kindness as a doctor dealing with Gary Cooper's situation in *Casanova Brown* (1944).

She would star again on the stage, but in films, she rarely had other than character roles. However, this attractive, now middle-aged actress continued to make her presence felt in the limited running-time that was now her lot. On post-war return to England, she appeared three more times on the London stage and nabbed a couple of good character roles in films: as a nurse who is not what she seems in the thriller *Bedelia* (1946), and the spinsterish and disapproving sister in *Escape* (1948), but work was not plentiful for returning ex-pats.

In 1951, she did what may be her finest work on film, in one of those unjustly scorned British 'B' movies. This was in *Private Information*, in which she played Charlotte Carson, who takes on the local government which has shut its collective eyes to the shoddy inadequacies of a housing estate. Jill had the chance here of a full-length part and fifty-odd years later she is still impressive to watch in it: short of stature, middle-aged, forthright, devoted to her children, she convincingly confronts and scores a victory over the corrupt council. Everything she does in this film is heartfelt and thoughtful: she makes an ordinary woman with the bit between her teeth someone to cheer for.

There were two more brief but telling character roles in US films in the '50s: as Frau Schindler, who suicides early in the Cold War thriller, *Night People* (1954), and, incisive as ever, as the mother of *A Man Called Peter* (1955). After a couple of episodes of TV's *The Adventures of Robin Hood* in 1956, as Queen Eleanor, she retired and threw her very considerable intelligence into various theatre-related charities. She was for years the Chairman of the Welfare Committee of the Actors' Charitable Trust, which looked after Denville Hall, and was much involved in the re-design of the building. There were so many loos, for fear of the residents' being caught short, and they were referred to as 'Jillies'. I remember her recalling a famous actress whose sister had to be asked to leave Denville because she would keep smoking in bed and setting fire to the bedclothes. Her other charity was the Theatrical Ladies' Guild, whose Patrons were Princess Alice of Athlone and Athene Seyler, whom she later sent me to meet.

When I first went to England in 1958, having written to her c/- one of her charities, she invited me to visit and I had the memorable experience of drinks in the back garden of her St John's Wood house, with George and Mercia (Swinburne) Relph as the other guests. They kindly drew this callow youth out about Australia, whereas I wanted to go on listening to the clatter of great names being dropped – Edith, Johnnie, Gladys, Michael, Gwen, etc – and there were several references by Jill to Larry, whom she once endearingly described as a 'silly arse'.

In the years that followed, I always saw her at least once when I'd go to England. Jill could never quite believe my interest in her films. It could have been anyone who gave me that lesson about art and life, but the fact remained that it *was* Jill. In after years it was interesting to me to track down what else she'd done – and to feel egoistically gratified that someone important to me as a child was in fact so good actress. When I'd try to draw her out about this or that film, she'd usually say: 'Are you sure I was in that? What did I play? Was I any good?' It wasn't just a matter of tactful manners to give a firmly positive answer to that last question.

The conversation was quite wide-ranging: she was sharply intelligent with an interest in what was going on in the world at large. Conservative in politics as she said she was, she nevertheless despised the behaviour of people like John Wayne who named names during the McCarthy anti-communist witch hunts. Talking about plays once, my wife mentioned how impressed we'd been by Peter Brook's gym-set *Midsummer Night's Dream*. 'Oh', said Jill, 'the *Dream* will always be for me the way Vivien Leigh played it [as Titania, in 1937].' This remark, matter-of-factly made, seemed to me to point to that generosity of spirit I mentioned earlier, and this was borne out in the way she never made any public comment on the break-up of her marriage to Olivier or discussed him with any of the myriad biographers. 1 never raised the name of Laurence Olivier with her: I was interested in her for her own sake, not for this connection, and, when she mentioned him, as she did, it was without the slightest rancour.

The last time I saw her was in Wimbledon Hospital just a few days before she died at home. There was something very admirable, very straight, about her that compelled respect and liking. She had a good deal of pain in her last years, but it was mainly from sources other than herself that one heard this. Once, in a letter, she wrote that she was feeling better (after a lung cancer treatment) and had just 'cut the garden hedge, a bit crookedly. But as long as I don't have to use my brain I'm all right'. In fact, she went on using that very well-stocked 'brain' to the end of the life she lived with courage and style.

She fixed my attention when I was eleven and retained it for the next forty-odd years, and 1 dedicated my 1992 interview book on British cinema, *Sixty Voices*, to her memory. 2008 was the centenary of her birth, and she deserves to be remembered, not just as a footnote in other people's lives, but in her own right.

Senses of Cinema, Issue 73, December 2014.

56

THE CHOICE FRUIT OF *THE MANGO TREE*

It's not as though there was nothing else going on in Australian cinema in the 1970s, but the combination of period piece, eye-catching locations, literary adaptation and coming-of-age theme surely conjures up a good deal of that crucial decade. Even in that climate, though, Kevin Dobson's *The Mango Tree* (1977) wasn't very popular. It was securely set during World War One, picturesquely located in Bundaberg and surrounding cane-fields, was derived from Ronald McKie's award-winning 1974 novel, and its ostensible concern was the rites of passage undergone by young Jamie Carr.

The film version, produced by Michael Pate, former actor who had had a sturdy career as actor here and in the US, certainly looks great as the camera tracks through waving cane-fields or the dusty streets of Bundaberg. But the film, easy as it is to watch, just can't seem to keep its mind on any one thing for long enough and this may well be because Christopher Pate, Michael's then 25-year-old son, simply can't command the attention needed for us to see the narrative's grab-bag of events as contributing to his emergence from adolescence – and it doesn't help that he looks as if he's well past school age.

So why have I remembered this film so vividly? Essentially because it enshrines one of the most luminous performances by an actress in Australian film. She is the celebrated Irish-American Geraldine Fitzgerald, here playing Grandma Carr who has had the raising of orphaned Jamie. The sequence of her death has stayed with me for the 30-odd years since I first saw it, and re-viewing it for this purpose I feel vindicated in my earlier judgment. Fitzgerald, long a great beauty, had been in films since the early 1930s, had done impressive and distinctive work in Hollywood without ever quite being a major film *star*, and had won great acclaim in the theatre in plays as diverse as *Our Town* and *Long Day's Journey into Night*. In 1974 she had a heartbreaking few minutes in Paul Mazursky's *Harry and Tonto*: had the casting director for *The Mango Tree* seen this and registered the capacity of this woman to imbue whatever she did with a profound sense of inner belief and truth of feeling?

Grandma Carr has become ill after helping to nurse casualties of the 1919 flu epidemic, but has recovered sufficiently to announce that she and Jamie will have a formal dinner, telling him to see to sherry and port and to open a bottle of wine. She dresses elegantly for the occasion with jewellery – silver drop earrings and pendant – setting off the high-collared black dress, and hair braided and pulled back from the face still beautiful in its seventh decade and its look of lived-in, shrewd-eyed wisdom. There is an element of *tour de force* as she tells a story of her past, of how a bushranger had appeared at her mother's door with a rifle, of a man so handsome she wished she'd gone away with him, and of how he was killed the next day. The director has been wise enough to leave the camera on her for the extent of this tale and at its end, sitting upright against a vertical beam and pronouncing herself 'utterly content', she quietly dies.

The sequence lasts only a few minutes but its potency derives in part from the way it is fed by our recalling the previous episodes in which Fitzgerald has commanded the screen, not by flamboyant technique but by the quiet fullness of her understanding of this generous-spirited woman. For instance, in a brief episode with a young woman of dubious reputation, Mrs Carr's liberality and respect for otherness are touchingly but unsentimentally rendered in Fitzgerald's performance which is an amalgam of her uniquely throaty delivery, the calm dignity of her over-all demeanour, the wise eyes and the wide, amused mouth. The film is not *about* her but it is she one remembers as she stamps her scenes with authority and rich humanity.

Senses of Cinema, Issue 55, July 2010.

57

OBITUARY

Sir John Mills

John Mills, very deaf and almost blind but still chipper, was appearing on chat shows and contributing cameo roles until he was in his mid-nineties. It was as if he'd discovered that one of the secrets of a happy life was to keep doing the work you loved for as long as people asked you – and in his case they'd gone on asking for more than 70 years. But it wasn't just the length of his career or even its diversity that was remarkable: he seemed, too, to be held in almost unique personal and professional esteem by his colleagues, while never losing the public's regard.

His first professional appearance was in the chorus of a 1929 revue and he returned to the stage often. Notable high spots included *Cavalcade* (Noël Coward became a sort of mentor) in 1931, Terence Rattigan's *Ross* (as T.E. Lawrence) on Broadway (1961) and Charles Wood's *Veterans* (1972), opposite John Gielgud in a play whose verbal frankness shocked their fans. He also starred in two plays by his second wife Mary Hayley Bell (they were married for 64 years) – *Men in Shadow* (1942) and *Duet for Two Hands* (1945) – and did some exceptional television (including *Ending Up* in 1990), especially in later life. But his real glory was his incomparable film career.

He was short and slight, pleasant-looking rather than film-star-handsome – unlike such contemporaries as the strapping Stewart Granger, the saturnine James Mason or the sexily ambiguous Dirk Bogarde. Granger and Mason had long Hollywood careers and Bogarde deliberately turned himself into a 'European' actor, but Mills remained a *British* star – essentially, an *English* one. He made sorties to Hollywood, but his career truly belongs to Denham, Pinewood and Ealing, not to L.A.

In the 1930s he was already a reliable light leading man, whether in musicals (*Car of Dreams*, 1935), adventure (*Brown on Resolution*, 1935), historical romance (*Tudor Rose*, 1936) or crime thrillers (*The Green Cockatoo*, 1937), working over the decade's genre range with increasing assurance. But it was the war that made him a star.

Invalided out of the Royal Engineers in 1941, he played a series of services roles: in *In Which We Serve* (1942), *We Dive at Dawn* (1943), *This Happy Breed* and *Waterloo Road* (1944) and *The Way to the Stars* (1945). Here he honed a new kind of hero for British cinema – an everyday chap, honest and decent, who could be counted on to rise undemonstratively to the challenge of dangerous occasions. Unthreatening, he could be your good-natured elder brother or your sister's boyfriend or your best friend; he could also, however, be handy with his fists when moral duty called (*Waterloo Road*) or trusted to deliver bad news sensitively (*The Way to the Stars*).

Often in uniform throughout the 1950s, when the filming of wartime exploits became a British cinema staple, Mills rang subtle enough changes on the stiff upper-lip stereotype not to seem merely repetitive, and is very fine as the nerve-stretched alcoholic captain in *Ice Cold in Alex* (1958). Other notable achievements include his definitive Pip in David Lean's *Great Expectations* (1946), in which he provides a compelling centre around which a cast of eye-catching eccentrics prances. His own favourite role was that other upwardly mobile 'hero', bootmaker Willie Mossop in *Hobson's Choice* (1953), holding his own against Charles Laughton's pyrotechnics. And he slid effortlessly into such character roles as the shabby private detective in *The End of the Affair* (1954), the captain pushed into neurotic rage in *Tunes of Glory* (1960), and the father at last acknowledging that he loved his dead mate best in *The Family Way* (1966). Festooned with honours (knighted in 1976), he won a Supporting Actor Oscar for his grotesque turn as the village idiot in *Ryan's Daughter* (1970); virtually anything else in his career is more deserving.

He also produced (and starred in) two late-1940s films – *The History of Mr Polly* (1948) and *The Rocking Horse Winner* (1949) – but told me: "I wasn't a very good producer because I was always dying to get on the floor." In 1965 he directed his younger daughter Hayley in one of her less successful films, *Sky West and Crooked*, having featured with her in the trim thriller *Tiger Bay* (1959) that launched her career. In later decades, like other acting knights, he appeared in cameos in large-scale enterprises such as *Young Winston* (1971) and *Gandhi* (1982), as well as playing a mute 'Old Norway' in Kenneth Branagh's *Hamlet* (1996).

In uniform or mufti, in period or contemporary, in lead or character roles, he became the most durable film star that British cinema ever produced. He made it look easy but kept us interested by imbuing a likeable surface with less predictable possibilities.

Sight & Sound, June 2005.

58

MERLE OBERON

'She walked in beauty ...'

Perhaps it was a matter of being caught young. I first saw Merle Oberon when I was about 12 or 13 when *A Song to Remember* (Charles Vidor, 1945) came to rural Victoria some years after a very long run at Melbourne's Savoy Theatre. I have never forgotten how she looked in that, and every time I've seen it since it brings back that indelible, life-changing image she imprinted on my young mind. Hers was a face of great delicacy, exquisitely oval, framed with lustrous dark hair, with eloquent eyes and bright red lips – and she was unforgettably dressed in pale grey trousers, scarlet waistcoat, generous bow-tie, black cutaway coat, and grey top hat on first appearance. As novelist George Sand, she swung down a Parisian street (that's Paris, Hollywood) with 'friend' Liszt, and came into a café where Chopin (Cornel Wilde) and his mentor/teacher Professor Elsner (Paul Muni) sat at a table. She said little in this scene, but as she and Liszt (Stephen Bekassy) move on to their own table she inclined her head to look provocatively at Wilde to say, 'I hope you will like Paris, Monsieur Chopin. I'm sure Paris will like you.' Simple words of courtesy maybe, but on Merle's lips charged with subtle sexual promise.

Curiously, *A Song to Remember* has never become a cult classic. Perhaps it goes in for too much 'dignity' and high-mindedness rather than camp excess. It is quite often very silly and its depiction of Chopin as a political refugee from Poland under the heel of 'tsarist swine' who composes for the sake of the motherland, even to the point of endangering his health, doesn't bear close inspection. The one thing that people recall when it is mentioned is 'the blood on the keys' when Chopin is about to collapse at the end of a patriotically inspired concert tour. But for me the great moments in this film all involve the fabulous Merle at the very peak of her beauty, the film having been made when she was about 33. I think of the recital she has arranged at the mansion of the Duchess of Orléans. Everyone has been expecting Liszt to play and the lights have been turned down to satisfy who knows what artistic whim associated with him. At open windows listening menials are whispering 'Ssh! Liszt!' As the pianist's performance draws to a close, Merle, her hair now swept up the better to reveal her incomparable forehead and her body encased not in trousers but in a swirling long white gown, walks down the aisle between the rows of the audience, holding a candelabra aloft to reveal that the performer was none other than her protégé Frédéric (aka Frederick) Chopin. This is a turning point in his fame and she carries off this epiphanic moment with stunning assurance and poise, until she stands beside him at the piano. Every budding composer surely needs such a patroness; my guess is that few have had one who looked like Merle.

There's an even bigger climax when she turns on him in wild apologia, her eyes blazing with anger, with 'No one knows this human jungle better than I'. We know she (i.e., George Sand) is a writer but the film is not very interested in, say, *La Mare au Diable* (neither was I when it was prescribed for French I at Melbourne University a few years later), and it was nothing like as memorable as Merle's outburst. 'No one knows this human jungle better than I. Who ever fought more bitterly to survive in it? To have had some talent and ambition and to be a woman – in the eyes of men something slightly better than a head of cattle. I wore men's trousers, to remind them I was their equal …' etc. I'm quoting that from memory but am pretty sure I haven't made any mistakes. Merle was ablaze with gender-based fury (why haven't the feminists lit upon this flare-up?) – and alight with sexual challenge. Anyway, she lures Chopin away from the distractions of Paris to her island fastness, predicting alliteratively, 'You could write miracles of music in Majorca'. All does not go smoothly on the island: the rain is incessant and Frédéric becomes very chesty. Merle is getting testy with him; perhaps, incredibly, he is not paying her enough attention, and she orders him to 'Stop this so-called polonaise jumble you've been working on for days' and pay more attention to her. After all, she has given him – in her own words – 'what artists have been crying out for down the ages': that is, solitude in a picturesque setting with someone who looks like her.

Well, the damp climate has played havoc with his chest and, bravely defying advice, he undertakes the fund-raising tour for beleaguered Poland that leads to the-blood-on-the-keys, after an extensive montage of concert halls and iconic monuments of cultured Europe. Merle is having her portrait painted when old Professor Elsner, who has always been wary of her, dodders in and says that Frédéric is dying and that he has asked to see her. Without a tremor of her matchless profile, she simply says: 'Frederick was mistaken to ask for me … Please continue

Monsieur Delacroix.' Not many actresses could carry off a line like that as if they meant it – and without laughing aloud.

There were a lot of other beautiful women in films when I was first getting interested in films – and in beautiful women. There were gorgeous redheads like Rita Hayworth, Maureen O'Hara and Geraldine Fitzgerald, and brunettes like Ava Gardner and Jane Greer, all predating the more obvious sexiness of Monroe a few years later, and all staying clearly with me over five decades. But Merle was something else: the challenging eyes, the forehead, the handsome bosom, the sheer elegance, the romantic intensity with which she imbued all she said and did.

It used to be thought that Merle was born in Tasmania and this myth was not exploded until after her death. In fact, she was born in India of mixed British-Indian parentage, and, when she went to racially-conscious England in the 30s, she suppressed her Eurasian heritage in the interests of pursuing a career. All this suppression is by now well-documented, and it's a bit surprising that she was able to maintain this secrecy about her background. As late as 1980 my son was working as dogsbody in a big Australian firm when an elderly Indian colleague told him about having been involved in a Calcutta dramatic society with Merle in the late 20s and very early 1930s. But such people, and there must have been plenty who remembered her, remarkably kept their counsel and never in her lifetime contradicted the Tasmanian myth. The racial mix, of course, accounts in no small measure for the astonishing uniqueness of the beauty.

After several tiny, uncredited roles in British films of the early 30s, she got herself noticed in Zoltan Korda and Leontine Sagan's *Men of Tomorrow* (1932) and even more thoroughly noticed the following year in brother Alexander Korda's *The Private Life of Henry VIII*. Not having for some years now seen this epoch-maker (for British films, not just for Merle), I've never forgotten how she, as doomed Anne Boleyn, asks as she comes up for execution ('Chop and change,' as a lady-in-waiting rather crudely says), 'Will my hair sit straight when my head falls?' She manages to invest her few moments with a touch of real poignancy, which is as much due to the contrast between her youthful perfection and the hideous cruelty of the axe as to Anne's historical situation.

By now, following the international success of *Henry VIII* and *The Scarlet Pimpernel*, in which she was a ravishing Marguerite to Leslie Howard's Percy Blakeney, Hollywood had Merle in its sights. In Goldwyn's 1935 romantic melodrama, *The Dark Angel*, she won an Oscar nomination as the woman whose lover is blinded in World War 1, but it was really William Wyler who made her a star with a world-wide following. In fact, in a reversal of the received wisdom about how Hollywood takes nice natural British actresses and turns them into artificial glamour pusses, Wyler somehow 'naturalised' Merle, who, notwithstanding how breathtaking she looked, was in danger of becoming a resident 'exotic' in British cinema. Never an actress of exceptional range, she nevertheless held her own with a scene-stealing Miriam Hopkins ('very bitchy' Merle recalled thirty years on) in *These Three*, adapted from Lillian Hellman's play about the dangers of gossip and the possibility of lesbianism among teachers at a girls' school. Sam Goldwyn, apprised that the play touched on lesbians, is reputed to have said merely, 'Make 'em Nicaraguans'.

But it was her next film for Wyler that cemented her reputation as an international star. She played Cathy in the film version of Emily Brontë's passionate *Wuthering Heights* (1939). Looking at this sixty years later, I must say how impressed I was not merely with the beauty, here exhibited in both 'natural' wind-swept mode and in the 'civilised' couture of her residence at Thrushcross Grange, having settled for dull Edgar Linton when her heart and soul belonged elsewhere (that's how they talked in 1930s Hollywood – and in Emily Brontë), but also with the quality of performance she brought to bear on Cathy. She would later say that Spencer Tracy had told her that the Oscars would never again be worth attending to when she wasn't nominated for Cathy. That may be an extreme reaction but she does exhibit an emotional range that was not often asked of her.

We see her in ecstatic profile as she contemplates running away with Heathcliff (Laurence Olivier); she is persuasively furious with Edgar (David Niven) and then rips off her fine-lady clothes to run out on to Penniston Crag, where it must be said she does her best with some dreadful dialogue. 'Let the world stop right here … Standing on this hill with you, this is me forever.' However, she does differentiate convincingly between the romantic child of nature in her scenes with Heathcliff and the conventional lady of the manor at Thrushcross Grange. In one of the scenes set in the latter, Merle suggests intimations of her later imperiousness as she treats the now rich Heathcliff with icy dismissiveness. She contrasts effectively with that other great beauty, Geraldine Fitzgerald, as Edgar's sister Isabella, who reveals the shy eagerness of *her* infatuation with Heathcliff. And she is finally both exquisite and touching as she lies on her deathbed, her face irradiated as Heathcliff arrives. Olivier has a fine brooding presence but Merle's unflinching delivery of the film's often excessive dialogue (by Ben Hecht and Charles Macarthur, who should have known better) can sometimes leave him sounding stagey by comparison.

To see what I mean by Wyler and Hollywood's having 'naturalised' her, one needs only to look at some of her 1930s British films. Some of these British roles are really charming, particularly that in *The Divorce of Lady X* (Tim Whelan, 1938). The film is saucily engaging piffle, certainly, but Merle in Technicolor was a great bonus, and she showed a feeling for romantic comedy that she would hardly ever again get so good a chance to exercise. Other British films of the period such as *Over the Moon* (Thornton Freeland, 1939) and the embarrassing flag-waver *The Lion Has Wings* (Adrian Brunel, Brian Desmond Hurst and Michael Powell, 1939) are best forgotten, and show little of the fruits of the burgeoning Hollywood career which had made her a compelling romantic star.

However, it must be said that, apart from the Wyler films and *A Song to Remember*, Hollywood hardly ever gave her anything very worthwhile to do. She ages convincingly as the eponymous *Lydia* (Julien Duvivier, 1941), vacillating between three suitors (it seems restrained of her that there were only three); she has some touching moments with Gladys Cooper and Roland Young at the end of the all-star story of a house, *Forever and a Day* (Edmund Goulding *et al*,1943), showing that she could wear glasses with impunity; she dances the can-can in *The Lodger* (John Brahm, 1944) and shows off a pair of very shapely legs in doing so; but the rest of the 40s films require a high level of devotion to the Oberon allure. She struggles with screenplay and quicksand in a minor *noir* thriller, *Dark Waters* (André De Toth, 1944); swishes her way through *Temptation* (Irving Pichel, 1946) as Ruby Chepstow, a divorcée of murderous bent in period London and Egypt ('Men are just begging to be lied to … so I lie', says Ruby); did her romantic best in a couple of really sudsy romantic dramas, *This Love of Ours* (William Dieterle, 1945) and *Night Song* (John Cromwell, 1948), and in a truly preposterous fantasy romance as the Princess Delarai ('Heaven was in her Eyes … And her lips were Paradise', the publicity promised') who ends up as wife to Aesop (of 'Fables' fame) in *Night in Paradise* (Arthur Lubin, 1946). Post-war Hollywood had other things on its mind than the lush romantic drama that was Merle's forte.

No matter. In the 1950s, when she was just 40, she played a couple of character roles that seemed to suggest a new career. In short order, she played the Empress Josephine to Brando's Napoleon in *Désirée* (Henry Koster, 1954), and the patroness of Sigmund Romberg (José Ferrer) in *Deep in My Heart* (Stanley Donen, 1954). Though Jean Simmons had the title role and superior billing in the former, Merle created, in her first character role, a potent sense of the woman of fine feeling who senses her time is passing and that a younger woman is displacing her, and contrived to be not just surpassingly elegant but surprisingly moving as well. In *Deep in My Heart*, as Sigmund Romberg's influential friend Dorothy Donnelly she again cedes romantic pre-eminence to a younger actress (is there anyone else alive who has now heard of Doe Avedon? What was Ferrer/Romberg thinking of?), and she dies gracefully on a chaise longue. As in *Désirée* there is a new authority in her playing. The sexy challenge of her earlier years is still there but now allied to a new maturity, which seemed to point to a possible new career direction. This didn't eventuate, and maybe the famous beauty got in the way of developing other gifts more fully.

The astonishing thing about the legendary beauty was how it seemed to keep adjusting itself to the decades. Even in the mid 60s, and *her* mid 50s, there is a still palpable sensual quality, especially in *Hotel* (Richard Quine, 1967) as a duchess who succumbs to blackmail to protect her husband's name. The first glimpse of her is of her feet as she mounts the hotel's back stairs after being involved in a motor accident. Gradually the camera makes us privy to the fact that her figure (encased in 'gowns' by Edith Head) is still a thing of beauty, the face miraculously resisting time's imprints and fully exposed with the lustrous black hair pulled back and up in an ambitious cluster. She is the most vivid character in this multi-story plot derived from Arthur Hailey's novel, and she is the only thing that makes it worth sitting through the trash of *The Oscar* (Russell Rouse, 1966) in which she guest-stars as herself.

Her other significant appearance in the '60s was in the documentary *The Epic That Never Was*, in which she and others (Emlyn Williams, Flora Robson, etc) recall the aborted filming of *I, Claudius* of 30 years earlier. Producer and future husband Alexander Korda called a halt to this production, starring Charles Laughton, Merle and Robert Donat, when Merle was involved in a motor accident of her own, though she expressed the view that, if all had been going well, he wouldn't have abandoned the film. The surviving footage is stunning, partly for Laughton's histrionic feast as the shy and awkward Claudius – and for Merle as Messalina, flitting sumptuously through Denham's Rome as Messalina, in flowing diaphanous gown, and refusing to marry lumpish Claudius because 'My family has other plans.' Well, for all we know that's how they talked in ancient Rome. What remains on film makes one wonder if director Joseph Von Sternberg could have done for her what he did for Dietrich?

Because of her supposed Tasmanian origins, there were frequent references in the Australian papers to her movements. In one of these reports, she was said to be staying at London's Savoy Hotel in 1955, so I took advantage of having a reliable address to send her a letter. To my surprise and gratification, she not merely replied but, unasked too, enclosed a large handsome signed photograph of herself – which I still have, and will of course leave to the nation. In 1969, there was an account in the Melbourne *Herald* of a proposed film, *Private War of Mrs Darling*, about an illiterate Scots woman who takes on the bureaucracy in the matter of tearing down (or was it putting up?) a bridge in rural Scotland. 'Now, could I really play an illiterate woman?' she asked – asked *me*, that is. And that brings me to the happy climax of nearly a quarter-century of adoration.

With wife and children, I was in America on a Fulbright grant for the northern academic year of 1970–71. A student at Trinity Grammar, where I had been teaching, had passed on to me an article from *Life* magazine in 1967 about Merle's idling her life away in Acapulco, in a house called 'El Ghalal' ('from an ancient Mexican-Indian phrase meaning "to love"'), with bouts of entertaining visiting royalty. I thoughtfully filed this piece, with its provocative title, 'In a Swinging Resort the Star Is Merle Oberon' (3 April 1967). When I knew we were going to America, I wrote to her at 'El Ghalal', suggesting that she and I should take advantage of our being in the same continent for once to meet. To my surprise and huge gratification, I had a reply saying she'd 'be delighted to meet' me and giving phone numbers and addresses. After an exchange of letters, one of which from her charmingly included my wife and children in the invitation, I finally secured these latter in a motel room in San Antonio and made my way south of the border. This jaunt was finally conducted alone because my wife (who looked like Merle when we were married) generously, if sardonically, felt 'A man's gotta dream' and, less generously but more pragmatically, looking at our kids, decided they were only moderately well-behaved and would probably knock over a valuable artefact or catch a disease.

Merle's chauffeur arrived at my hotel to transport me to the House of Love. Over precipitous and lumpy roads we arrived at the Pagliai mansion (Merle was then married to Italian industrialist Bruno Pagliai), to be met at the door by the lady herself. After, as I say, nearly a quarter-century of helpless adoration, it seemed scarcely possible, but there she was, looking fabulous in, my diary says, pink slacks and shirt, with long dark hair hanging loose, the face a thing of olivine perfection and the figure as gracefully sculpted as ever. She escorted me through the house to sit beside the pool, shaded with banana trees and palms, and to absorb the stunning vista of the bay. She had been having trouble with architects (the house was put up for sale shortly afterwards), servants (so hard to get decent staff in Mexico) and health. As to the latter, she'd been diagnosed by her doctor over the phone as having hepatitis, and, while there was no one I'd rather have caught it from, I was hoping it wasn't contagious. I began to feel I should leave in case she was getting tired, but she insisted she wasn't and I stayed nearly three hours, during which some of those unsatisfactory servants plied us with cool drinks. She offered lunch but this seemed too much for someone who was meant to be unwell.

I'm glad I hadn't read some of the stories about her, or Charles Higham and Roy Moseley's 1983 biography, *Merle*, before the visit: they certainly would have punctured my more or less innocent vision of this miraculous beauty. They might also have lessened my wife's willingness to send me off alone on this pilgrimage. As it was, I simply sat there drinking in the beauty – and enjoying the talk. She was relaxed, kind, well-informed and had lots of firm opinions (see earlier references to Tracy and Miriam Hopkins); she liked talking about her films and those of others and was neither the conventional charmer nor the bitchy socialite the gossip columns sometimes suggested. She probably had a higher opinion of *A Song to Remember* than most critics would feel able to share, but who cared about historical verisimilitude when Merle was on screen? And she warded off potential criticism (as if I were about to offer any!) by praising Columbia's ogre-boss, Harry Cohn, for buying up a Polish film about Chopin just so that he could reproduce one scene. This scene was the one I've mentioned above involving Liszt, Chopin and candelabra. When I asked if I could take some photos of her, she said yes, and added that 'Prince Philip was here only a week or so earlier with such a cunning little camera, no bigger than your finger.' My resulting photos are only a little blurred, and are in fact as good as you could expect from a shaking hand.

While I was there, I urged her to get back to the movies which so sorely needed her in grungy 1970, and I strongly recommended that she enlist the support of George Cukor to direct and Henry Fonda to co-star with her in a screen version of Henry James's *The Ambassadors*. She wasn't familiar with this subtle and glittering work but I assured her she was born to play Madame de Vionnet who so effortlessly captivates men across a wide age-spectrum. On return to Michigan, I sent her a copy (she wrote thanking me for 'the Henry James book'). She was unusually absent from the gossip columns over the next few months and I pointed this out to my wife who simply, if perhaps not wholly kindly, said, 'Don't be silly, she's at home with a tutor trying to read *The Ambassadors*.' The other roles I wanted her to play were the title role in a version of Angus Wilson's *The Middle Age of Mrs Eliot*, though I didn't quite like to name it in case it seemed rude in the face of her ageless beauty, and Jocasta in *Oedipus Rex*. I mean, how many woman are old enough to be your mother but ravishing enough to make you want to marry them? In the event, of course, she followed none of my suggestions but made an ill-fated comeback in *Interval* in 1973, divorced her industrialist husband, and married her co-star, Robert Wolders, who as my wife pointed out to me, again not all that kindly, 'is even younger than you are.' This last film, a May-December love story in which she played December and he played May. It was unkindly reviewed and has never come my way. Is there anyone out there who …? [Since I wrote this, my daughter has found me a copy on e-bay.]

Merle has been dead now for nearly thirty years, and I've met quite a number of film stars since, several of them quite gorgeously beautiful, but I suppose that having been caught young by Merle's dark charms helps account for the fact that none has ever dislodged her image from my mind. It was worth taking up a Fulbright for the chance to meet her – and to feel my youthful infatuation had been vindicated. I still feel this every time I re-see, say, *Lydia* or *Dark Angel*, and, sensing the need for another viewing of *A Song to Remember* coming on, I recently acquired and watched a DVD. I can only say my youthful judgment was spot-on. She established for me a standard of subtly sexy beauty that no other screen star has surpassed. Others may have things in common with her, but not all these elements are to be found in any *one* other. She may not have been the screen's greatest actress, but, hell, *anyone* can act.

Senses of Cinema, 10 February 2009.

CPSIA information can be obtained
at www.ICGtesting.com
Printed in the USA
JSHW031209300420
5413JS00002B/65

9 781925 523416